KT-134-449

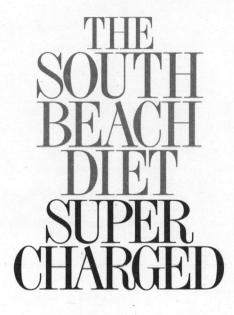

THE SOUTH BEACH DIET SUPERCHARGED

OTHER BOOKS BY
DR ARTHUR AGATSTON

The South Beach Diet

The South Beach Diet Cookbook

The South Beach Diet Good Fats/Good Carbs Guide

The South Beach Heart Programme

For more information on the South Beach Diet,
go to: www.SouthBeachDiet.com/Supercharged

THE SOUTH BEACH DIET SUPER CHARGED

FASTER Weight Loss and Better Health for Life

Dr Arthur Agatston

with Joseph Signorile, PhD

RODALE

This edition first published by Rodale 2008
an imprint of Pan Macmillan Ltd
Pan Macmillan, 20 New Wharf Road, London N1 9RR
Basingstoke and Oxford
Associated companies throughout the world
www.panmacmillan.com

ISBN 978-1-9057-44-27-5

Copyright © 2008 Dr Arthur Agatston

All rights reserved. No part of this publication may be reproduced, stored in or introduced into a retrieval system, or transmitted, in any form, or by any means (electronic, mechanical, photocopying, recording or otherwise) without the prior written permission of the publisher. Any person who does any unauthorized act in relation to this publication may be liable to criminal prosecution and civil claims for damages.

5 7 9 8 6 4

A CIP catalogue record for this book is available from the British Library.

Printed and bound in the UK by CPI Mackays, Chatham ME5 8TD

This book is sold subject to the condition that it shall not, by way of trade or otherwise, be lent, re-sold, hired out, or otherwise circulated without the publisher's prior consent in any form of binding or cover other than that in which it is published and without a similar condition including this condition being imposed on the subsequent purchaser.

Notice
This book is intended as a reference volume only, not as a medical manual. The information given here is designed to help you make informed decisions about your health. It is not intended as a substitute for any treatment that you may have been prescribed by your doctor. If you suspect that you have a medical problem, we urge you to seek competent medical help.

The information in this book is meant to supplement, not replace, proper exercise training. All forms of exercise pose some inherent risks. The editor and publisher advise readers to take full responsibility for their safety and know their limits. Before practising the exercises in this book, be sure that you equipment is well maintained, and do not take risks beyond your level of experience, aptitude, training and fitness. The exercise programme in this book is not intended as a substitute for any exercise routine that may have been prescribed by your doctor. As with all exercise programmes, you should get your doctor's approval before beginning.

Mention of specific companies, organizations or authorities in this book does not imply endorsement by the publisher, nor does mention of specific companies, organizations or authorities in the book imply that they endorse the book, its author or the publisher.

Websites and telephone numbers given in this book were accurate at the time the book went to press.

Visit **www.panmacmillan.com** to read more about all our books and to buy them. You will also find features, author interviews and news of any author events, and you can sign up for e-newsletters so that you're always first to hear about our new releases.

We inspire and enable people to improve their lives and the world around them

To South Beach dieters everywhere

who have achieved a healthier way of life

And, as always, to my wife, Sari,

and sons, Evan and Adam

CONTENTS

PART I
Living The South Beach Diet

PART II
The South Beach Supercharged Fitness Programme

PART III
Supercharged Eating on The South Beach Diet

PREFACE

This book is a celebration and an affirmation. It is a celebration of the success of the South Beach Diet and it is an affirmation of the wide acceptance of the healthy eating principles we have continued to advance since the original South Beach Diet book was published in 2003. These principles are simple: choose nutrient-rich, high-fibre carbohydrates found in vegetables, fruits and whole grains; good, unsaturated fats; lean sources of protein and low-fat dairy.

This book also introduces a unique metabolism-revving exercise programme that works. The programme is based on the proven science behind interval training and core functional fitness.

For several years, readers of the original book and many of my patients have requested an update on the South Beach Diet. While the basic principles of the diet have not changed and are unlikely to change, volumes of new research have furthered our understanding of the importance of these principles. In fact, a major theme of mine when I speak to doctors and lay groups around the country is that the diet debates are over. We have progressed beyond the low-fat versus low-carb wars. We are at the point where there should no longer be confusion regarding the best diet approach for sustained weight loss and optimal health.

There is now a consensus of expert opinion that it is not the relative amounts of carbohydrate, protein and fat that are important but their quality. Today, the basis of an optimal diet and the South Beach Diet are one and the same. In fact, the healthy eating principles we stand by can be applied to almost anyone's particular dietary needs. Our diet principles are reflected not only in the most recent government recommendations but also in the guidelines of the many other organizations devoted to promoting good health.

We have learned a great deal over the past 5 years about how South

Beach dieters can best apply our healthy eating principles to their hectic everyday lives. We have learned about the pitfalls that some dieters experience and we have developed effective strategies to help them overcome these problems. One of these pitfalls is what I like to call the 'You Can Never Be Too Thin' syndrome, in which people who have reached a healthy weight and look good still want to lose more weight. I explain why this is a problem that can lead to yo-yo dieting and even more weight gain (and what you can do about it), beginning on page 67. We have also learned more about why some dieters plateau at a particular weight, and what they can do to successfully rev up their metabolisms and continue their weight loss successfully. Furthermore, we have learned a great deal in recent years about how individual nutrients in foods and drinks can protect your health. These include the phytonutrient resveratrol, which is found in one of my favourite foods (dark chocolate) and perhaps in one of yours (red wine).

Today we also know more about how and why the epidemics of obesity and diabetes have occurred, and ongoing research has taught us that the right diet is even more important than we thought just 5 years ago. In fact, in dozens of recent studies, the presence of belly fat has been convincingly associated with inflammation and appears to be a common denominator behind many of the diseases of the Western world. These fascinating new findings are helping us all better understand how to improve our own nutrition and health, along with that of our families.

One criticism of the first South Beach Diet book was that we did not include more on exercise. While I have always been a strong believer in the health benefits of exercise and said so in the original book, in 2003 I didn't feel that I had important new fitness information to communicate. At the time, our patient studies were based on dietary changes alone in order to show the efficacy of the diet and I didn't want to dilute our exciting new approach to healthy eating. Today, thanks to some eye-opening personal experiences, I do have important and exciting new fitness information to offer in the form of a unique three-phase exercise programme that dovetails perfectly with the three phases of the diet itself. To create the programme, I consulted two outstanding exercise specialists: Joseph Signorile, PhD, a well-known professor of exercise physiology at the University of Miami and Kris Belding, a Miami-based Pilates teacher who has worked with my wife, Sari, and me for several years.

I have always considered the South Beach Diet and my goal to make it a lifestyle a work in progress. As new information becomes available, we do not hesitate to integrate it into our programme. Naturally, as science marches forward, new developments in health, nutrition and fitness may supersede or conflict with our current knowledge. But even as new knowledge must influence our thinking, the core mission of the South Beach Diet remains consistent: to help you live happier and healthier lives.

My ability and that of my colleagues to successfully treat our patients has improved exponentially during my 30-year medical career. Practising medicine is more gratifying for me today than ever before because of the advances in medical and nutritional science. I am thankful that I have the opportunity to share some of this important information with you in this new book.

Dr Arthur Agatston

ACKNOWLEDGMENTS

It is impossible to thank all of the people – friends, doctors and partners – who have supported the South Beach Diet and influenced my work over the years. However, I would like to acknowledge those who have participated personally in the development and creation of this book.

First, I want to extend my deep appreciation to the South Beach dieters who have contributed their moving success stories to these pages. Your achievements are an inspiration.

I would also like to thank my collaborator, Dr Joseph Signorile and my Pilates teacher, Kris Belding, for helping me develop the South Beach Supercharged Fitness Programme for this book.

Special credit also goes to Marie Almon, my nutrition director, who has worked with me for many years counselling South Beach dieters and who has contributed greatly to the new meal plans and recipes. In addition, thanks go to Mindy Fox for developing the delicious dishes and to Samantha Cassetty, of SouthBeachDiet.com, for her nutrition advice.

At Rodale, I would like to thank publisher Liz Perl and my long-time editor and friend Marya Dalrymple, who has truly been a partner in the creation of this book. I would also like to acknowledge test kitchen manager JoAnn Brader, project editor Hope Clarke, photographer Thomas MacDonald and the best art director ever, Carol Angstadt.

Finally, I must once again credit my friend Linda Richman for making a phone call so many years ago and uttering seven life-changing words: 'My doctor needs to write a book.'

Above all, and always, I thank my wife and partner, Sari, and sons, Evan and Adam, for their constant support, enthusiasm and love.

PART I

Living
The South Beach Diet

Changing the Way We Live

The South Beach Diet was always intended to be more than just a diet. In fact, it was originally developed to help my cardiac and diabetes patients lose weight in order to prevent heart attacks and strokes. As a cardiologist, I have always felt that the South Beach Diet is less about dieting and more about living a long, healthy and active life. I wrote the original book in 2003 because I wanted to help change the way we eat. Now I have a new goal: I want to change the way we *live*, not only by helping people eat healthily and lose weight, if necessary, but also by helping them become more fit. We must begin to overcome the poor eating habits and sedentary lifestyle that are making us fatter and sicker every year.

Over the past several decades, we have witnessed an unexpected epidemic of obesity in the West. In the UK, nearly 25 per cent of adults over the age of 16 are obese and a third of our children are either overweight or obese. Moreover, a statistical report produced for the UK National Health Service in January 2008 shows that 60 per cent of men and over 70 per cent of women in the UK fail to meet the recommended weekly levels of physical activity. The results have been catastrophic.

This epidemic of obesity is causing an array of health problems that is much broader than we doctors ever imagined. Beyond the cosmetic concerns that pervade our culture, the list of real problems arising from our toxic lifestyle is getting ever longer. A partial list includes – and you may want to sit down for this – heart attack, stroke, prediabetes, diabetes, many types of cancer, Alzheimer's disease, macular degeneration, arthritis, osteoporosis, psoriasis, acne, depression and attention deficit disorders. And this is just a sampling.

It also appears that if we do not reverse the health course that we are on, the cost in human and economic terms will reach crisis proportions. Our poor diet and sedentary lifestyle are already exacting a steep toll in terms of mortality and money. And as the baby boom generation gets older, these health costs are likely to continue to soar.

The good news is that now that we better understand what's happening to us, we can start to create solutions.

A Sedentary Lifestyle

In order to develop strategies to halt and reverse the epidemic of obesity, we must be aware of the trends that have gradually but inexorably brought us to the crisis situation we are in today. I have found in my practice that by putting patients' current problems into a context they can understand, they can more easily become co-operative partners in moving towards solutions. Perhaps because I have a history degree (not all doctors have biology degrees), I also find that tracing today's health problems back to their original roots is fascinating.

The truth is that while our bad diet and unhealthy lifestyle have been many decades in the making, the toxic changes in the way we live have really accelerated in recent years. Our DNA is designed to live, eat and exercise the way our hunter-gatherer ancestors did and it hasn't changed substantially since that time. But we no longer live in the wild. We don't have famine in this country to keep us thin. We no longer burn calories hunting and gathering our food.

On top of that, a completely sedentary lifestyle has gradually crept in, invention by incredible invention. Due to the march of technology, we sit in front of computers both at work and at home. Machines and gadgets lift, move and carry things for us. We communicate by e-mail and many of us don't even walk around the office to chat with colleagues as often as we used to! While studies document how much less physical exertion we're doing, we really don't need research studies to appreciate the trend. All we have to do is look around.

The preponderance of labour-saving devices, from tractors and fork-lifts to remote controls and the personal computer, has had a major impact on the number of calories we expend daily at home and at work. These devices have also had devastating effects on our muscles, bones, tendons and ligaments. Sitting bent over at a computer for most of the day is simply not good for our health. In Chapter 5, 'Boomeritis: The New Epidemic!' I talk about these evolving physical problems and their solutions. And in Part II of the book, I present the South Beach Supercharged Fitness Programme. Not only will this 20-minute-a-day programme help you burn more calories even when you're not working out, it will also strengthen the key core muscles in your abdomen, back, pelvis and hips. It's your core muscles that help you avoid the back pain and other muscle problems that so often result from our sedentary lives.

Missing Our Nutrients

Our unhealthy lifestyle is made even worse by our poor diet. Since man began growing fields of grain about 10,000 years ago and developed the ability to cultivate fruits and vegetables, the nutritional content of our foods has seriously deteriorated. This is because we tend to breed plants for hardiness, taste and aesthetics, not nutrients. Today, the fruits and vegetables we find in most supermarkets are larger, sweeter and better-looking than those our ancestors gathered. The problem is that they also have less fibre and fewer vitamins, minerals and other nutrients than is optimal for our general health – not to mention our waistlines. Luckily, more and more of us are embracing organic foods, traditional fruits and vegetables and sustainable farming methods, all trends that are bringing food back to its more natural and nutritious state. In Chapter 7, 'Supercharged Foods for Better Health', I recommend some foods with powerful nutritional benefits that can help you stay healthy and avoid the host of chronic and degenerative diseases currently affecting so many of us.

Over-processed Food

Beyond our desire to cultivate and produce food almost exclusively to please our tastebuds, other social and technological trends have affected our food supply for the worse. A few generations ago, our great grandparents walked to local markets on a daily basis to buy whatever produce they didn't grow themselves, as well as fresh bread and other food for their families' next meals. They could only travel to local markets and take home what they were able to carry. With the advent of the automobile and the home refrigerator, however, it became possible to travel further to shop and people could take home enough food to feed their families for a week or two. But for that to be possible, foods had to have longer shelf lives. This led to supermarkets and to food processing, which, unfortunately, removed important nutrients while adding substances like sodium and trans fats to prevent spoilage. In a sense, we began digesting our food in factories instead of in our intestines.

It's only now that we are appreciating the deleterious effects these technological 'advances' have had on our weight and on our health. In Chapter 3, 'A Diet You Can Live With . . . For Life', I discuss the health and character of a Mediterranean society that thrived without many of our modern advances and I show you how we can learn from this remarkable example.

We Must Act Now

If you're like me, you find how we got into this sad state not only depressing but scary. But there is hope if we take action today. Because we finally understand so much of what has gone wrong, we can use our advanced technologies to turn things around. We now know that our increasing waistlines, poor physical fitness and worsening health are not different problems but rather, part of the same problem. We now know that what's good for our waistlines is also good for our hearts, our brains and our general health.

We must ask the food industry, including traditional and fast-food restaurants, to help make healthy food more convenient and convenient

5 YEARS of SUCCESS

Deborah M., aged 43: We Are Healthier People because of the Way We Live

It was 2003 and my partner had very high blood pressure that wasn't being controlled, even with medication. I was very overweight and knew that we both needed to make a change. The South Beach Diet had just come out and I went to the bookshop to look over a copy. The first thing I turned to was the recipe section. It was great. I love to cook and was thrilled that I didn't have to give it up.

After reading the book, I realized that I ate too many bad carbs all day, such as crackers and biscuits. Once I stopped eating enriched white flour, I noticed a complete change in everything about me, including my mood and energy levels, and I started losing weight. Within a year, I lost 20.4kg (45lb) and my partner lost 9kg (20lb). Although he still takes medication for high blood pressure, it's under control.

Now I'm the go-to girl at work for healthy-food questions. When we have company lunches, everyone knows they can count on me to bring in something healthy. I have learned how to take bad carbs out of a recipe and replace them with good carbs. I am passionate about telling people to read food labels! Don't be fooled; buy only whole-grain products. If it says 'enriched white flour', find something else.

In 2005, we decided to foster a child and an 11-year-old boy came to live with us. He was overweight and already taking medication for high blood pressure. He lived on junk food. We took him to a doctor, who told us that he shouldn't go on a diet – he should start living a healthy lifestyle. I decided to give him the same healthy food my partner and I were eating, but I told him he could eat as much as he wanted. He also started exercising. Simply by eating the right foods and being more active, he started losing weight fairly quickly. By the end of 4 months, he was off the blood pressure medication and by the time he left us 18 months later, he had lost 13.6kg (30lb). While living with us, he learned how to read food labels and make good food choices. I hope he continues to live a healthy life. My partner often jokes that I should open my home to people who want to lose weight.

I am happy with my weight loss but even happier that my partner and I are healthier people because of the way we live and eat. I am a true believer in the South Beach Diet way of life.

food healthier. We must supply our schoolchildren with nutrient-rich meals and make nutrition education and physical education integral parts of our schools' curricula. We must reinstate the family table and, despite our busy lives, try to provide fresh foods for our children on a regular basis. We must also create communities and workplaces where good food and exercise opportunities are readily available. These steps will make for healthier, happier, more motivated and more productive citizens. I guarantee it.

In the chapters that follow, I explain the lifelong benefits of adopting a healthy diet and fitness programme. And in Parts II and III, I offer the specifics on how to get there. Whether you have 4.5kg (10lb), 45kg (100lb) or no weight to lose, whether you are active or inactive, helping you to become healthy and fit – for life – is the mission of this book. So read on and learn more. We can beat the epidemic of obesity. And we can all become part of the solution.

The Basics of the South Beach Diet

Recently, an Associated Press story about the New York City subway system caught my eye. According to subway officials, a leading cause of subway delays is crash dieters who faint on the platform or on the train. That's right – crash dieters who pass out and require medical help are a top cause of transport delays. Clearly, these people are not eating properly and they're certainly not following the South Beach Diet!

On the three phases of the South Beach Diet, you will eat three meals a day and at least two snacks. You will eat until you are pleasantly full and you will not walk around feeling dizzy or hungry. We don't want you to skip meals or snacks. You'll be eating satisfying portions of real food, including nutrient-rich, high-fibre carbohydrates (vegetables, fruits and whole grains); lean sources of protein; good unsaturated fats and low-fat dairy products. You can eat dessert on even the strictest phase of the diet (in fact, we recommend it) and enjoy an occasional glass or two of wine with a meal after the first 2 weeks. South Beach dieters do not faint from lack of food on the underground, on the street or anywhere else.

The goals of the South Beach Diet are to help you lose weight safely

THE SOUTH BEACH DIET PHASES
IN A NUTSHELL

In Part III of this book, 'Supercharged Eating on the South Beach Diet', beginning on page 147, you'll find all the tools you need to get started and proceed through the diet's three phases. But I want to give you a quick overview right here, so you'll understand its foundation.

Phase 1: This is the shortest and strictest phase of the diet, lasting only 2 weeks. Phase 1 is for people who have a substantial amount of weight to lose or experience significant cravings for sugary foods and refined starches. During this phase, you'll jump-start your weight loss and stabilize your blood sugar levels to minimize cravings by eating a diet based on healthy lean protein (fish and shellfish, chicken and turkey, lean cuts of meat and soya); lots of vegetables and plenty of salads; beans and other pulses; nuts; low-fat cheese; eggs; low-fat dairy and good unsaturated fats, such as extra-virgin olive oil. You'll enjoy three satisfying meals a day plus two snacks and you'll even be able to have some dessert. What you won't be eating are starches (bread, pasta and rice) or sugars (including fruits and fruit juices). While this may seem hard at first, your cravings will soon disappear and you won't feel hungry all the time. Remember that in just 2 weeks, you'll be adding many of these foods back into your life. Also keep in mind that exercise during this and all of the phases of the diet is important to your overall health and will improve your results.

Phase 1 gives positive reinforcement because you lose weight fairly rapidly over the 2-week period, but the main purpose of this phase is to stabilize blood sugar and eliminate cravings. You then have much better control over what you eat. And while the rapid weight loss is exciting and gives you the incentive to keep on losing, it's important to move on to Phase 2 to begin more gradual weight loss and the evolution from diet to lifestyle.

and stay healthy and fit for the rest of your life – and never walk around feeling famished and light-headed.

The South Beach Diet is not a high-protein, low-carbohydrate diet, nor is it a low-fat diet. It is a nutritionally sound diet that consists of a wide variety of wholesome foods and teaches you how to make better food choices for life.

Phase 2: People who have 4.5kg (10lb) or less to lose, who don't have problems with cravings or who simply want to improve their health can start the diet with Phase 2. If you're moving on to Phase 2 from Phase 1, you'll find that your weight will continue to drop steadily (although more slowly) and your cravings will subside. You'll gradually re-introduce many of the foods that were off-limits on Phase 1, including more good carbohydrates, such as whole fruits, wholegrain breads, wholewheat pasta and brown rice, as well as some root vegetables (like sweet potatoes). You'll even be able to have a glass of red or white wine with lunch or dinner on occasion. Don't be discouraged by your slower weight loss during this phase. Your goal is to reach a weight that's healthy for you, achieve permanent weight loss and develop a healthy lifestyle. Otherwise, it's just a quick fix.

Phase 3: This phase begins once you reach your healthy weight. The principles of Phase 3 are guidelines for the way all of us should be eating, even those who've never had a weight problem. At this point in the diet, you'll fully understand how to make good food choices while maintaining that healthy weight. You'll have learned the pecking order of foods (from good to not so good). You will know to choose a higher-fibre, nutrient-rich sweet potato over a baked white jacket potato. You'll know to choose brown or wild rice over white rice, blueberries over watermelon and overall maximize your consumption of healthy fruits, vegetables and whole grains. You'll be able to easily monitor your body's response to particular foods and you'll find yourself naturally making the right choices most of the time. Remember, once you reach Phase 3, no food is completely off-limits. You can enjoy a decadent dessert on occasion and will probably find you've satisfied that sweet tooth after just a few bites.

Choose the Good Carbs

Do you know the difference between a good carbohydrate and a bad one? Many of my patients didn't until we published our original diet book 5 years ago. In fact, until fairly recently, even many medical professionals did not know much about how carbohydrates differ. For instance, it turns out that fibre plays a very important role in what makes a carbohydrate good.

The concept of dietary fibre relating to disease was first introduced by Dr Denis Burkitt, a British army surgeon who served in Africa in the 1960s, but its role in nutrition did not become widely appreciated until the early 1980s. That's when Dr David Jenkins, of the University of Toronto, introduced the concept of the glycaemic index, a method of classifying carbohydrates based on their potential to raise blood sugar levels, which is in part due to the type of starch, sugar or fibre they contain. (I discuss the glycaemic index in more detail in the next chapter.) Additionally, it wasn't until the last decade that we realized that high-fibre good carbs are also great sources of literally thousands of micronutrients known as phytochemicals, including the antioxidants that are essential for preventing disease and simply keeping us healthy.

When it comes to fibre, it's important to know that there are two types – soluble and insoluble – and both will help you achieve your weight loss goals. Soluble fibre is found mainly in vegetables, fruits, pulses, barley, oats and oat bran. It slows down digestion, so food stays in your stomach longer, making you feel satisfied longer. Insoluble fibre is found mainly in wheat, especially in wheat bran and other whole grains. It speeds up the movement of food through your intestines, thereby helping to prevent constipation.

Unfortunately, as I noted in the last chapter, fibre is often removed from grains during processing to produce a smoother texture and to extend the shelf life of breads and other baked goods. Without fibre, processed grains become essentially chains of glucose (sugar) molecules known as starches, which are devoid of nutrients. These starches are rapidly digested and converted into the simple sugars that can cause a sudden spike in blood sugar. In fact, a piece of white bread will raise your blood sugar faster than a teaspoon of table sugar will. That's why highly processed baked goods and sugary low-fibre cereals are amongst the worst carbs you can eat.

Let's say you typically start your day with a bowl of sweetened cereal or a Danish pastry. Your breakfast is largely free of fibre and nutrients and is converted into simple sugars very quickly. When your blood sugar rises, your pancreas (a small, flat organ that lies behind your stomach) responds by producing insulin, the hormone that facilitates the movement of blood sugar and fat from the bloodstream into your cells. This is a crucial step that ensures that the energy you consume in the form of food gets into your body's tissues, where it is burned, stored or incorporated into hormones in order to keep you functioning and healthy. But when you consume a meal of nearly pure starch or sugar, your pancreas has to produce more insulin than it normally does. Once that additional insulin kicks in, your blood sugar falls abruptly. While you may feel satisfied and energized for a while, relatively soon after your meal, when the sugar is cleared from your bloodstream, your sugar high rapidly becomes a sugar low. And as your blood sugar drops, you feel tired, grumpy and hungry again.

It's due to these exaggerated swings in blood sugar that many people are walking around much of the time in search of another sugary or starchy snack – a quick fix – to relieve their food cravings. Over time, this cycle will disrupt your metabolism, making you susceptible to a condition called prediabetes or metabolic syndrome. (I will tell you more about prediabetes in later chapters.) Already a quarter of the world's adults are affected by this condition, which, if left untreated, can cause an increase in heart attacks and strokes and eventually lead to full-blown diabetes.

Choose the Good Fats

More than a decade ago, when I first began suggesting to my heart patients that they should eat more good fats, it was tantamount to committing medical heresy. Today, nutrition experts unanimously agree that good fats are important. This is great news, especially for people who have suffered on very low-fat diets that left them feeling unsatisfied. In fact, diets that severely limit fat have proven very difficult to stay on. We need good fats because they're essential for building cell membranes; for nerve, heart and brain health (fats compose 60 per cent of the brain); and for nearly all of the body's basic functions. In addition, fats slow the digestion of carbohydrates and make food taste better, helping you feel satisfied. However, you do have to be careful about which fats you consume. Just as all carbohydrates are not the same, all fats are not the same. Some are good, some are bad and some are really terrible.

Good fats are the unsaturated fatty acids our bodies need to survive. Unsaturated fats are either monounsaturated or polyunsaturated. Mono-unsaturated fats can be found mainly in olive, peanut, avocado and rape-seed oils. There are two types of polyunsaturated fats – omega-3s and omega-6s. Omega-3s are found in some nuts; flaxseed and other seeds; and all seafood, especially oily cold-water fish such as salmon, tuna, sardines and herring. Omega-6 fats are found in corn, sunflower and sesame oils and also in grains. Both omega-3s and omega-6s are called essential fatty acids because they are required by the body and must be obtained through food sources or supplementation.

Omega-6 fats are dependent on interactions with omega-3s for their optimal health benefits, but omega-6s are considered good fats only when consumed in moderation and in proper proportion with omega-3s. A normal ratio of omega-6s to omega-3s in a healthy diet should be about 2–4:1. Currently, the ratio of most Western diets is more like 10–20:1, largely due to increased over-use of processed oils and the increase in consumption of grain-fed beef as grains contain a lot of omega-6 oils. (Grass-fed cattle and wild game, which eat a more natural diet, have relatively more omega-3s.) When too many omega-6 fats are consumed, they tend to be pro-inflammatory, whereas omega-3 fats are anti-inflammatory. Because we are getting too many omega-6s and not enough omega-3s, as a society we have, in a sense, become hyper-inflamed. And, as more studies are showing, this constant state of inflammation can cause or exacerbate a range of health problems, from heart attack and cancer to Alzheimer's disease.

Although I don't generally recommend dietary supplements (I prefer that you get your nutrients from whole foods), I make an exception when it comes to omega-3s. In fact, to make up the shortfall, I recommend a fish oil supplement for most people, especially those who don't eat fish at least twice weekly.

The two active ingredients to look for in omega-3 or fish oil supplements are EPA (eicosapentaenoic acid) and DHA (docosahexaenoic acid). If you read the supplement label, you will see the amount of these nutrients listed in milligrams (mg). You should take between 1,000 and 2,000 milligrams of EPA and DHA daily, with the approval of your doctor. For some conditions, such as a severe elevation in triglycerides, higher doses are recommended. Interestingly, DHA is present in large quantities in the brain and has been added to many brands of infant formula since 2002.

We do need to be a little careful, however, even with the good fats. As good as they are, they are also calorie dense and should be consumed judiciously during all phases of the South Beach Diet. I suggest that you limit added oils to approximately 30ml (2tbsp) per day (no, you don't have to eat your salads dry!) and limit nuts to about 30g (1oz) a day. While many nuts do contain good fats, it's too easy to unconsciously eat too many.

Avoid the Bad Fats

Bad fats include saturated fats (often referred to as animal fats), which are found primarily in fatty cuts of beef, lamb and pork; in poultry with the skin and in full-fat dairy products. There are also plant sources of saturated fats, including coconut, palm and palm kernel oils, but the jury is still out on how bad they are. In fact, research suggests that some of these plant oils may have health benefits. The *really* bad fats are trans fats, which are created when manufacturers add hydrogen to vegetable oil – a process called hydrogenation – to increase the shelf life and stability of foods. Trans fats can be found in hard margarines (but not in most soft margarines or vegetable oils), lard, foods fried in hydrogenated oils and many packaged snack foods containing hydrogenated or partially hydrogenated oils.

Most bad fats, especially the trans fats, deserve their bad reputation. We've known for some time that a high intake of saturated fats from animal sources is linked to a greater risk of heart attack or stroke because these saturated fats raise bad LDL (low-density lipoprotein) cholesterol. And we now know that trans fats not only increase LDL, they also reduce good HDL (high-density lipoprotein) cholesterol and may even play a role in metabolic problems, obesity, infertility and many other health problems of the Western world. Increasingly there are moves to make consumers more aware of the trans fat content of their food. In the US, the Food and Drug Administration (FDA) has from 2006 required food manufacturers to list the amount of trans fats on packaging. In the UK

5 YEARS of SUCCESS

DANNY S., aged 42: My Insurance Policy against Weight Gain

I was one of the first people to go on the South Beach Diet; in fact, I was a story in Dr Agatston's first book. I'm delighted to be able to share my continued success.

I actually went to Dr Agatston about 8 years ago because I had to lose weight – I was 185.5cm (6'1") and weighed over 118kg (260lb). I was 35, and although my health was okay, I realized that if I didn't do something about my weight, I could easily develop a problem in the future. I lost 27kg (60lb), and I've kept it off. The diet is my fallback, my insurance policy against weight gain. It definitely saves me from ever going back to that high weight. If I do put on a few pounds or find that my cravings have returned, I go right back on Phase 1 for a few days, lose the weight, and reinforce my healthy eating principles.

Once I began losing weight, I began to work out. I had never done any regular exercise before. I suddenly felt so much better, so much more alive and limber, that I no longer thought it would be a challenge to go to the gym. Now I weight train three times a week and do cardio five times a week.

The diet taught me what triggers my overeating. I know that bread is a huge problem for me, so I've learned to moderate it. I'll only eat bread – mostly wholemeal – in the morning. I rarely eat white bread. And there are a lot of other things besides a sandwich that I can have for lunch. If you're really addicted to something, the desire doesn't go away immediately, but you can learn how to control it. The good thing about the South Beach Diet is that you don't have to give up any foods completely once you've reached your goal weight. It doesn't make sense to deny yourself something for the rest of your life. The diet showed me that it's possible to take off the weight you need to take off and then maintain it. If you do put a few pounds back on, it's not the end of the world. You can go back on the right phase and take them off.

and Australia, food manufacturers are encouraged to list the amounts where they claim foods to be low in trans fats, to assist consumers in making healthier choices.

Choose Lean Protein

Protein foods are digested slowly and do not produce the spike in blood sugar that stimulates hunger and overeating. They also satisfy you, so you won't be walking around feeling hungry all the time. On the South Beach Diet, you can eat lean cuts of beef, lamb and pork; skinless white meat chicken and turkey; game meats; fish and shellfish; soya products; beans and other pulses; eggs and fat-free and low-fat dairy products. The amount of protein you require varies, depending on your age, activity level and any illness you may have. Young athletes, for example, need a lot of protein, while older, sedentary individuals require less. For people with kidney problems, protein may have to be severely limited.

Some people have asked me how a cardiologist can recommend that people eat red meat even though it contains saturated fat. I'm not advising anyone to eat a steady diet of high-fat cuts, such as brisket or rib-eye steak or to eat red meat daily. Lean cuts of meat, however, are excellent sources of protein, iron, zinc and B vitamins. And, in terms of maintaining a healthy weight, it's far more preferable to eat lean meat than to gorge on highly processed refined carbs.

This doesn't mean that the South Beach Diet isn't for vegetarians. Many vegetable sources of protein, such as soya and pulses (beans, lentils, chickpeas and so on), are very satisfying. Vegetarians will also benefit from eating good monounsaturated and polyunsaturated fats, as well as good carbohydrates, from the wide variety of fruits, vegetables, pulses and whole grains we recommend.

Go High Fibre

I've already talked a bit about fibre, but I can't say enough about it. That's because one of my goals as a cardiologist is to get people to eat more fibre-rich foods. I have no doubt that if they did, there would be far fewer cases of obesity around the world. Why? As I noted earlier, high-fibre foods slow the rate of digestion of starches and sugars, which blunts the swings in blood sugar that lead to cravings. It's not surprising, then, that people who consume higher amounts of fibre gain less weight over a period of years. They just aren't hungry all the time!

In addition to helping people maintain a healthy weight, fibre also plays an important role in combating a number of diseases. At one time, people were advised to load up on fibre as a means of preventing colon cancer. This belief was based on research that showed that countries with the highest rates of dietary fibre consumption had the lowest rates of colon cancer. While later studies put this theory into doubt, fibre does appear to protect against heart disease and type 2 diabetes. A major US study at Harvard University of more than 40,000 male health professionals found that those who ate lots of dietary fibre – especially cereal fibre – had a 40 per cent lower risk of coronary heart disease, compared with men who ate the least fibre. A study of female nurses, also conducted at Harvard, found that fibre had the same heart-healthy effects on women. And numerous studies have linked fibre consumption to a reduced risk of diabetes (see page 77 for one example).

Today, government guidelines in the UK recommend eating 15g (½oz) fibre for every 1,000 calories consumed daily. That adds up to about 25–35g (1–1¼oz) per day, depending on how many calories you take in. But most of us don't get anywhere close to this amount. In fact, according to the British Nutrition Foundation, the average daily intake is a *total* of 15g of fibre. That's why I always remind people to keep eating plenty of fibre-rich whole fruits and vegetables, pulses and whole grains.

· · · · · · · · · · · ·

Now that you understand the value of good carbs, good fats, lean protein and fibre, you can see why they're the mainstays of the South Beach Diet. You'll find it's easy to incorporate healthy nutrients into your meals by choosing what appeals to you most from the Foods to Enjoy lists in Part III. You can follow our suggested Meal Plans for Phases 1 and 2 verbatim or use them to inspire meals of your own.

You now have the tools to eat great food, look great and feel great. You'll find it easier than ever to follow a healthy diet as a lifestyle.

3

A Diet You Can Live With . . . For Life

When we originally published the South Beach Diet in 2003, some people asked me about long-term studies documenting its value. Others questioned whether anyone can successfully stick to a diet. And over the ensuing years, some articles were written claiming simply that 'diets don't work'. This can certainly be true, unless the diet teaches you how to make better food choices and evolves into a healthy, sustainable lifestyle.

In that regard, I like to point out a diet and lifestyle experiment that lasted hundreds of years with remarkable success. It involves the inhabitants of the Greek island of Crete. Of course, the people of Crete didn't know they were part of an experiment. They didn't know they were on a diet or participating in an exercise programme. They didn't weigh their food or count calories, carbs or fats (in fact, their diet was relatively high in fat). They didn't go to the gym. And they certainly weren't walking around hungry. In fact, they were quite satisfied with a wonderful range of food choices. Yet even with this seeming lack of regard for diet and exercise, they were not overweight and they enjoyed low rates of heart disease, diabetes, cancer and other diseases.

How did they accomplish this? They were simply surrounded by a wide variety of fruits, vegetables and whole grains. There were ample quantities of lean meats and fish. They consumed plenty of fat, but it was predominantly healthy Mediterranean oils, in particular olive oil. And there was, in fact, a great deal of exercise in the form of long walks and vigorous exertion as part of their daily routine. They were happy and healthy without working at it or even thinking about it. Unfortunately, today the Western lifestyle has found its way to Crete and its men and women are showing it – in both their abdominal girth and their health profile.

Why Are We So Fat?

In the UK and the US, our epidemic of obesity and diabetes really took off over the past 20 years and has continued at a steady pace to the present day. Coincidentally, the mid 1980s was when the UK Department of Health along with the Food Standards Agency (FSA), began to aggressively promote the benefits of a low-fat, high-carbohydrate diet. This was eventually reflected by the first national pictorial food model, the Balance of Good Health plate model, developed in 1994, which emphasized bread, potatoes, rice, pasta and cereals as the basis of a healthy diet. Fats and oils were to be used sparingly. Was this the wrong advice? Did it have a role in the fattening of the British population? I believe the answers to these two questions are yes and yes.

These recommendations were based on what was felt to be the best scientific evidence at the time. Much, if not most, of the nutritional research we have today was simply not available back then. In the US the rationale for the low-fat, high-carb approach was largely predicated upon population studies performed after World War II. The most influential were those conducted by Ancel Keys, PhD, a US physiologist. Dr Keys looked at the relationship between diet, blood cholesterol and heart disease in industrialized and non-industrialized countries. Industrialized countries, such as those in Western Europe and the US, had a high fat intake associated with high cholesterol levels and heart attack. Non-industrialized countries had low-fat diets, low cholesterol levels and low rates of heart attack.

A glaring exception in the non-industrialized category was the Greek island of Crete, which, as I noted above, had a relatively high-fat diet, yet a low rate of heart disease. But Crete was considered a fluke and ignored at the time. So the UK, along with the US, went on a low-fat, high-carbohydrate diet and got increasingly fatter.

How did we go so wrong?

At the time of the national recommendations, the thought was that the diet depicted in the Balance of Good Health plate would mimic the diet composition of the non-industrialized world, where there was almost no obesity or heart disease. The problem was that in the national recommendations, no distinction was drawn between good carbs and bad carbs or between good fats and bad fats. While sugar was not recommended, starches (the so-called complex carbohydrates) were. It was simply not known at the time that low-fibre starches, such as white bread and potatoes, raised blood sugar just about as fast as simple sugars did, or in other words, they had what's known as a 'high glycaemic index (GI)'. As for fats, studies showing the overall health benefits of good fats (such as omega-3-rich oils), including their positive effects on the heart, had not yet been performed.

In response to the conventional – and misguided – wisdom of the time, the food industry began to produce reduced-fat baked goods, including cakes, biscuits and pastries made with refined white flour and varying amounts of sugar. In order to avoid the use of saturated fats in these products, much of the fat was replaced by vegetable oils. However, to give these foods a longer shelf life, a more solid consistency for baking and acceptable texture in the mouth, the oils were hydrogenated or partially hydrogenated vegetable oils which caused the formation of the harmful trans fats I talked about on page 15. These are directly associated with heart attack, stroke, diabetes and other serious health problems.

Ironically, although trans fats were created as a healthier alternative to saturated fats, they turned out to be worse. For years, most of us thought we could eat these high GI, trans fat-laden foods with impunity. We were mistaken. And as a nation the UK got fatter.

How Eating Can Make You Hungry – And Fat

Thanks to ongoing research in the science of food, nutrition and diabetes, by the early 1990s, I had a pretty good idea of where our diet had gone wrong. It became clear that as a society, in our attempt to limit fat, we were consuming ever-higher amounts of bad carbohydrates – in other words, more of the sugary sweets and refined starches that are essentially devoid of fibre and other nutrients. This was causing exaggerated swings in our blood sugar, which resulted in cravings for more refined carbs and the constant hunger that I described in Chapter 2.

The reason we were so hungry all the time also became clearer when I learned about the glycaemic index, a measure of how the carbohydrates in an individual food can affect blood sugar. The foods that keep blood sugar nice and stable – the ones that don't cause dramatic blood sugar swings – are those that are low on the glycaemic index. These include whole grains, most vegetables and low-sugar fruits (such as berries), which are digested slowly, making you feel full and satisfied for a longer period of time. Fibre is a major determinant in establishing a food's glycaemic index, but there are other factors as well, such as the degree to which a food is processed, how long it's cooked and its acidity. However, as useful as the glycaemic index can be for guesstimating how certain foods will affect your blood sugar levels, it doesn't tell the whole story. We have learned a great deal more about food and how it works in our bodies since the glycaemic index was first identified. The expanded Foods to Enjoy and Foods to Avoid lists in this book reflect this growing body of knowledge.

It's no wonder that back then my patients were getting fatter as they filled up on the high-glycaemic carbs (the pastas, breads and cereals made from white flour) that we were mistakenly recommending as a substitute for fatty meats and full-fat dairy products. Once I understood more about the glycaemic index, however, it didn't take me long to see that these essentially fibreless, starch-laden foods were making patients hungrier due to the swings in their blood sugar.

And, of course, the hungrier they got, the more they ate and the more weight they gained. It was an endless cycle. And as they got fatter, they also became prediabetic and diabetic. Because of new research in this area,

I also began to understand that there were as many misconceptions about these diseases as there were about what constitutes a good diet.

Misunderstood Prediabetes

Most people mistakenly associate all diabetes with a lack of insulin, the hormone produced by the pancreas that clears sugar (glucose) and fat out of the bloodstream and moves it into the cells after meals. Type 1 diabetes, formerly called juvenile diabetes, is characterized by the inability of the pancreas to make enough insulin. But in prediabetes, which often leads to type 2 diabetes, the problem is not too little insulin, but the resistance of cells to the hormone's effects. In fact, in prediabetes, blood insulin levels actually remain high after a meal until the excess insulin finally opens the floodgates, allowing glucose to move from the bloodstream into the cells. This results in a rapid fall in blood sugar, which is known as reactive hypoglycaemia because the reaction or blood sugar drop (hypoglycaemia), comes sooner after a meal than a normal, gradual drop would. It's why the insulin resistance associated with prediabetes only exacerbates the already exaggerated swings in blood sugar and consequent cravings caused by bad carbohydrates. And it's why prediabetics are almost always hungry again soon after a meal and tend to gulp down their food to bring up their sagging blood sugar.

Prediabetes typically occurs in individuals with a genetic predisposition to accumulating belly fat. In fact, you can recognize people with prediabetes on the street. They're the ones walking around with large bellies and relatively thin arms and legs. They also tend to have high blood pressure, low levels of good HDL (high-density lipoprotein) cholesterol and high levels of triglycerides (a fat-storage molecule found in blood and fat cells).

But how does prediabetes lead to type 2 diabetes? Over time, your pancreas tends to burn out from the stress of producing extra insulin to overcome the insulin resistance of your tissues and clear sugar and fat from your blood in a timely manner. It is at this point that your sugar remains high for many hours after a meal and type 2 diabetes is diagnosed.

IT WASN'T STRESS THAT MADE US FAT

Many overweight individuals, including many of my patients, believe that their food cravings have to do with stress rather than blood sugar swings. They're embarrassed by their lack of willpower and assure me that it's the fight with the boss or the spouse, the 2-hour wait in traffic or the children's bad report cards that made them wolf down that giant muffin, handful of sweets or piece of chocolate cake. Even some scientists have suggested that the current obesity epidemic is due to the psychological stresses of living in modern times.

While I acknowledge that some people do overeat to compensate in times of stress, I take issue with those who believe it's the cause of our obesity epidemic. I like to point out that stress didn't just begin recently and we didn't start getting really fat in Europe until the last decade. We were enjoying unprecedented wealth and a high standard of living. This was also the period when the character of our food supply changed and our physical activity rapidly declined, largely due to increased use of the personal computer and other labour-saving gadgets.

The point is, it was in the midst of peace and prosperity that we became so fat. With what we know today, it's clear that it was not our psychological state, but what we ate and how sedentary we became that was the primary cause.

During the prediabetes phase, most people's fasting blood sugar is borderline, normal or even low. For this reason, many of my patients initially believe that their risk of heart attack and stroke increases only if they become diabetic. This belief is wrong! During the prediabetes phase, when fasting blood sugar is still normal, insulin resistance is present and it takes longer to clear fats and sugar from the bloodstream. It's that extra fat hanging around after a meal that often penetrates the walls of the blood vessels supplying the heart muscle, brain and other organs. This is the origin of the atherosclerotic plaque that clogs these vessels and eventually leads to a heart attack or stroke. And, yes, this can and does occur during prediabetes, well before type 2 diabetes is diagnosed.

Again, this is relatively recent information. Prediabetes was first described in the US in 1988 by Dr Gerald Reaven, of Stanford University and we're still learning about the havoc it wreaks on our blood vessels and overall health. I talk more about the origins and the health implications of prediabetes in Chapter 6, 'Bye-Bye Belly Fat'.

Creating the South Beach Diet

Armed with the conviction that our problem was not too much fat or too many carbohydrates in our diet, but the wrong fats and the wrong carbs, I decided to try a good-fats, good-carbs diet on myself and on my patients. I also chose to recommend lean sources of protein that didn't have excess saturated animal fat.

I decided on a three-phase approach, with each phase having a distinct purpose. The first phase would be strict and last just 2 weeks. It would jump-start the diet and get rid of cravings. While studies had shown the positive psychological effects of early rapid weight loss, we intentionally did not want this rapid weight loss to continue for too long. Not only would dieters miss out on key nutrients in fruits and whole grains but over time, rapid weight loss would become counter-productive. For this reason, we designed the second phase for slower weight loss, so that my patients could learn how they reacted to whole grains and whole fruits as they gradually re-introduced them. It would be an educational stage and a transition from diet to lifestyle. The third phase, or maintenance phase, would become a permanent, healthy lifestyle and a guide for the way we should all eat, whether or not we need to lose weight or improve our blood sugar and cholesterol levels. Because studies showed that well-timed snacks help prevent the sugar lows that can bring on cravings in the late morning, late afternoon and/or evening, I included what I called strategic snacking on all the phases, but especially the first phase of the diet.

I felt that this approach was not only a true departure from the nationally recommended low-fat, high-carb diet at the time, but also from the then-popular low-carb, high-fat diet and severely fat-restricted diets. I didn't want to give my heart patients a high-fat diet that included liberal amounts of saturated fat that might accelerate their heart disease, nor did I want to severely restrict total fat. First, in my experience, patients had great difficulty adhering to such a diet. Second, with a low-fat, high-carb diet, I had seen patients' good cholesterol decrease and their triglycerides and blood sugar shoot up. Third, I wanted my patients to have the benefit of good fats; studies had convinced me that they were good for both the heart and general health. In addition, having a certain amount of good fat in the diet made the food taste better and improved satiety and compliance.

The First South Beach Dieter – Me!

My interest in finding the ideal diet went beyond concern for my patients, however. In fact, it was a little bit selfish. I'd had my own bad experience with the low-fat, high-carb approach and had gained weight due to what I now realize were very poor choices when it came to carbohydrates. I had even developed my own middle-aged fat-storage depot where my once-trim belly used to be. Furthermore, I found I was running out of steam in the late afternoon, which often led me to a mad dash to the doctors' lounge, where I would inhale a low-fat (but sugary) muffin and a cup of coffee to help me make it through the rest of the day. I now realize that this was a sign of reactive hypoglycaemia due to insulin resistance and that the refined carbs and sugar I was eating only exacerbated the problem.

So I designated myself as the first candidate for my new diet. I was amazed to observe my belly fat start to disappear in just 2 weeks and I quickly felt energized. I no longer needed to make those late-afternoon dashes to the doctors' lounge to hike up my falling blood sugar.

With the confidence and excitement that resulted from my own experience, I recruited Marie Almon, at that time the chief clinical dietitian at Mount Sinai Medical Center in Miami Beach, to help me develop meal plans for each phase of the diet, based on the principles of nutrient-dense, fibre-rich carbohydrates; healthy fats and lean sources of protein. When this was accomplished, we began counselling patients, explaining the three phases and handing out photocopies of the Foods to Enjoy and Foods to Avoid lists and the meal plans.

I was amazed by my patients' success. After years of frustration with the low-fat diet, I was now witnessing wonderful results as their belly fat seemed to melt away and their cholesterol improved, triglycerides dropped and prediabetes and early type 2 diabetes reversed. I was also surprised and gratified to learn that my patients were mailing and faxing their photocopied diet guidelines to friends and relatives around the country. (Of course, this was before e-mail!)

The South Beach Diet Goes Prime Time

Because of the diet's success, we began sharing our results at national meetings. First we reported consecutive cases and then we undertook a small clinical trial. We compared our good-fat, good-carb approach to what was then called the American Heart Association (AHA) Step II Diet, which was very low in fat and high in carbohydrates (it has since been supplanted).

Of a group of 60 overweight participants, half went on our diet and the other half went on the AHA Step II Diet. After 12 weeks, five of the low-fat dieters had dropped out, but only one of the South Beach dieters quit the programme. In the end, the South Beach dieters lost nearly twice as much weight as the low-fat dieters and actually had greater improvements in their blood fats. Notably, their blood triglycerides improved dramatically. Just as I had, they lost a lot of belly fat (which was significant when measured by their waist-to-hip ratios; see 'Why Your BMI Can Be Misleading' on page 64). The low-fat dieters did not have the same success.

In Spring 1999, after we presented our results at a national meeting of the American College of Cardiology in New Orleans, a Miami TV station asked me if they could offer the South Beach Diet to their viewers. I said fine and hundreds of South Floridians went on the diet and lost weight. The response was incredible and the South Beach Diet series became an annual event for the TV station for 3 consecutive years. I continued to prescribe the diet to my patients and people urged us to write a book. Its publication in 2003 seems like yesterday.

Scientific Support: The Diet Debates Are Over

In the 5 years that have passed since the publication of the original book, we have received thousands of testimonials documenting people's good

living THE SOUTH BEACH DIET

Jen P., aged 43: Now I Love Life and All the People in It

I have found a new life with the South Beach Diet. In April 2006, I was 41 years old, 1.68m (5'6") and 70kg (154lb). I weighed 13.6kg (30lb) more than I had before I got married in 1997. I was smoking two packets of cigarettes a day and drinking a whole pot of coffee before 10 a.m. for an energy boost. I never ate breakfast and I never exercised. My meals consisted of fast food and anything processed that I could eat on the run. My cholesterol was 7.4, and that was with medication.

Then two things happened that made me take stock of my life. First, my grandmother died. She had been living with my mother with the help of hospice care, but I helped take care of her the last week of her life. I had been very close to my grandmother and this was very difficult for me. Then, just 3 weeks later, my father died suddenly of a stroke. His death was shocking so soon after the loss of my beloved grandmother.

Following the funerals, I felt a strong, overwhelming need to live and cherish every moment of every day. I decided I needed a complete overhaul of my lifestyle. My supervisor at work told me that she was on the South Beach Diet, and it was working really well for her, so I decided to give it a try. I bought the book and followed the Phase 1 guidelines to a T. I lost 3.6kg (8lb) during those initial 2 weeks and had more energy than I'd had in years. I started walking outside. I could go only a mile or so at first, but I did it every day until I had the strength to walk 5–8km (3–5 miles) on some days. My speed increased, too.

results on the diet. You will find stories like Jen P.'s (above) throughout this book. There have also been numerous scientific studies reaffirming our healthy eating principles, including, notably, the importance of good fats and good carbohydrates.

And there's much more going on. In the US, food manufacturers are now required by law to list the amount of trans fats on their food labels, and in the UK and Australia it is encouraged that they do the same. In New York City, restaurants are currently banned from using most frying oils containing artificial trans fats for cooking and will have to eliminate

I knew it was time to stop smoking. Being on the diet made it easy because I already had a refrigerator packed with raw vegetables to munch on. Also, I could always walk when I felt the urge to smoke. I did it – I stopped smoking and never gained back an ounce. I continued to lose 0.5–1kg (1–2lb) a week while on Phase 2 and tried another type of exercise. I bought a bike and rode it on a bike trail we have in town. I hadn't been on a bike in more than 20 years and now I can ride the whole trail nearby, which is 35.4km (22 miles). I also bought a kayak and some dumb-bells, exercise videos and a treadmill so I could walk when the weather got cold.

In 2 months, my cholesterol went from 7.4–4.0. My doctor couldn't believe it. Six months later, with my doctor's permission, I went off my cholesterol medication completely.

I also joined a gym for the first time and love all the exercise classes. I'm always telling people on the SouthBeachDiet.com message boards about my exercise routine. We also share recipes all the time. I actually learned how to cook from those wonderful people.

I met my goal of losing 13.6kg (30lb) more than a year ago. It took about 7 months and I have been working hard at maintaining it. Sometimes I'll regain a few pounds, but then I just go back to eating like I did when I was on the first couple of weeks of Phase 2 and the weight comes right off. It's very simple.

Another added benefit of the diet is that I've made new, healthy friends at work, at the gym and in my neighbourhood. I wasn't a very pleasant person to be around before South Beach. Now I love life and all the people in it. I didn't just find a new lifestyle with the South Beach Diet – I found life!

artificial trans fats from all their foods by July 2008. This awareness is gradually spreading throughout the rest of the Western world. When we watch TV today, we see more and more advertisements for whole grain foods. And the terms *good carbs, good fats* and *glycaemic index* are now common in both the media and our daily conversations. These are all clear signs that the diet debates – and diet confusion – are over.

Here's just a small sampling of the scientific studies that support our diet philosophy.

Low fat a failure. In 2006, the Women's Health Initiative Dietary

Modification Trial in the US reported the results of a 7½-year study involving nearly 49,000 women between the ages of 50–79. One group followed a low-fat diet, decreasing their fat intake to 20 per cent of calories. They were informed that the diet was not intended to promote weight loss and were encouraged to maintain their usual energy intake by replacing fat calories with calories from other sources. The other group, the control group, received diet-related education materials and continued to eat a normal, higher-fat diet. Researchers found no benefit to the low-fat diet in terms of cardiovascular health, nor did it reduce the occurrence of breast or colorectal cancer.

Mediterranean diet a winner. In 2006, a Spanish study (the PRED-IMED Study) divided 772 adults at high risk of cardiovascular disease into three groups. One group ate a low-fat diet, while the other two ate a Mediterranean-style diet that, like the South Beach Diet, was rich in fruits, vegetables, whole grains, seafood, lean meats and good fats. One of these two groups was allowed additional olive oil (1litre/1¾pints) per week and the other was allowed additional nuts (30g/1oz) per day. The results: both groups following the Mediterranean diet had better blood sugar, better blood pressure and better ratios of good HDL to bad LDL cholesterol than those in the low-fat group. Those following the Mediterranean diet also had a reduction in C-reactive protein, a measure of inflammation, in their blood. (You can read about the health implications of inflammation in Chapter 6.)

Low-glycaemic best against insulin resistance. Studies comparing the low-glycaemic approach to other diets have confirmed our good results. In a US study in 2007 led by nutrition pioneer Dr David S. Ludwig, at Children's Hospital, Boston, 73 obese young adults were placed on either the standard low-fat diet or a low-glycaemic diet. All the participants were tested before the study to determine whether they were high-insulin secretors, which would mean that they would be especially sensitive to high-glycaemic foods. These same people would be likely candidates for prediabetes (metabolic syndrome). After 18 months on the diet, the high-insulin secretors lost more than 5.5kg (12lb) on the low-glycaemic diet. Those on the low-fat diet lost only 1.18kg (2.6lb). Those following the low-glycaemic diet also lost more body fat and remarkably, did not regain any weight. Both the high-insulin secretors and those with normal insulin response did better on the low-glycaemic diet than on the low-fat diet in terms of two important numbers: their HDL, or good cholesterol, went up and their triglyceride levels went down.

Support from around the world. In a 2007 Australian study, researchers at Children's Hospital at Westmead in Sydney, Australia, reviewed six randomized control trials from Australia, France, South Africa, Denmark and the US, comparing low-glycaemic diets with other diets. They found the low-glycaemic diets to be more effective in terms of overall weight loss and a decrease in body fat. Furthermore, those on the low-glycaemic diets had a greater reduction in overall cholesterol and bad LDL cholesterol.

* * * * * * * * * * * *

I could cite many other studies, but they all tell the same story. Health-care professionals universally agree that our focus should be on nutrient-dense, fibre-rich carbohydrates; healthy sources of unsaturated fats; low-fat dairy products and lean sources of protein. The principles of the South Beach Diet are here to stay.

Over the past decade, the South Beach Diet has helped millions of people lose weight. For many, following the diet was the first step towards adapting a healthy way of life. Many of them also went on to engage in some form of regular physical exercise, often for the first time in their lives (I wish they all had).

There's no question that being active is key to maintaining a healthy weight. And the good news is that even the busiest individuals can fit exercise into a South Beach Diet lifestyle. Just as I have learned more about the nutritional value of certain foods in the last 5 years, I have also learned what type of exercise is best for revving up your metabolism and speeding weight loss. And working exercise into your life is a lot easier than you might think. Just turn to Chapter 4.

living THE SOUTH BEACH DIET

Louisa O., aged 38: Lost 50 Pounds of Pregnancy Weight

I've been struggling with my weight problem since I was young. I'd tried all kinds of diets: the string bean diet, the cabbage diet, the soup diet. You name it, I'd tried it. They all worked for a while, but I always gained the weight back.

I gained 22.6kg (50lb) during my pregnancy and I couldn't seem to take it off. After 3 years of breastfeeding, I was still 18kg (40lb) overweight. I was wearing US size 14 (equivalent to UK size 18) and couldn't fit into anything smaller than an XL. I love fashionable clothes and looking good and I wasn't able to find anything I liked in my size. I looked years older than I was.

I was miserable about my weight. I had been invited to a wedding and told a friend of mine that I didn't even want to go because I was so depressed about how I looked. She gave me a copy of *The South Beach Diet* for Mother's Day. She had been on the diet herself and told me how great it was. I told her that diets didn't work for me and that I didn't want to bother with it. She encouraged me to read the book so I would understand why this diet was different and healthier than the ones I had been on before.

I read the book and I finally learned what I had been doing wrong. I was eating too many starchy carbs – white rice, white pasta, white potatoes and white bread – and very little protein. I decided to try the diet and see if I could lose the weight before the wedding. I found the diet easy to follow. I started eating lots of vegetables and lean protein, like white meat chicken and lean pork, as well as whole grains, including brown rice, wholemeal bread and wholewheat pasta. I found I wasn't always starving like I was on other diets. That was the best part for me.

It was pretty easy to lose the 18kg (40lb). I was not only eating tasty food, but it was healthy. I now weigh 64kg (140lb) and I'm wearing an American size 8 dress (UK size 12)! And I haven't regained the weight.

Today I follow Phase 3. On the South Beach Diet, you acquire new habits and you learn which foods are healthier for you. I've learned to make better choices. I even enjoy some dessert now and then. But I still eat lots of vegetables and lean protein.

I love myself again. Everyone comments about how great I look and how much weight I've lost. I am happy, I have energy for my daughter and I have regained my self-confidence.

4

Supercharge Your Metabolism

My patient Susan, who was prediabetic, had lost more than 9kg (20lb) on the South Beach Diet. Although she looked and felt a lot better, she wasn't happy. She still wanted to lose another 2.3–4.5kg (5–10lb) but was having difficulty doing so. No matter what she did, she couldn't seem to lose more weight. She asked me, 'Couldn't I just go back to Phase 1? I had no trouble losing weight back then!'

I strongly advised against it. Phase 1 is designed for people with cravings and substantial weight to lose, not for someone like Susan, who had only a few pounds left to shed. More important, Susan's cravings were gone and her blood chemistries were normal. In cases like hers, cutting back on calories and once again limiting nutritious food choices like fruits and whole grains could be counterproductive and potentially lead to yo-yoing (see page 41).

If Susan wanted further safe weight loss while continuing to follow the healthy eating principles of the South Beach Diet, she had only one option: she had to burn more calories. And the most efficient way to accomplish this was by engaging in the most efficient form of regular exercise. That meant more or better exercise and that was exactly what Susan *didn't* want to hear. She was already getting up at 6 a.m. to spend, as she put it, 'one long, tedious hour' walking on her treadmill before getting her children off to school and going to work.

'Don't tell me I have to spend more time on the treadmill', Susan complained. 'I just can't get up any earlier!'

Susan was pleasantly surprised when I explained that she didn't have to spend more time exercising to burn more calories. She could actually jump-start her metabolism and burn more calories in *less* time by making some changes in her exercise routine.

I told Susan that doing more of the same wasn't going to work. Her body had become accustomed to operating at her new weight and her current activity level, as often happens after a period of successful dieting. In fact, the most common complaint of dieters is what they call hitting a plateau. I'm sure many of you have experienced it.

Depending on our intrinsic metabolism, we all have different set points where our weight will plateau, even though we may be doing exactly the same thing we've been doing all along to lose weight. There are, of course, those lucky people who are born with a naturally high metabolic rate and who never have to diet or worry about hitting plateaus – they're the people we all love to hate because they seem to be able to eat anything and not gain weight. It simply doesn't seem fair!

Susan, like most of us, wasn't so lucky. Her problem was that her metabolism was stuck in neutral. Her body had adjusted to her need for fewer calories, so she was neither gaining nor losing.

Her only healthy and sustainable solution was to change her exercise routine and shift her metabolism into a higher gear. In other words, since Susan did not inherit a fast metabolism, she would have to rev it up herself.

Do More with Less

I advised Susan to switch to an interval training programme. In interval training, you alternate between short bursts of intensive effort and easier recovery periods, as opposed to working at a steady, continuous and potentially monotonous pace. While this book focuses on walking, just about any form of exercise can be done in an interval training mode, including swimming, running, cycling, elliptical training and even strength training.

Here's the advantage: When you work at a higher intensity for part of the time, you end up burning far more calories and fat in less time than you would if you were working out at a steady pace. And there's a bonus: with interval training, the higher the intensity of the exercise, the longer the afterburn; that is, you will continue to burn more fat and calories after you've completed your exercise session. As you become more fit and develop more lean muscle mass, you increase your basal metabolic rate even further. This means you'll burn more fat and calories while you're going through your daily activities and even while you're resting.

Don't let the term *higher intensity* scare you. It's true that you may be working harder than you're used to for short periods of time, but you will have plenty of time to recharge during the easier recovery periods. Interval training is not just for the very fit. It works just as well for people who are not as fit and is even being used to help cardiac patients and people with lung disease get back in shape. That said, I do recommend that you talk with your doctor before embarking on this or any exercise programme, especially if you haven't been exercising.

Susan was also missing another important component of fitness – a core-strengthening programme to develop the muscles in her back and abdomen and increase her overall strength and flexibility. Susan's treadmill workout focused on her cardiovascular system, but she needed to do something more to further improve her muscle tone and bone density.

Due to a natural decrease in hormones and to reduced physical activity, both men and women tend to lose muscle and bone as they age. For women, this drop in hormones occurs fairly abruptly during menopause and typically causes a drop in metabolic rate. Consequently, postmenopausal women invariably find it much tougher to maintain their weight.

For men, the drop in hormones – what is called andropause – is more gradual, but it too results in a slower metabolism and weight gain with age.

In both men and women, decreased hormone levels and decreased

(continued on page 38)

living THE SOUTH BEACH DIET

Barbara P., aged 58: Making Giant Leaps One Small Step at a Time

I had always been a yo-yo dieter, but I had reached a point where I finally had my weight under control. I was slim, I looked good and I felt good about myself. Then about 4 years ago, I broke up with my boyfriend and I lost it. I began eating everything fattening I could get my hands on. I'm over 1.70m (5'8"), so it took a while for the weight to become noticeable. But 22.6kg (50lb) later, when I weighed 89kg (195lb), I looked terrible. I had a beautiful wardrobe but didn't fit into any of my favourite clothes. I was six sizes larger than I had been and the worst part was that I had to buy clothes I didn't like at stores I didn't enjoy shopping in. The funny thing is, I never stepped on a scale. I didn't want to know what I weighed. I pretended it wasn't happening.

Friends don't tell you you're getting fat; they don't know what to say. But a close friend of mine who had lost weight gave me a copy of *The South Beach Diet*. I didn't open it. I was seeing a therapist and he kept after me about my weight. He became my conscience. We talked about control issues. I now realize that I had just given up – for me, weighing 89kg (195lb) was basically throwing in the towel.

You can't imagine how devastating it is not to feel good about how you look. How you feel about yourself, your sense of attractiveness or lack of attractiveness – spills over into all aspects of your life.

It took a while for me to deal with my weight. I took it one step at a time and sometimes they were pretty small steps. About 3 years ago, I was visiting some friends in Florida and it was swimming costume time. I think that's when it finally dawned on me how my life was really being controlled by my weight. I saw and felt what I had done to myself and where it was all going. There wasn't a remote possibility that I was going to put on a swimming costume. I thought, *Here I am, I'm not that old, I'm a pretty attractive woman and I can't wear a swimming costume.* And I'm not talking about a bikini; I mean a plain old one-piece. I realized that I was really messing myself up big time. I took that first step – literally. I went to the hotel gym and walked on the treadmill for a short time. I felt pretty good afterwards and when I got back to New York, I joined a health club, hired a trainer and began working out regularly. I had a coupon for the health club hanging on my refrigerator for about a year but never did anything about it. I took it off the refrigerator and used it.

I finally reached the point where I was ready to read *The South Beach Diet,* which had been lying around my house for about a year. Once I started it, I couldn't put it down. With every page, I gained new insight about food and eating. Like, what's a good carbohydrate? I learned what foods I could eat and what I should avoid. I used to think that I shouldn't eat bread, but I learned that you can eat bread as long as it's 100% wholewheat, wholemeal, whole grain or another high-fibre type, which digests more slowly than white bread. The glycaemic index was a new concept for me. I learned how nutrition affects how the body works. I learned about my metabolism, like how to speed it up. I used to think that if you don't eat, you lose weight. I was completely wrong. I learned that if you don't eat, your body thinks it's being starved and your metabolism slows down. I didn't know any of this before.

I started making changes in how I ate a little at a time. I learned not to let myself get hungry, because when you get too hungry, you tend to want to eat more. I learned that you have to keep your blood sugar levels even to prevent cravings. To this day, I always walk around with healthy snacks. I carry small bags of nuts such as almonds or walnuts and little cherry tomatoes or low-fat cheese wedges because I don't want to get hungry.

I didn't actually go on the diet right away; I just incorporated a few things. I wasn't ready to give up sugar yet, so when I went to Starbucks and ordered my usual cappuccino, I asked for skimmed milk instead of full-fat. That was my big concession when I weighed 89kg (195lb)! I realized that that was okay; I didn't feel deprived. I was ready for the next step. I remember thinking, *I don't need to eat a sandwich for lunch. Maybe I can have just the meat and a salad.* Or instead of eating white bread, I ordered wholemeal bread. When I started taking off a little weight just by doing these simple things, I was motivated to keep going. I saw that this was very do-able and it wasn't making me unhappy. That's when I decided to go on Phase 1 and really do the diet as written.

It took 2 years, but I took off all the weight I'd gained. I fit into my old clothes again. I wear tight, sexy jeans and can still wear sleeveless tops. I feel like my old self. I've just made another big step – I posted my profile on Match.com. I feel good about myself and I'm ready to start a new relationship.

I walked into a friend's office recently and she said, 'You look better than you've ever looked.' She's a straight-shooting woman. It was a very exciting moment.

physical activity also diminish the quantity of muscle (and bone). Since muscle requires more calories to maintain than fat, less muscle means fewer calories burned, which further slows metabolism. By maintaining your muscle mass with exercise, you can help overcome the natural decrease in metabolic rate.

That's why, as you age, it's so important to keep your metabolism revved up. If you want those muscles to be metabolically active – if you want to burn more fat and calories – you must use them. I therefore recommended that Susan follow the South Beach Supercharged Fitness Programme described in Part II. Before she could protest that she was already pressed for time, I showed her how she could do an even more effective cardio and calorie-burning programme in half the time she was already spending on the treadmill (and achieve core fitness and greater overall muscle tone on alternate days).

The Weight Melted Away

Here's how we transformed Susan's 1-hour treadmill programme into a fat-busting, calorie-devouring interval training programme. I instructed Susan to cut her treadmill time back to about 20 minutes every other day. Instead of walking at a constant pace for her entire workout, as she had been doing, she should mix it up. That is, after a warm-up, she should alternate short bursts of walking very fast with recovery periods of slower walking. (See page 109 to get started on Phase 1 Interval Walking.)

Depending on the workout goal for the day, Susan could do several fast-slow intervals within 20 minutes. As her endurance improved, she would be able to spend more time doing fast spurts and less time in the slower recovery periods, gradually adding more repetitions if time permitted. In addition, she wouldn't be bored: When you do interval training, your workouts vary so they're more interesting and the time seems to fly by.

Another benefit of the programme was that on alternate days, Susan would strengthen her core muscles, which she had been neglecting by doing only cardio.

Susan was sceptical but agreed to give it a try.

When I saw Susan about a month later, I didn't have to ask how she was doing. I could see the good results with my own eyes. That last unwanted weight 4.5kg (10lb) was fading away. And, thanks to the core component of the programme, Susan was standing straighter and looking stronger and more toned.

The Conventional Wisdom Is Wrong

At this point, many of you may be thinking, *This contradicts nearly everything I've been told about exercise.* And you're right, it does. In the past, we believed that the best way to burn fat was to work at your training heart rate, which is about 60 per cent of your maximum heart rate. Once you knew your training heart rate, you were told to take your pulse or wear a heart-rate monitor during exercise to make sure you maintained that level. You were also told that you needed to work for at least 20 minutes before you started burning fat. We now know that this simply is not true.

Interval training is not new. Endurance athletes like marathoners and professional cyclists have used this technique for years to help them perform at higher levels. But now there is growing evidence that interval training can also be a huge boon to non-athletes who are trying to lose weight and improve their fitness. An abundance of good science supports interval training as a great way to burn fat and calories and research also shows that it provides better results than working at a constant moderate pace for longer periods of time.

In a Canadian study conducted in 2007, researchers had women in their early twenties do an interval training programme consisting of 10 sets of 4 minutes of hard cycling with 2 minutes of rest between each set. After seven 1-hour sessions over 2 weeks, all eight women in the study showed a 36 per cent increase in fat burning. This finding held true for women who were fit, as well as for those who were less fit. So much for the myth that you can't burn fat working at a high intensity! The women also showed a 13 per cent improvement in cardiovascular fitness, which means their hearts and lungs were more able to send oxygen to working muscles, which is important whether you are working out or simply going about your daily activities.

Burning calories is critical to shedding pounds and maintaining a healthy weight. And on the calorie-burning front, interval training is the clear winner. A landmark US study conducted by Darlene Sedlock, PhD, and her colleagues at Purdue University found that it took only 19 minutes for a high-intensity exercise group to burn the same 300 calories that it took a low-intensity group 30 minutes to burn. Even more interesting, the high-intensity group continued to burn more calories long after the exercise period ended, compared with the low-intensity group.

In another US study, conducted jointly by Baylor University and the University of Alabama, researchers compared continuous low-intensity exercise performed for 60 minutes to a high-intensity interval training programme alternating between 2-minute periods of work and recovery, also for 60 minutes. The participants were eight women between the ages of 23–35. Researchers found that the interval training protocol burned 160 more calories per day than the low-intensity training method or about 800 calories more per week when the exercises were performed five times a week.

The point is that if you want to burn more calories, you need to work out with greater intensity. But don't worry, we're not telling you this so you feel compelled to get on the treadmill for an hour a day. In fact, we've already seen some excellent results with women we've put on our 20-minute-a-day Interval Walking programme. Not only have they lost excess pounds, but they've lost them in trouble spots like the waist and hips.

Studies also reveal that interval training is more effective for normalizing blood sugar and correcting bad blood fats (such as LDL or low-density lipoprotein, cholesterol and high triglycerides) than conventional exercise, making it ideal for cardiovascular health. This means that interval training is a wonderful choice for people at risk of developing prediabetes and diabetes. And it's particularly effective for burning away belly fat; the dangerous visceral fat that is the bane of many men and women in mid-life.

There's yet another reason interval training is preferable to conventional training: It prepares you better for living in the real world. Consider this. Do you take your training heart rate when you leave the house in the

HOW YO-YO DIETING
WORKS AGAINST YOUR METABOLISM

The human body is designed to combat adversity. While this was good for our prehistoric hunter-gatherer ancestors, it's not necessarily good for us when it comes to dieting. Hunter-gatherers faced frequent periods when food was scarce. What saved them from starvation was that during times of famine, their metabolisms switched into low gear, permitting their bodies to run on fewer calories.

Unfortunately, this innate survival mechanism doesn't help modern dieters, especially those who are impatient and want to take off a lot of weight very quickly. When people go on severely restricted, low-calorie crash diets, they do lose a lot of weight at first. But then the survival mechanism kicks in. Their metabolisms slow down and weight loss stops or becomes much slower, which is exactly what they don't want to happen.

Furthermore, when caloric intake is drastically restricted, it's not just fat that's burned to maintain blood sugar levels and provide energy; it's also protein from muscle and bone. Muscle requires more calories to maintain than fat does. When we have less muscle, we burn fewer calories, even at rest.

And this is just the beginning of a sad cycle for many people. It's impossible to stay on a low-calorie, high-deprivation diet for a long time. We just get too hungry. To feel better, we eventually break down and start eating normally. When this happens, we start piling on the pounds, gaining more weight than we carried before because our metabolisms have slowed. When we get fat again, we freak out, go back on the low-calorie diet and – you guessed it – inadvertently slow our metabolisms down even more. The cycle repeats itself over and over again. And we get fatter and fatter.

We call this cycle yo-yo dieting. You lose weight quickly, gain it back again and then have to lose it all over again, only to regain again – in spades. Each time you yo-yo, you decrease your metabolic rate and ultimately wind up working against yourself.

The bottom line: deprivation diets don't work. Gradual weight loss does. By making the healthy food choices on the three phases of the South Beach Diet, you never starve yourself; you keep your metabolism working efficiently and you lose weight slowly, steadily, safely and permanently.

morning and stay at that level for the whole day? Of course not. You're constantly speeding up and slowing down as you go about your activities, whether you're getting up from a desk, running for a bus or chasing after a toddler. Our lives are actually built around interval activities. Therefore, an ideal fitness programme should prepare you for the kinds of physical demands you encounter every day. And interval training does just that.

How Interval Training Works

How does interval training work? It switches your metabolism into high gear and increases your demand for energy (calories) so that you burn more calories and fat. Think of your body as a car. When you drive in stop-and-go traffic, you burn a lot more petrol than when cruising along at a constant speed. With petrol prices so high these days (let alone our desire to use less fossil fuel), that's the last thing you want to do when you're driving. But it's exactly what you *do* want to do to burn maximum calories and fat during exercise. And that's how interval training works. Every time you work hard and then slow down, you waste energy and use up calories. And what it's costing you are those extra, unwanted pounds.

Debunking Those Exercise Myths

Many of you have heard metabolism mentioned in connection with weight loss, but unfortunately, few people actually understand what metabolism is all about. If you want to look great in your swimming costume, fit back into your 'thin' clothes, prevent diabetes and maintain a healthy weight for life, you need to know how to make your metabolism work for you, not against you. So bear with me while I give you a brief lesson on metabolism.

In a manner similar to how your car runs on petrol, your cells run on a substance called adenosine triphosphate or ATP, which is made in all the cells of the body. You need energy from ATP to run your body's systems as well as to perform your day-to-day work. ATP is, in a sense, your only energy source and it's replenished by the food you take in daily, as well as the fuel stored in your body as fat or glycogen (the storage form of sugar). ATP is what's converted into the energy you need to contract your muscles and perform all of your bodily functions. Using ATP for energy is analogous to burning coal in a furnace to run a steam engine. The burning coal heats the water that makes the steam that propels the engine.

At the peak of endurance training, athletes like Lance Armstrong require roughly 6,000 to 9,000 calories a day to keep their muscles working for extended periods of time. It seems like these elite endurance athletes must spend most of their non-exercise, non-sleeping time eating just to keep up with their training muscles' demand for energy. For most of us, however, all the fuel we need for a regular exercise and weight loss programme is easily consumed in the healthy meals and snacks we should be eating every day.

Another key point to understand about metabolism is that there are two types and each one burns different fuels. Aerobic metabolism requires oxygen to make ATP and can use both sugar and fat as fuel. Anaerobic metabolism doesn't use oxygen to make ATP and burns sugar and a compound known as creatine phosphate, which is made in the cells, for fuel.

If the words *aerobic* and *anaerobic* are familiar to you, it's because we also use them to categorize different types of exercise. Aerobic activities (sometimes called cardio), which can be done for a long duration, include walking, cycling, rowing and working out on a treadmill or an elliptical trainer. Since these are done at a relatively low intensity level, you can usually maintain your performance using the aerobic systems of the body. Therefore, by breathing more deeply and more frequently and having your heart beat faster, you can deliver sufficient blood and oxygen to supply your muscles' needs without accumulating excessive waste products that can fatigue your muscles. Anaerobic activities, such as weight-training, skipping and sprinting, work muscles at a high intensity and consequently require energy faster than the aerobic systems can supply it, even though they're working as hard as they can. The result is that your working muscles rapidly build up waste and tire out. Therefore, anaerobic exercise cannot be sustained for long and you're forced to reduce activity to a level where aerobic metabolism once more dominates.

There are several misconceptions about exercise in general, and anaerobic exercise in particular. One of the biggest myths is that you can burn fat only by doing aerobic exercise. This idea is based on a misinterpretation of the fact that fat is an aerobic fuel and it has led to a second, more insidious myth: when you work at a high-intensity anaerobic level, such as during interval training, you shut down your fat-burning machinery. This is simply not true; it's based on a misconception about how your metabolism operates. We were once taught that the body can be in only one mode of metabolism at a time – either aerobic (burning sugar and fat) or anaerobic (burning sugar and creatine phosphate).

In reality, as you exercise, your body slides freely between aerobic and anaerobic metabolism. Depending on the activity, your body may favour one type over the other, but it's never exclusively in aerobic or anaerobic mode. You're never actually burning just sugar, fat or creatine phosphate. You're burning all three fuels simultaneously. But, depending on your activity, you're burning more of one than another.

When you do interval training, you're repeatedly moving from high-intensity work to low-intensity work and you're also moving along the metabolic spectrum. You can't maintain a high-intensity level for too long because you'll get tired. Tiredness occurs for several reasons: first, you rapidly burn through your high-energy fuel, creatine phosphate, while you're still burning sugar and fat. Second, your muscles make lactic acid and a number of waste products, which contribute to fatigue. So, to cope with this fatigue, you slow down and move into your low-intensity recovery period. During this recovery period, you're not only burning off lactic acid as fuel, you're also using fat and carbohydrates aerobically to replenish creatine phosphate and ATP. This allows you to do the next high-intensity spurt and continue to burn more fat and calories.

The really exciting news is that with every additional interval, you burn an even higher proportion of fat. This is because with every subsequent interval, you require more and more oxygen for both the work and recovery portions. This means that you slide further and further towards the aerobic systems and use both fat and carbohydrates to rebuild the creatine phosphate and ATP needed for the next interval. However, you can still maintain higher levels of activity than would be possible during aerobic training at a constant pace, because the recovery periods allow

FRINGE BENEFITS

Okay, you know that exercise can boost your metabolism and help you burn more fat and calories. But here are some other wonderful benefits you can get from working out.

Enhanced sex. If you want to get in the mood, get out your running shoes. Numerous studies have linked regular vigorous exercise with more frequent sexual encounters and enhanced sexual enjoyment for both sexes. A 2003 study of male health professionals found that men over the age of 50 who were physically active reduced their risk of erectile dysfunction by 30 per cent. A Canadian study conducted at the University of British Columbia found that 20 minutes of intense exercise appeared to stimulate sexual response in women. About 15 minutes after the workout seemed to be the optimal time. Maybe couples should consider doing their workouts together!

Increased energy. Think you're too tired to exercise? The problem could be that you need to get off the sofa. American researchers at the University of Georgia analysed 70 different studies on the impact of exercise on more than 6,800 subjects. The bottom line: 90 per cent of the studies reported that when sedentary people completed a regular exercise programme, they experienced more energy and less fatigue, compared with people who did not exercise.

Better brainpower. Around the age of 40, the human brain begins to shrink, causing age-related changes in mental function, such as memory problems. Until recently, we believed that an ageing brain couldn't make new brain cells. We now know that it's possible to make new brain cells well into old age, but there's one catch: you have to work at it. Specifically, you have to do your cardio. An American study of 60–79-year-olds conducted at the University of Illinois found that when people did 1 hour of aerobic exercise three times a week, their brains actually grew. More brain cells translate into better mental function – yet another reason it's smart to exercise.

Longer life span. Exercise can add years to your life, according to a 2005 study published in the *Archives of Internal Medicine*. Researchers examined the medical records of more than 5,200 men and women who participated in the Framingham Heart Study, a groundbreaking study that has gathered information on diet, lifestyle and health over a 40-year period and is still ongoing. People with even moderate levels of physical activity gained up to 1½ years of life and those who did more intense exercise lived, on average, 3½ extra years. My belief is that not only did the more active people live longer, but they probably enjoyed a much better quality of life.

replenishment of ATP and creatine phosphate and removal of waste products. The bottom line is that more energy is used, with more and more of it coming from the aerobic use of fat. And one last happy thought: *the more you train, the more fat you burn during recovery.*

As good as it is, intense interval training isn't for everyone. It must be customized for people with certain orthopaedic problems or serious heart conditions. Again, my advice is to check with your GP before starting this or any other exercise programme.

And please, before you do any exercise, read the next chapter, 'Boomeritis: The New Epidemic!' to make sure that you're exercising safely.

Boomeritis: The New Epidemic!

From my discovery of baseball at the age of 5, I have always loved sports and have played just about all of them. Unfortunately, as I got older and spent more time in the surgery and at the hospital, basketball, softball and touch football gradually faded into oblivion, except for occasional games with my two sons. My major athletic endeavour became tennis, which I played competitively in my youth and spent summers teaching. I also jogged on a regular basis (and had for years) and did short spurts of ice hockey (yes, ice hockey in Miami), karate and rollerblading. About 10 years ago, I gravitated to golf. I had to give up some of the more taxing sports because as I got older, I tended to get nagging injuries – particularly shoulder, low-back and knee pain. I was not alone. Not surprisingly, the preponderance of such injuries amongst baby boomers like me has come to be known as boomeritis.

About 3 years ago, I began doing core training with Kris Belding, the Pilates teacher who designed the core functional fitness part of our exercise programme, and I was amazed at how much better I felt. My overall strength and flexibility greatly improved, I felt younger and I stopped experiencing the boomeritis aches, pains and injuries that previously seemed to occur on a regular basis. And I finally fulfilled one of my mother's long-time admonitions: 'Stand up straight!'

While I was at home in Miami Beach, I had no trouble following my usual exercise and diet routine. But like so many people who travel a lot for business, I wasn't always as diligent on the road and occasionally gained a few pounds during my travels. (I didn't always follow my own advice about being prepared with healthy snacks.) Also, I found it difficult to put enough time into a cardio workout that was necessary to complement my core training.

Fortunately, about this time, I was lucky enough to meet my collaborator on this book, Joe Signorile, PhD, who teaches exercise physiology at the University of Miami. Joe told me about the benefits of interval training and convinced me that I could burn more calories and achieve a higher level of fitness in a shorter period of time than I was currently spending on my workout. While I had heard about interval training for competitive endurance athletes, I was unaware of its potential benefits for the rest of us. I reviewed the scientific literature he suggested and was convinced that interval training for non-athletes was an important advance.

The beauty of interval training – which, as I explained in the last chapter, involves doing short bursts of high-intensity exercise followed by an easier recovery period – is that you can do it wherever you are and adapt it to any activity.

As fate would have it, about the same time I met Joe, my friend and patient Mel was raving about his experience with boxing. I knew that Mel had boxed as a teenager and I was surprised to hear that at the age of 72, he was back in the ring, albeit with a trainer. Mel's partner, a former professional dancer, and I had been trying to get him to do regular exercise for years, but he was quickly bored by conventional workouts. I was delighted when I heard that he had kept up with his boxing lessons for more than a year – and it showed. His energy level had increased immensely and his blood chemistries, blood pressure and weight all reflected the benefits of his time in the ring.

Those of you who are unfamiliar with boxing may not know that it's one of the most demanding of all sports. In fact, boxing is possibly the ultimate in interval training, with 2-3-minute rounds of intense exercise followed by a rest period.

I had always heard that boxers are amongst the fittest of all athletes and was curious to give boxing a try as a way to work intervals into my own cardio programme. I was referred to Luis, a fabulous boxing trainer and began working with him. But before I go further, let me put in an important disclaimer. What I did with Luis was baby boomer boxing: Luis held up hand pads and directed me on when and how to punch them. He was not allowed to punch me back!

What I learned was a progressive choreography, where my skills and fitness improved at a fast pace. Within a few months, I was 'floating like a butterfly' around the ring. I was also clearly burning more calories in less time than during my previous long jogs or walks at a steady pace.

I was thrilled with my progress and improved fitness. But then I made a big mistake that led to injury, pain and an unfortunate break from exercising. In fact, it's what inspired me to write this chapter of warning for my fellow boomers.

At the end of our sessions in the ring, Luis and I would do some classic boxing exercises using a medicine ball. This was fine until I did a repetitive move of lifting, throwing and catching the heavy ball over my head. Almost instantly, I felt a sharp pain in my left shoulder. But instead of stopping at that point, I disobeyed the advice I always give to my own patients: I ignored the pain and continued with the over-the-head exercise. Over the next few days, the pain in my shoulder got worse.

When I went to the doctor, I didn't even have to see him before my problem was identified. His partner, who was assisting him, was recording my medical history. When she heard about my medicine ball escapade, she immediately told me that she often heard her partner advising patients my age (and even those quite a bit younger) not to lift weights overhead – and especially not repetitively. It was now clear to me, even before it was confirmed by the doctor and an MRI, that I had joined the crowd of my peers who had sustained a rotator cuff injury.

The orthopaedic doctor explained that, with age, there is simply less room within the shoulder joint because of normal calcification that occurs as the result of general wear and tear, and this room is compromised even more when we lift weights overhead. The result is trauma within the joint that tears the rather delicate rotator cuff muscles. This injury at least temporarily ended my nascent but promising boxing career. It also put a major crimp in my golf swing and the quality of my Pilates training. Fortunately, I didn't require surgery and after about 6 months of regular visits to an outstanding physical therapist, I returned to pain-free exercising.

As I described my experience to many of my patients, it seemed that half of the men and a third of the women I saw had also experienced rotator cuff problems. Many had required surgery and almost all had learned the 'nothing heavy overhead' lesson. I was really sorry that I hadn't had that important piece of information earlier, when it could have saved me from my own injury.

During the time that my exercising was severely limited, I noticed another ailment. My wrist was hurting. Was this arthritis? No. It was carpal tunnel syndrome, a problem many of us boomers and pre-boomers develop by spending long hours typing on computers. In an informal survey of my patients and friends, carpal tunnel syndrome, like rotator cuff injuries, seemed to be occurring in epidemic numbers. And a quick review of the medical literature confirmed how common carpal tunnel syndrome has become in our post-industrial society.

I'm not telling you these stories to discourage you from exercising. The alternative is far worse. Being sedentary increases your risk of developing many of the illnesses known to man and woman, including arthritis, cancer, heart disease and Alzheimer's. I'm telling you this so you don't make the same mistake I made. If I had known not to lift heavy objects repetitively over my head, I'd still be boxing today. The problem wasn't the sport; it was the way I trained for it.

It doesn't matter what activity you're doing. You could be playing tennis, lifting weights, jogging or ballroom dancing. If you do foolish things like ignore pain (as I did), do too much before your body is ready, ignore previous injuries or don't train properly for your sport or activity you will get into trouble.

An Injury-Prone Generation

As more and more baby boomers try to stave off the effects of old age by engaging in various modes of exerciese to stay fit, there's no question they are becoming increasingly vulnerable to injury. A positive desire for physical health has ironically produced a generation more susceptible to injury than ever.

One reason for this is that many people who have not exercised for years or who have never exercised before and who are poorly conditioned, have suddenly decided to make up for lost time. They join a gym and start running at full pelt on a treadmill or lifting too-heavy weights with a vengeance, or they go for long jogs outside on hard pavements.

On one hand, it's wonderful that so many people are inspired to start or increase a fitness programme. On the other hand, this enthusiasm needs to be tempered with appropriate caution: whatever form of fitness you pursue, it's a good idea to begin slowly so you don't get injured. There's a reason our fitness programme, which you'll learn about in Part II of this book, is a three-phase programme. During Phase 1, which you do for 2 weeks (or longer, if need be), you gently ease into an exercise routine, making sure your body is ready before you move on to the next phase. Once you're in Phase 2, you will become stronger and more flexible, ready for an even more challenging workout. And once you've mastered Phase 3, you will know how to work your body in a safe, healthy way and you'll be able to integrate the concepts of the programme into your own fitness regime, if you like.

Too Much, Too Late

I'm a cardiologist who sees people every day who have heart disease or who are at risk of it. But sometimes I feel more like an orthopaedic doctor. I always take an exercise history from my patients because it is such

living THE SOUTH BEACH DIET

Diane and Mark C., both aged 58: A Diet We Can't Stop Talking About!

My partner, Mark, and I have been following the South Beach Diet for more than a year and we are so excited about our weight loss. We never stop talking about the diet. Over the past year, I have lost 17.3kg (38lb), dropping from 73kg (170lb) to 60kg (132lb). My partner lost 22.6kg (50lb) from 109kg (240lb) to 86.4kg (190lb). I started the diet first and within 2 weeks shed 3.6kg (8lb). Mark said he'd never go on a diet, but when he saw how well I was doing, he decided to join me. He lost an incredible 10kg (22lb) over the first few weeks and believe me, we didn't starve ourselves.

I am a big eater, so the puny servings that most diets call for don't satisfy me. But on the South Beach Diet, I ate until I was satisfied and it sure worked for me.

Before going on South Beach, my partner was quite the junk-food junkie and a big beer drinker. Diets were never for him. He hated them. Today he's a totally reformed eater and thrilled with his results. He's good about following the principles of the South Beach Diet. Sometimes he'll ask, 'Am I allowed to eat this?' He now realizes that he can have his cake and eat it, too, but not all the time and not so much.

I had tried many diets but always ended up gaining more weight than when I started. This time, it's different. I actually went on an 11-day cruise and didn't gain an ounce but ate very well. I had eggs for breakfast and ate nuts and vegetables when I was snacking or hungry. For dinner, instead of having the ship's decadent desserts, I'd ask for some fresh berries. The most amazing thing about the South Beach Diet is that it isn't complicated and you can always eat well no matter where you are.

Mark and I are both 58 and we had always heard that it's harder to lose weight as you get older. The South Beach Diet made it easy.

an important part of their cardiac status. What I invariably hear is a litany of complaints characteristic of boomeritis: low-back pain; rotator cuff pain; hip, knee, wrist, ankle and neck pain; tennis elbow; Achilles tendinitis and shin splints are the most common ailments cited. The good news is that almost all of these are preventable.

The problem is that many people – even the very fit – are not doing the right exercise for their bodies, especially their mid-life bodies. For example, I see far too many knee and hip injuries in my practice, often amongst runners. In fact, I have rarely seen a baby boomer who runs regularly on hard surfaces who has not experienced knee, hip and/or low-back problems. Many of these people continue to run even though their joints are tender and painful. I tell them that they can keep their running shoes, but it's time to do more joint-friendly exercise, at least part of the time.

I also see a fair number of people who simply overdo it when it comes to exercise. Instead of giving their bodies a needed break, they keep pushing themselves harder and harder, further and further, to the point of injury. You can get away with running for miles every day on a hard surface when you're in your teens or twenties, but by the time you reach 40, I don't recommend it. The human body was never meant to sustain that kind of beating. (If you do want to continue running, I urge you to do an interval training programme and run fast for only short periods of time, with adequate recovery periods. And, if possible, avoid hard surfaces.)

And it's not just runners and middle-aged athletes who are exposing themselves to overuse injuries. Let me share another of my personal boomeritis experiences. About 10 years ago, I attended the annual American College of Cardiology meeting in New Orleans. I stayed at a hotel about a mile away from the convention centre where the meeting was held. I walked there and back, and then walked for miles within the convention centre. Great exercise! Two days into the meeting, as I hiked back to my hotel, I began to notice pain and tenderness in my shins, which seemed to get worse with every step. Just as I thought I couldn't walk any further, I spotted a shoe-shine stand and decided that I needed a shine and a rest. As I sat down, I complained to the shoe-shine man that my shins were really aching. He observed the thin-soled loafers I was wearing and quickly made the diagnosis of shin splints. (I was clearly not the first conventioneer who had sought refuge at his stand because of shin pain.)

Dr Shoe Shine quickly prescribed a well-known brand of rubber-soled shoes. Though I had long ago learned to wear thick-soled running shoes when I jogged, it had never occurred to me that I should be wearing them for walking, or that shin splints wasn't a malady suffered only by runners. I bought the recommended shoes and have walked long distances at many heart meetings since without a recurrence of shin pain. Still, too many others continue to pound the pavement one way or another without proper precautions and they're paying the consequences.

It's not surprising, then, to learn that experts are predicting that the number of knee- and hip-replacement surgeries will soar as baby boomers reach their later decades. A US study published in 2007 estimates that there will be 3.48 million total-knee replacements performed in 2030, a 673 per cent increase from the number performed today. The study also predicts that there will be 572,000 hip replacements performed in 2030, a 174 per cent increase from today's number.

This does not mean that you should not exercise.

While it's true that many of these spare parts will be going to ageing athletes who have overworked their joints through the years, even more will be replacing the severely arthritic joints of people who may not have done *enough* exercise. A sedentary lifestyle can lead to being overweight or obese and that too puts undue stress on the hips, spine and knee joints. Even a small amount of weight loss can save your knees a lot of wear and tear. With every step you take, you impose a force of from 3–6 times your body weight across each knee. A 2005 study published in *Arthritis & Rheumatism* in the US found that for every pound (0.5kg) of body weight lost, there's a 1.8kg (4lb) reduction in stress to the knee joint. Considering that you work your knee joints every time you stand or walk, the lighter the load, the better. The point is that overdoing it, as well as doing nothing, will lead you to the same operating theatre. This is why everyone needs to incorporate joint-friendly exercise and recovery periods into their fitness routines and the earlier the better.

Smart Fitness

As it happens, many, if not most of the boomeritis complaints I see in my surgery, including rotator cuff injuries and low-back pain, aren't the result of sports injuries. Rather, they occur in people who are just going about daily chores, like bending over to strap a child into a car seat or picking up a bag of groceries. While some of these injuries are simply the result of weak core muscles and poor flexibility, I also see these problems occurring in the fittest of my patients – or at least the ones that look to be the fittest.

This gets me to another important point. Many people who think they're doing smart workouts may be doing themselves more harm than good. Conventional weightlifting, sometimes called classic gym, can be counter-productive because it tends to isolate muscle groups and train them in a manner that is not naturally functional. In other words, the workout does not mimic everyday human activities and it usually neglects the core muscles. The result is muscles that may look good in the mirror or on the beach, but aren't much help when it comes to injury prevention or performing active sports or day-to-day tasks.

The best exercises you can do to prevent boomeritis injuries are called functional exercises. These exercises, which are similar to movements you execute in your daily life, require you to use several muscle groups in one fluid movement. That's why, in addition to cardio conditioning, our fitness programme emphasizes functional fitness to strengthen your core and peripheral muscles. For example, when you lean over to pick up a child or lift heavy bags of groceries from your car, you're not using just your arms and legs. If you did, you'd be overusing these muscles, leaving them vulnerable to injury. When you bend over to pick something up, you're engaging all your muscles, including your legs, mid-line, back and arms. The core muscles support all your other muscles and help you maintain strength, good posture and balance.

You may be surprised to learn that as a cardiologist, I place as much importance on core-strengthening exercises as I do on cardio conditioning. Because this type of exercise promotes stability, strength and flexibility, it's essential for preventing injury and maintaining a healthy weight. And if you suffer an injury and you're in pain, you're not going to do an effective cardio workout – or any workout at all. In my practice, I see all too many patients who are no longer able to exercise due to injury.

The importance of functional fitness has only recently become appreciated. During my travels, I visit many gyms or fitness rooms associated with the hotels where I stay. I have noticed that more and more of the people who are exercising, with or without a trainer, have incorporated functional fitness into their workouts. I am pleased to find both women and men lifting hand weights while sitting on exercise balls, or using pulley-type machines or standing on balance boards, which all require them to engage their core muscles as they work other parts of their bodies.

Watch the Core Busters

Of course, our ancestors didn't have to worry about setting aside time to perform muscle-flexing and strengthening exercises to maintain fitness. They accomplished this while going about their everyday routines. Anthropologists tell us that cave dwellers had remarkably strong muscles and bones, thanks to their normal daily activities. Hunting and gathering was hard work. Stalking and killing prey and finding and picking fruits and vegetables provided a full-body workout. And if you injured your back, you might not survive. Even our very recent ancestors were more physically active than we are. Before society became industrialized, just getting through the day was physically challenging for both men and women. Chopping wood, tending the garden, scrubbing floors, washing clothes on a board or a rock and hanging them up to dry – all involved full and functional body movement.

Today we drive to work, take a lift to our offices and sit at our desks all day long. We now use the remote control not just for our TVs but for our sound systems, DVD players, lights and even curtains. Our children aren't running around after school, climbing trees and playing sports like they used to, because they're home playing video games. Our modern civilized world has created what I call core busters because they prevent our core muscles from getting the activity they were meant to experience. Muscles that aren't used become weak and stiff and weak, stiff muscles lead to further inactivity, a sluggish metabolism and eventually, injury.

Stop Sitting, Start Moving

We all need to be more aware of the core busters in our everyday lives. Exercising for a few hours a week is great, but we also need to think about what we're doing the rest of the time. Are we just sitting around or are we active and moving? Do we walk up the stairs or take the lift? Do we flag down a taxi when we could walk? It turns out that the movements we do throughout the day – both consciously and subconsciously – burn calories. And these calories really do add up.

Dr James A. Levine, from the Mayo Clinic in the US, has popularized a concept called NEAT, an acronym for 'non-exercise activity thermogenesis'. NEAT reflects all the calories we burn when we are not sleeping, eating or doing formal exercise. In a study published in 2005 in the journal *Science*, Dr Levine and his colleagues compared NEAT in two groups of people who did not formally exercise. Half were thin and half were obese. He found that the thin subjects who frequently got up from their desks to walk around or stretch, paced while talking on the phone or just fidgeted were on their feet during their normal daily routines for 2 more hours than the obese subjects. This translated into burning 350 extra calories per day, enough to explain the difference in weight between the two groups.

In another interesting perspective on the importance of NEAT, William L. Haskell, PhD, of the Stanford Prevention Research Centre in the US, estimated that spending 2 minutes per hour sending e-mails rather than walking through the office to speak with a colleague resulted in a 4.5kg (10lb) weight gain over 10 years. Wow! Maybe switching my surgery to paperless by using electronic medical software wasn't such a good idea after all.

The unfortunate fact is that over the last 100 years, the proliferation of labour-saving devices, from the automobile to electronic software, has decreased NEAT 500–1,000 calories weekly. This has clearly played an important role in our obesity epidemic. The impact of NEAT on our society, while disturbing, presents an important opportunity. We need to plan our workplaces and daily routines better to make up for the energy expenditure we have lost because of the activities we no longer do.

NEAT is wonderful news for people who believe that the only way to stay trim and fit is to run marathons. Walking when you could be riding, standing when you could be sitting and moving when you could be keeping still are easy ways to stay slim and strong for life.

More important, maintaining a healthy weight and doing the right exercise is your best insurance against boomeritis. Following the South Beach Diet and the South Beach Supercharged Fitness Programme can help you achieve both of these goals painlessly. And when your partner or a friend tells you to sit still and stop fidgeting, just say, 'No'.

6

Bye-Bye Belly Fat

If you've had trouble zipping up your favourite pair of jeans lately or had to loosen your belt a notch or two, then beware. Your expanding waistline could be increasing your odds of having a heart attack or stroke. In fact, it could even kill you.

One of the most important benefits of the South Beach Diet is that as you lose excess pounds, you also lose girth, especially around your midsection. Women tell me with great pride that for the first time in years they can wear dresses with waistlines, and some even boast that for the first time in their lives, they can wear bikinis! Men are equally thrilled that when they take off their shirts at the beach, they can show off tight abs instead of a bulging belly. While this is great news for those interested in the cosmetic effects of a diet, it's even better news for those concerned with avoiding a heart attack and improving their general health.

Walk down a busy city street almost anywhere today and you will readily observe that not all overweight people have the same body shape. Some look more like pears and others look more like apples. If you'd been keeping track of overweight individuals over the past few decades, you couldn't help but notice the shocking increase in overweight, apple-shaped people. In these individuals, excess fat is concentrated in the belly, whereas in pear-shaped people, most fat is concentrated in the hips and thighs. Ever since French doctor Jean Vague first distinguished the android (apple shape) form of obesity from the gynaecoid (pear shape) form in 1947 and observed a connection between apple-shaped obesity and the development of diabetes, hypertension, gout and atherosclerosis, research has continued to demonstrate that the health implications of body shape are more important than we thought, even a few years ago.

It turns out that belly fat is different from fat that accumulates directly under your skin. Belly fat is the fat within the abdominal cavity – it's the fat attached to organs such as the stomach, liver and intestines. These internal organs are called viscera and that's why the fat that attaches to them is known as visceral fat. Visceral fat is like an endocrine organ, producing hormones and other chemicals that have a spectrum of biological effects on the body. And as we shall see, it is these hormones and chemicals that are slowly killing us.

The Proliferation of Apples

Why are the US and the UK populated by so many more apple-shaped people, and why should we care? It turns out that the proliferation of apples around the world is a human survival mechanism gone awry. Understanding this mechanism will help you appreciate what has caused the fattening of these two nations, how it is hurting our health and what can be done about it.

For early humans, the accumulation of fat during times of feast acted as a fuel reserve that could be called upon for survival during famines. If this fuel reserve was concentrated in the belly, leaving the arms and legs leaner, then a person could still run and hunt without limitation. Consequently, it would be a survival advantage to eat more than normal hunger dictated when food was plentiful and build up this fatty fuel reserve. To use a contemporary analogy, early man protected himself by filling up an accessory petrol tank in his belly. When food was abundant in the summer and autumn, he might fill up the tank by consuming more than was required for his immediate needs. Then he could gradually empty the tank as needed during the winter months, when food was scarce.

This survival mechanism worked fine for millennia, but today most of us live in the midst of a constant feast, without intervals of famine. The hunger that once helped us to store fat in order to survive continues unabated. The result: we've become fatter and fatter and fatter and many of us also have become prediabetic and diabetic.

You may be wondering why in the midst of this constant feast, we aren't all overweight apples. The reason is fascinating. It turns out that the genes that encourage fat storage – what are called thrifty genes – aren't distributed equally amongst societies around the world. Those societies that have experienced subsistence living punctuated by famine in recent times have a generous dose of thrifty genes. If they move from their traditional diet and lifestyle to a Western diet, however, they almost always become obese.

One such society that has been extensively studied is the Pima Indians in the south-west United States. For centuries, these people barely survived in desert conditions. Their ability to store fat easily when food was available and use it in times of scarcity was a crucial survival mechanism. But in the later 20th century, when the Pimas moved from their traditional lifestyle to a Western one, they experienced a horrible epidemic of obesity that continues to this day. This, in turn, has led to devastating rates of diabetes, early heart attacks and strokes. Today Asian Indians who move to the West and adopt a fast-food diet have the same problems. But they no longer have to move to experience obesity and diabetes. In New Delhi (and even Beijing), where Western fast-food restaurants are beginning to proliferate, these health problems are becoming more and more common.

But what about our friends who seem to be able to wolf down large amounts of chips and sugary drinks and remain thin? Well, these individuals were born with fewer thrifty genes and are blessed with a genetically rapid metabolism – a great boon in modern times. (If it makes you feel any better, in prehistoric times, these genetically thin people may not have survived.) So, depending on our genetic heritage, we each have a different propensity for accumulating belly fat and becoming an apple or a pear.

The Yin and Yang of Belly Fat

Why is belly fat a problem beyond the cosmetic? Overall, the hormones and other substances produced by visceral fat are pro-inflammatory. At first glance, this would seem to be good, since inflammation is an important means of fighting disease. For example, if you cut yourself or are invaded by harmful bacteria, your inflammatory response is called upon first to stop the bleeding with the formation of a blood clot, then fight any invader by mobilizing white blood cells to neutralize the bacteria or wall off a foreign body. In appropriate amounts, visceral fat and the inflammatory substances it produces are essential for survival. In fact, when it's not present in adequate quantity, such as in starving Third World children or those malnourished from cancer or another chronic disease, the inflammatory and immune response under-performs, increasing the risk of infection and death.

When Our Fat Stays Turned On

What happens if we persistently have excess visceral fat? What if our inflammatory response is turned on when we don't need it? What if it's on all the time? Because we have become a country of apples and our excess belly fat is continually pouring out inflammatory substances, we are now seeing its unfortunate effects. We're discovering that there are additional inflammatory chemicals produced by this excess fat, and we're learning more and more about how they affect the body.

One such substance that's frequently mentioned in medical news is C-reactive protein (CRP). This protein particle can easily be measured in clinical practice with a blood test known as the high-sensitivity CRP (hs-CRP) test and although not routinely carried out in clinical practice in the UK, research studies have shown the protein particle to be elevated when there is infection in the body. Alhough lower in prevalence than in the US population, CRP is found in dangerously high levels in the UK in people with belly fat, prediabetes and diabetes.

Dr Paul Ridker and his colleagues at the Centre for Cardiovascular Disease Prevention at Harvard University in the US, who did the initial research on CRP, have taught us that elevated levels of CRP are a risk factor for heart disease and that chronic inflammation is intimately involved with atherosclerosis, the build up of fatty plaque in our arteries leading to the blockages causing heart attack and stroke. But we are only now realizing that the scourge of inflammation goes well beyond affecting heart and blood vessels. In recent years, we have learned that inflammation appears to be a common denominator behind numerous other diseases, including diabetes, Alzheimer's, macular degeneration, asthma, arthritis and many forms of cancer. Belly fat and inflammation also appear to play a role in such common conditions as acne and psoriasis.

Belly Fat = Inflammation

Why should inflammatory substances be associated with belly fat? It turns out that an inflammatory response requires energy. If early man was starving, he could not afford the energy expenditure needed for an inflammatory response. All his energy was required just to bring blood and nourishment to his organs. This trade-off meant he was vulnerable to death from injury or infection and it is probably why our inflammatory response became associated with belly fat. The presence of belly fat in our forebears ensured the fuel reserve that was required for the protective inflammatory response. The fact is, humans were never intended to be carrying around the excess fat so many of us are lugging around today.

So how does this early survival mechanism translate to how we live today? The presence of excess belly fat in such a high proportion of our population is unprecedented. Because we never before had so many inflammation-producing apples, we didn't understand the extent of the health implications until recently. Just look at heart disease deaths, which had been decreasing over past decades due to improved treatments and better prevention. This favourable trend appears to be reversing itself in our younger age groups. A study published in the November 2007 *Journal of the American College of Cardiology* showed that in Americans between the ages of 34–55 – the very ones who've had the greatest exposure to processed and fast food – deaths from heart disease are on the rise (so are incidences of prediabetes and type 2 diabetes, two other diseases directly associated with belly fat). Thus, it appears that our sedentary, fast-food lifestyle is

WHY YOUR BMI CAN BE MISLEADING

Body mass index (BMI) is a formula for measuring optimal weight. It uses your height to adjust for your weight as it compares you to other individuals and populations. For instance, two men may weigh 90kg (200lb), but if one is 1.62m (5'5") and the other is 1.85m (6'2"), then weight alone is obviously a very poor predictor of which one is in fact overweight. BMI is the most common method of classifying normal versus overweight versus obese individuals. If your BMI is between 18.5 and 24.9, you're considered to be in a healthy weight range for your height. If your BMI is between 25 and 29.9, you're considered overweight. And, if the figure is 30 or greater, you're considered obese. To determine your BMI, just use one of the quick BMI calculators available on the Web.

While BMI has been a more helpful measure of obesity than weight alone, when it comes to comparing obesity rates in two different cities or areas, it can be a misleading indicator of health in individuals. That's because BMI does not take into account the distribution of body fat. Remember, fat concentrated in the belly is much more dangerous than fat concentrated directly under the skin. For instance, you might have a professional athlete with a great deal of muscle mass who has an elevated BMI but little belly fat, or a severely overweight person with a high BMI who has fat predominantly concentrated under the skin. Both of these people may well be at low risk of prediabetes, diabetes and heart disease. Conversely, you can have someone with a normal BMI who carries a dangerous amount of visceral fat in a pot-belly. That person's BMI might be normal because of thin arms and legs and little weighty muscle – but that person is nevertheless at increased risk of heart disease and many other diseases as well.

So if BMI can't accurately predict if your fat is dangerous, what is a more accurate measure? The answer is your waistline. Two waist measures are commonly used: One is your waist circumference measured where it's smallest, usually just above your belly button. (The waistline circumference cut-off for the diagnosis of prediabetes in a woman is 87.5cm (35in); in a man, 100cm (40in).) The second measure is the ratio of your waist circumference to your hip circumference – known as your waist-to-hip ratio. To find it, measure your hips at the widest part of your buttocks, then divide your waist circumference by your hip circumference. For example, if your waist is 85cm (34in) and your hips are 80cm (32in), divide 85 by 80 (34 by 32); your waist-to-hip ratio would be 1.06. If your ratio is greater than 0.95 for men or 0.8 for women, you fall into the apple-shaped category and it's time to do something about it.

trumping even our impressive gains in the treatment of the number one killer of men and women. If things continue as they are, when the current XL generation gets older, matters will be even worse.

The Diabetes – Belly Fat Connection

I cited this statistic before, but I want to mention it again: Today, nearly a quarter of the world's adults between the ages of 40–70 are prediabetic. The prevalence of prediabetes has tripled over several decades and today most patients in coronary care units are prediabetic or diabetic.

The cause of these burgeoning problems goes back to our fat-storage survival mechanism, which, rather than being life-saving, has become harmful in modern times. As it turns out, it's the accumulation of visceral fat that leads to insulin resistance, the condition in which the body produces enough insulin but the cells can't use it properly (the cells are in fact resistant to the action of insulin). As I noted earlier, insulin resistance causes the exaggerated swings in blood sugar that in turn cause hunger. Without periods of food scarcity, this hunger leads to further fat accumulation. And the more fat you store around your mid-section, the bigger your belly fat cells become. The problem is that insulin does not communicate effectively with swollen fat cells after a meal. As a result, the pancreas has to keep producing extra insulin to overcome the insulin resistance of these larger cells and move sugar and fat from the bloodstream into the tissues. Eventually the pancreas becomes exhausted and cannot produce adequate insulin. When this happens, blood sugar remains elevated after meals and type 2 diabetes is diagnosed.

Clearly, what helped man survive in the past is killing us today. Luckily, we now understand why, as a nation, we have got so fat and hyperinflamed. And luckily, we now know what to do about it.

Don't worry – I'm not suggesting that we all starve ourselves or try to imitate those times of food scarcity or famine. But in some ways, we all do need to eat more like our ancestors. This means consuming more fruits, vegetables, whole grains, healthy fats and lean protein. These are the basic tenets of the South Beach Diet and following them will reverse our accumulation of belly fat and its detrimental health consequences.

The other thing we must do is move more, the way our ancestors did. This means regularly doing aerobic (cardio) conditioning and functional core exercises. In fact, studies show that exercise is one of the most effective ways to get rid of visceral fat. In a US study conducted in 2005, 175 overweight men and women with mild to moderately bad blood fats (cholesterol and triglycerides) were randomly assigned to participate for 8 months in one of three exercise groups. The participants were instructed not to change their eating habits. One group exercised at a moderate intensity (40–55 per cent of aerobic capacity) for approximately 3 hours per week. A second group exercised at a high intensity (65–80 per cent of aerobic capacity) for 2 hours a week. The third group exercised at the same high intensity but for 3 hours per week. Both the 2-hour high-intensity group and the 3-hour moderate-intensity group showed no further accumulation of visceral fat. But the best news was that the high-intensity group that worked for 3 hours per week actually showed a significant decrease in visceral fat. And the bad news for couch potatoes: a control group that didn't exercise showed a significant increase in visceral fat, which means that if you do nothing to stop it, visceral fat just keeps on growing.

Another US study, published in 2006 in the *International Journal of Obesity,* found that a combination of diet and exercise – not diet alone – reduced the size of abdominal fat cells. This is an extremely important finding because swollen fat cells are the ones that become insulin resistant. Shrinking abdominal fat cells can help restore a normal insulin response, which will help prevent prediabetes.

What about Pears?

But what if you're a pear – a person who carries fat mainly in the hips and thighs? Will you respond as well as an apple to a proper diet and exercise? The answer, unfortunately, is no. It will, in fact, be harder for you to lose weight than it is for your apple friends, because like most pears, you have a slower metabolism due to your genetic make up, not your diet. That makes metabolism-revving exercise even more important for you.

But there's good news, too. As a pear, you are much healthier than your apple friends who may weigh the same as you. It turns out that overweight pears don't have the thrifty genes that lead to fat storage in the belly.

A Word about Metabolic Rate

While most of the epidemic of obesity has been due to activation of the fat-storage survival mechanisms discussed above, this is not the cause of all obesity or overweight. Even before we began this unintentional experiment of eating the wrong foods and avoiding exercise, there was still a percentage of Westerners who were overweight. Many claimed that they didn't overeat, and it turns out that many of them were telling the truth. In contrast were the food-guzzling types who never gained a pound. The fact is, we all have different metabolic rates and these rates do affect whether we gain weight readily or not. This point was made quite clearly in a famous Canadian study of twins.

In the study, 12 sets of identical twins were overfed by 1,000 calories a day, 6 days a week, for 100 days. The amount of exercise was carefully monitored and exactly the same for all. In other words, all the participants had the same energy intake via food and the same energy output via exercise. By the end of the study, each set of twins had gained virtually the same amount of weight, but between different pairs, the weight gain varied from about 4–12.7kg (9–28lb). This study proved that a major contribution to weight gain is metabolic rate, which is largely genetically determined. It's an important fact for dieters to understand, because your metabolic rate will affect how you respond not only to diet, but also to exercise. But don't be discouraged if your metabolism is slow. It doesn't mean you should throw in the towel and stop trying to lose weight. You'll just have to be a little more conscientious about maintaining our diet principles and work a little harder at your exercise routine.

The 'You Can Never Be Too Thin' Syndrome

I can't tell you how often the discussion of metabolic rate comes up in my cardiology practice. Let me share a typical patient story. A 52-year-old woman I'll call Karen comes to see me with a family history of diabetes and heart disease and the additional complaint of post-menopausal weight

living THE SOUTH BEACH DIET

Alan J., aged 52: Finding His Own Fountain of Youth

In May 2006, my cardiologist told me the results of my latest blood work and they weren't good. My lack of exercise and love of beer, fried foods and lots of ice cream had finally caught up with me – I had a beer belly to show for it. I weighed 113.6kg (250lb) and my blood sugar was 8 – that was much too high. I'm 1.87m (6'3"), so I always thought I could eat whatever I wanted and get away with it. Even a trip to the A & E for chest pains 3 years earlier wasn't enough to make me take care of my health. I thought that all I had to do was take medication for my blood pressure and cholesterol and I would be fine. I was wrong.

My cardiologist told me that I was a 'sugar cookie away' from entering the prediabetes stage. I immediately thought back to when I was in the A & E. I saw a man whose leg was so black that I thought he was a burn victim. The nurse told me that he would be losing his leg the next morning, thanks to diabetes! When my doctor told me I was a candidate for prediabetes, I was finally scared enough to take action.

My doctor had been trying to get me to read _The South Beach Diet_ for more than a year, but I resisted because I thought it was just for women. But that day, I followed my doctor's advice and finally got a copy. The book made a lot of sense, explaining why some foods do what they do to your body. The testimonials gave me hope that the diet would work for me. So, like any other red-blooded male, I immediately decided to start the diet – in a week! That gave me 6 more days to go on a farewell binge, in which I'd eat all my favourite foods. In that week I managed to pile on another 2.3kg (5lb) and my waist grew another 2cm (1in) or so to 105cm (42in).

gain. Her blood chemistries show evidence of prediabetes and she experiences frequent cravings. I put her on the South Beach Diet and recommend regular exercise.

Karen loses 6.8kg (15lb) over the next 6 months. Her cravings have disappeared and she feels great. When I see her at her next visit, I remark that she looks wonderful and I proudly tell her that her blood chemistries have completely normalized.

I was really afraid of Phase 1 and saying good-bye to all my comfort foods *and* beer. What really helped was keeping the book close to hand to refer to when I needed it, along with the support of my partner in making all those Phase 1 recipes work for me. My quiche cups, vegetable juice, turkey wraps, cheese sticks and all the others became my new best friends. In no time at all, I was learning all kinds of new things, like the fact that chicken doesn't always come in a bucket and that fish is not a fried brown fillet served on a bread roll with tartare sauce and chips.

Now that I no longer came home from work and downed a few beers to unwind, I had a lot more time on my hands. I decided to go to the gym after work. Bad knee and all, I figured out that a simple walk on the treadmill would be a good way to kill 30 minutes. I was surprised to find out that walking felt so good, I wanted to do it every night.

After just a few weeks, I'd lost 11.4kg (25lb)! By October, when I had my follow-up at the cardiologist's, it was obvious that the diet was working. My blood sugar was down to 5, which is very good and my weight was 96.8kg (213lb); a big improvement. In December 2006, I hit my personal goal of 88.6kg (195lb) with a 90cm (36in) waist. Even though I treat myself to a couple of indulgences every month, I am maintaining my weight. You know why? Because I realized very early on that I didn't go on a diet. All I did was change the way I live my life. And it works.

Last week, I had an annual stress test and after pushing that treadmill to six levels to complete the test, my doctor looked at me in amazement and said, 'You have added 10 years to your life.' So, after 18 months and nearly 1,000 miles on the gym treadmill, I want to say thank you, South Beach Diet, for being my personal fountain of youth.

I'm expecting a response of pleasure based on the fact that Karen has achieved my goals – and what I thought were her goals. I'm also anticipating some gratitude for her wonderful blood chemistries. Instead, she says, 'That's nice, Dr Agatston, but I am still too fat. I need to lose at least another 2.3kg (5lb) and another cm (½in) here – and here' (she points to her hips and thighs). Karen's response is, unfortunately, the rule, not the exception. Too many women tell me the same thing. And it's due to the fact that our culture has set an unrealistic and disturbing ideal of what women should aspire to look like – what I like to call the 'You Can Never Be Too Thin' syndrome. I have deleted the 'too rich' part of this famous line (thank goodness my patients don't come to me with financial issues).

Because I have heard responses like Karen's so often, my answer is well prepared. I tell her again that she looks fine to me (and to my staff), but that if she wants to lose more weight or another centimetre (½in), she can. However, she should not do it by trying to further limit her calorie intake. Once patients have resolved their cravings and normalized their blood chemistries, further caloric restriction can lead to yo-yo dieting (see page 41) and regaining more weight than they carried before.

Karen's genetically determined metabolism has dictated where her weight has stabilized. So how can she lose more weight and sustain it as part of a lifestyle? She must increase her metabolic rate. This means an exercise programme that helps build and maintain muscle and bone mass while it burns calories. Adopting our fitness programme is an ideal way to accomplish this.

The Bottom Line on Belly Fat

So, let me try to put the health implications of belly fat into perspective. I firmly believe that the recent epidemic of obesity in the West is primarily due to the types of foods we are eating and to our sedentary lifestyle. Our disproportionate increase in belly fat is due to the survival mechanism of insulin resistance. This has particularly dire implications for our health because belly fat is simply more dangerous than fat found directly under the skin.

Luckily, if you follow the South Beach Diet principles, your belly fat simply melts away. Moreover, by following a regular exercise programme, you speed that weight loss and help maintain it as well. This is true even for those of you who are overweight due predominantly to a slow metabolism rather than insulin resistance. It's also true for those of you who look fine but just want to lose a few extra pounds.

It has been very satisfying for me to see how far we've come in just 5 years in understanding what has caused us to become fatter and sicker.

But even more gratifying is seeing how far we've come in learning how to prevent these problems by helping people become thinner and healthier for life.

living THE SOUTH BEACH DIET

Linda S., aged 56: My Partner's Health is Vastly Improved

My partner, Bill, and I began the South Beach Diet in January 2007 after his doctor told him that he was on the brink of developing type 2 diabetes. My partner is 1.75m (5'10") and weighed 131.4kg (289lb), which made him very uncomfortable. His blood sugar was too high and he had lots of belly fat, which we knew wasn't good. But it wasn't just the fear of diabetes that worried us. He has multiple medical conditions that were being aggravated by his weight – specifically, degenerative bone disease in his back and fibromyalgia, which causes severe muscle pain. He was taking a lot of medication to manage the pain. Both of us knew he had to do something different to improve his health.

At the time, I was about 11.4kg (25lb) overweight, weighed 79kg (174lb) and was a couch potato. I was disgusted with myself, so I decided to go on the South Beach Diet with Bill. When we started learning about the diet, we realized we were doing every-thing wrong. We ate a lot of prepared, processed foods: white, starchy foods were my favourites! And we didn't eat enough vegetables and whole grains. I'm not much of a cook and frankly, never liked cooking, but I began to experiment with some South Beach Diet recipes. We started eating more lean protein and vegetables . . . lots of vegetables . . . and we were really surprised at how good healthy food actually tastes.

Then we took the next step. We joined a local gym and started working out 3 days a week – a really big change for us. With all his medical problems, Bill had to be very careful, but he did what he could. The weight started to come off both of us. I've lost 11.8kg (26lb) and Bill has lost 25.5kg (56lb) and is feeling much better. In fact, he feels so much better that he's been able to cut his pain medication in half. *And his blood sugar is now normal!* There's no question that his health has vastly improved.

The funny thing about the South Beach Diet is that we found that healthy eating is more enjoyable than the way we used to eat. We don't feel deprived (at least most of the time!) and we know that we'll never go back to the way we used to be.

7

Supercharged Foods for Better Health

There has been a real revolution in the quality and depth of nutrition information and it's going to make you and your family and friends healthier. Until recently, we didn't know which foods had the most nutrients because many of the nutrients in fruits, vegetables, whole grains, good fats and other foods hadn't been discovered yet. Even the role of fibre, which is now known to be crucial to our health, was virtually unknown until a few decades ago. And the knowledge that vitamin supplements cannot compensate for a nutrient-poor diet is an even more recent development.

Thanks to this explosion of knowledge, we know that there are thousands of micronutrients working together in whole, unprocessed foods that help to maintain and optimize our health. Numerous studies have established that people who eat more fruits and vegetables have less chronic disease, including heart disease. We also know that to obtain the greatest benefits from fruits, vegetables, whole grains and other good carbohydrates, it's best to eat a wide variety of each. So let's explore some of the exciting new nutritional science that's driving this revolution.

Good Carbs, Great Benefits

When you reach your 100th birthday, you're going to thank me for urging you to eat lots of fruits, vegetables and other good carbohydrates. South Beach Diet favourites, such as berries, cruciferous vegetables (broccoli, kale, cauliflower), wheat and oat bran and even chocolate (my favourite) and red wine have all been making consistent headlines for their positive effects on our health.

Not only are fruits and vegetables chock-full of fibre, they're also great sources of vitamins, such as C and E; minerals, such as iron, magnesium and calcium; and phytonutrients, the good health-boosting chemicals found only in plants. Phytonutrients are concentrated in the pigments (often in the skin) that give fruits and vegetables their colour. To get the full palette, you need to eat a variety of brightly coloured fruits and vegetables every day.

In the worst-case scenarios, the Western diet leaves us overfed and undernourished. Our meagre consumption of fruits and vegetables is just one example of how we are starving ourselves of life-giving nutrients.

We are all advised to eat 5 portions of fruit and vegetables a day. Although recent surveys published by the FSA show that people are now more *aware* of the need to eat plenty of vegetables and fruit, the percentage of people meeting the government recommendations in the West is still very low. Ironically, our hunter-gatherer ancestors, who had to forage widely for their food, ate a much greater variety of fruits and vegetables than we modern men and women do, even though we only have to go as far as the nearest supermarket. What's even more shocking is that, despite all the miracles of modern medicine, there's some convincing evidence that the hunter-gatherers were, in many respects, healthier than we are. That's because, as the research shows, they did not suffer from the chronic and degenerative diseases that plague us today. Most likely this is because of the variety of whole foods they consumed. It's been shown that later societies, which depended on just one major source of nutrition, such as wheat or rice, were shorter in stature than early man, had weaker bones and often had clear evidence of nutritional deficiencies.

Plant Power

There are thousands of phytonutrients commonly found in foods and we have barely scratched the surface in understanding what they do. Studies show that many phytonutrients act as antioxidants, which protect us against cell-damaging free radicals, chemicals that are produced when we use oxygen to make energy. In excess, free radicals are pro-inflammatory and attack healthy cells and tissues, which can ultimately lead to heart disease, cancer, premature ageing, Alzheimer's disease, arthritis and numerous other ailments. Antioxidants help maintain the right level of free radicals in your body.

You can compare antioxidants, which are found mainly in the skin of fruits and vegetables, to the rust-proofing that's used on a car. If you lose the protection, your car rusts and ages prematurely. If we do not have adequate antioxidants in our diets, we in a sense start to rust and age like that car. Have you ever noticed that smokers seem to look older than people their age who don't smoke? Their skin is frequently wrinkled and they are often prematurely grey. In addition, smokers' muscles, bones and organs tend to age faster than those of non-smokers. Smoking is well known to stimulate the production of inflammatory free radicals. It could be said that smokers are rusting!

Phytonutrients do much more than protect you from premature ageing, however. They also have the power to:

Beat inflammation and improve sex. Take polyphenols, for example. These phytonutrients seem to be particularly good for heart health because they are anti-inflammatory and relax the blood vessels, which improves blood flow and lowers blood pressure. If you follow nutrition news, you know that there's been a great deal of buzz about pomegranate juice, which studies show may reverse atherosclerosis (hardening of the arteries) and even improve erectile dysfunction (it's all about the polyphenols and blood flow). I usually recommend that people eat whole fruits for their fibre rather than drink fruit juice, but in the case of pomegranates, I make an exception. That's because most people have trouble getting the pomegranate seeds out of the whole fruit and drinking the juice for its potent polyphenols has proven health benefits. I like mixing pomegranate juice, which can be quite tart, with sparkling water for a refreshing drink.

In addition to improving blood flow, the polyphenols found in black, white, green and oolong tea and red wine have several other health benefits. Tea can lower bad LDL (low-density lipoprotein) cholesterol and red wine can raise good HDL (high-density lipoprotein) cholesterol. One study even showed that regular ingestion of green tea, which is rich in a type of polyphenol called catechins, may decrease body fat and help weight loss. You can enjoy tea, caffeinated (in moderation) or decaffeinated, on all phases of the South Beach Diet, and can sip a glass or two of wine with a meal on Phases 2 and 3.

And for those of you who, like me, are chocoholics, I've saved the best news for last. Several studies have shown that dark chocolate can lower blood pressure, again probably due to the beneficial effect of its polyphenols on blood flow. I'm not giving you a licence to gorge on chocolate. But when you do enjoy it, it's best to choose brands of dark chocolate that contain the most cocoa and the least sugar. While you won't be able to eat dark chocolate on Phase 1, you can take heart in knowing that enjoying the occasional piece is allowed on Phases 2 and 3.

Protect the eyes and prostate. Carotenoids, found mainly in yellow, orange and red fruits and vegetables and in dark green vegetables, are another family of phytochemicals that have been studied extensively for their health benefits. Two carotenoids, lutein and zeaxanthin (both abundant in dark green vegetables), are associated with lower rates of macular degeneration and possibly cataracts. Another carotenoid, lycopene, found in tomatoes, pink and red grapefruit and papaya, has been associated with lower levels of prostate cancer.

Keep you sharp. Anthocyanins are potent antioxidants found in blueberries, purple grapes, plums, aubergines, cherries and red wine. If these antioxidants work as well in humans as they do in mice, eating these foods may preserve your brain well into old age. In a 2006 US study, a blueberry extract was fed to mice that had a genetic mutation causing them to develop the same kind of amyloid plaques found in the brains of human Alzheimer's patients. Eight months later, the mice performed as well on a maze function test as their normal peers, an indication that their brains were still plaque-free. These studies have also shown that rats fed blueberries showed fewer signs of physical and mental ageing than rats that did not eat blueberries.

Fight cancer. Cruciferous vegetables, including broccoli, Brussels sprouts, cauliflower, cabbage and kale, are chock-full of cancer-fighting phytochemicals, including indoles and isothiocyanates. Consumption of these foods has long been associated with lower rates of breast cancer. More recently, a 2007 US study published in the *International Journal of Cancer* found that people who ate the highest level of isothiocyanates daily had much lower rates of bladder cancer than those who did not.

These are just a few examples of the nutritional power of phytonutrients. Needless to say, there have been many attempts to isolate a particular phytonutrient from a food source and put it in supplement form. In fact, you'll find shop shelves full of supplements claiming to have harnessed the healing power of foods. The fact is, the studies on supplements have not yet yielded the same kind of positive health results as the studies of food. That's probably because when you remove a particular nutrient from a food, you also lose its potentially beneficial interactions with the food's other nutrients. My advice is that if you want to benefit from nature's pharmacy, you need to eat whole foods as nature made them.

Bread Can Be Your Friend

Many people new to the South Beach Diet, especially those who have been on high-protein, low-carbohydrate diets, are often taken aback when, beginning on Phase 2, they learn that they are allowed to eat bread, cereal and pasta – and not just on special occasions, but every day. They wonder how they can continue to lose weight and also eat these carbohydrates, which they erroneously believe are responsible for the West's obesity epidemic, not to mention our epidemics of diabetes and heart disease.

I can't say it often enough: All carbohydrates are not the same. The overly processed refined starches and sugary processed foods that have been stripped of their fibre content are guilty as charged. These are the true culprits in the promotion of prediabetes, diabetes and obesity. But whole grains are an entirely different story. There's a world of difference between whole and refined grains. Whole grains are composed of the entire seed of the plant – the bran, germ and endosperm. Refining typically removes the bran and germ, which contain B vitamins and other nutrients as well as fibre. It leaves the endosperm, which is mostly starch and it's the starch that converts rapidly into sugar during digestion.

When most people think of grains, they think of wheat, but whole grains include oats, barley, rice, quinoa, spelt and rye. If you've been denying yourself a slice of bread or a serving of rice or cereal, you can stop doing so if you choose the whole-grain versions, which are actually very good for you. In fact, when it comes to your health, whole grains can:

Fight diabetes and heart disease. Recent studies show that eating whole grains can actually lower the risk of diabetes and heart disease. In May 2007, a US study published in the *Archives of Internal Medicine* reported that eating 28g (1oz) of fibre daily in the form of grain products resulted in a 27 per cent lower risk of developing diabetes than did eating roughly half that amount. Researchers noted that it wasn't only the fibre that appeared to be protective, but also magnesium, a mineral found in whole grains.

In June 2007, another study, published in the *American Journal of Clinical Nutrition,* showed that eating whole grains can help prevent artery-clogging atherosclerosis. In the study, researchers measured the thickness of the carotid arteries of 1,178 men and women. This measurement is called intimal medial thickness and is a good predictor of heart attack and stroke. The people who ate the most whole grains had the best results on this test.

With growing awareness about the benefits of whole grains, many new whole grain products have appeared on supermarket shelves. There are now some wonderful wholewheat pastas, whole grain cereals and breads that really taste great and are loaded with nutrients, including plenty of fibre. But if consumers don't buy them, you can't blame food manufacturers for not continuing to offer them. In fact, food manufacturers prefer to refine grains for two reasons: first, refining grains extends their shelf life; second, according to the producers, consumers are thought to prefer the smooth texture of refined flours over the texture of whole grains. I urge you to prove them wrong.

Remember, when you buy wholewheat pastas, wholemeal breads and other products, be sure the label says '100% wholewheat' or 'whole grain', and look for breads that contain 3g or more fibre per slice.

Got Enough Milk?

Is it the calcium and vitamin D that make low-fat dairy foods a good choice? Or is it both of these nutrients and something else? Although the scientific community doesn't have the answer yet, there is mounting evidence that something in dairy foods protects the heart and fights cancer. So drink your milk and eat your yogurt to:

Lower blood pressure and prevent prediabetes. Several studies have shown a direct link between consumption of dairy products and a reduced risk of high blood pressure. And a 2007 study conducted in Cardiff at the University Hospital of Wales suggested that dairy products may do much more than that – they may also help prevent prediabetes, also known as metabolic syndrome. Researchers followed 2,375 men aged 45–59 for 20 years as part of a long-term health study known as the Caerphilly Prospective Study (CAPS). Those who consumed the most dairy products were less likely to suffer from metabolic syndrome. The researchers did not distinguish between low-fat and high-fat dairy foods, but as a cardiologist, I definitely do. We know that saturated fat, which is found in fatty meats, poultry skin and full-fat dairy foods, is associated with an increased risk of heart disease. And even though this particular study showed positive results for any kind of dairy, I don't advise people to use full-fat products. Furthermore, there is no need to. Thanks to a broad selection of reduced-fat cheeses, low-fat milk and fat-free yogurt, it's just as easy to buy these healthier products as it is to purchase full-fat versions. One of my new favourites and one we include in a number of recipes in this book, is fat-free Greek yogurt, which is thicker than regular yogurt. Honestly, to me it tastes like full-fat soured cream.

5 YEARS of SUCCESS

Ellen P., aged 48: I Never Feel Like I'm Denying Myself

Five years ago I provided a testimonial for Dr Agatston's first book. Now I'm thrilled that I can offer an update because I've kept off the weight I lost 5 years ago for my daughter's bat mitzvah. I no longer think of South Beach as a diet; I think of it as a lifestyle. I feel like I'm eating normally all the time, and I am. Living this lifestyle for all this time has been great for me. You don't have to count calories or weigh your food and you can eat what you like, not what someone tells you to eat. I have friends who are on different diets and they have to eat exactly what they're given every week – I could never do that. I like being able to plan my own meals and cook fresh food. If you follow the South Beach Diet lifestyle, you don't walk around hungry. I eat prawns, lobster and steak, but now I eat them with a big salad and lots of vegetables.

I've stayed on the diet because I like the way I look and I like the way I feel. The funny thing is, I used to be such a dessert person. I'd go out to lunch with friends and be the only one ordering the molten chocolate cake. Now I order fresh berries and I'm perfectly happy. I never feel like I'm denying myself and I still eat a decadent dessert on occasion.

Another thing that's helped me keep the weight off is water. Drinking water has become a way of life for me – no more sugary soft drinks. You'd be surprised by how many calories you save by just drinking water. I also snack a lot. I always liked to munch on something crunchy and I still do. But instead of crisps, I eat raw vegetables with a dip. It's very satisfying.

Today, when I cook for my family, I follow the principles of the South Beach Diet. I have two teenaged daughters. They really like eating this way and they do it because they want to. They love salads and prefer to snack on mozzarella sticks and fruit, just like I do. If we go to a family party together, I notice they head straight for the raw vegetables and dip, not the junk.

My children are proud of me. They say that their friends tell them, 'Your mum looks so young and slim, like you guys.' It makes me feel good because I'm going through a divorce and starting to date again. I'm amazed by how many men are asking me out.

Fight breast cancer. As I sit writing this chapter, a newly released French study of more than 3,600 women has shown a significantly reduced risk of breast cancer amongst women with the highest dairy intake. This is consistent with US studies that found that pre-menopausal women who consume higher amounts of calcium and vitamin D appear to have a lower risk of breast cancer.

The 'Good' Fats

I wish I could think of another word for *fat*. Despite all the recent studies confirming that certain types of fat found in fish, nuts and vegetable oils are essential for health, some of my patients are still sceptical when I tell them that fat can be good. In fact, good fats have been shown to:

Improve triglycerides, lower cholesterol and protect against diabetes. Let's start with nuts, which have had a bad reputation for years. I am a great proponent of eating nuts in moderation. While they are high in fat, it's good monounsaturated or polyunsaturated fat. In fact, the amount of fat varies from nut to nut, with chestnuts having the least and macadamia nuts the most (although 70 per cent of the fat in macadamias is monounsaturated). Consider walnuts, which are rich in alpha-linolenic acid (ALA), a heart-healthy omega-3 fatty acid that has been shown to help keep triglycerides, the bad fat associated with prediabetes, under control. Not only do walnuts help lower triglycerides, but the mono- and polyunsaturated fats they contain also help lower blood cholesterol when these nuts are substituted for saturated fat in the diet. Whenever I recommend nuts to South Beach dieters, I do add a word of caution: because they're high in calories and it's easy to eat more than a handful, you need to be careful about how many you consume during the weight-loss phases of the diet and even when you're on Phase 3. (See page 165 for specific advice.)

Decrease heart attack risk. Good fats can be great for your heart, especially the omega-3 fatty acids found in cold-water oily fish such as salmon, tuna and sardines and also in walnuts, flaxseed and some vegetable oils. One of the first and most impressive trials in the US to show this was the Lyon Diet Heart Study, reported in 1994. It tested the effect of the Mediterranean diet on 605 patients who had already suffered a heart attack. Those on the diet were told to eat more omega-3-rich oils from both plant and animal sources, especially in the form of a rapeseed oil spread. The results were pretty amazing: the dieters had a 73 per cent decrease in recurrent heart attacks and other heart-related problems. What really struck me, though, was that this was a far better result than we were getting at the time with our medications. Interestingly, the diet did this without significantly altering the patients' cholesterol values.

Today, as part of the South Beach Diet, I encourage people to eat fish several times a week, and with good reason. The overwhelming majority of studies have reported that fish consumption is associated with a lower risk of heart attack and sudden death. In addition, a high-dose omega-3-rich fish-oil supplement is particularly useful in patients with very high triglyceride levels. (If you are pregnant or breastfeeding, however, be sure to consult your doctor about which fish may be high in mercury or other contaminants and whether you can take an omega-3 supplement.)

Beat inflammation. Fish oil also appears to protect against inflammation. A 2005 study published in the *Journal of American College of Cardiology* reported that fish eaters have lower blood levels of inflammatory markers, such as C-reactive protein (CRP) and TNF-alpha, which are linked not only to heart disease but also to rheumatoid arthritis, psoriasis, asthma and other diseases caused or aggravated by inflammation.

In fact, the US Food and Drug Administration was so impressed with the heart-healthy effects of omega-3 fatty acids that in 2004, the agency issued a ruling that allowed food manufacturers to make the following claim on labels: 'Supportive but not conclusive research shows that the consumption of EPA and DHA omega-3 fatty acids may reduce the risk of coronary heart disease.'

As I've noted earlier, EPA (ecosapentaenoic acid) and DHA (docosahexaenoic acid) are most widely found in abundance in fatty cold-water fish. Consumers may find information on the amount of EPA and DHA on food packaging or through other labelling, including shelf labels, signs, posters or brochures displayed in close proximity to the fish.

Improve intelligence and mood. Omega-3 fats are not just important for maintaining heart health. As it happens, DHA is found in the brain in high concentrations, which could explain why fish have earned a reputation for being brain food.

Omega-3 also appears to play a positive role in mood and other brain functions. It's been shown that people who don't get enough omega-3 fats in their diet are at greater risk of depression, dementia and learning problems, including attention deficit hyperactivity disorder (ADHD), which can affect adults as well as children. So if you want to be happy, healthy and wise, keep eating these good fats and try to get your children to eat fish on a regular basis as well.

• • • • • • • • • • • •

As you'll soon discover, fruits and vegetables, whole grains, low-fat dairy and good fats – just some of the foods we recommend on the South Beach Diet – are a veritable food pharmacy! Because you're eating a diet that is abundant in vitamins, minerals, fibre and other key nutrients, you'll keep your body running at optimal levels both while you are losing and maintaining your weight. Not only will you look and feel terrific, but you'll be avoiding many of the chronic diseases so prevalent today.

PART II

The South Beach Supercharged Fitness Programme

Overview
of the Programme

The South Beach Supercharged Fitness Programme consists of two parts: Interval Walking and the Total Body Workout, which you will do on alternate days. By incorporating exercise into your daily routine, you will not only supercharge your diet and lose weight faster, you'll tone your body, take inches off your waistline, rev up your metabolism and get off those frustrating weight loss plateaus. And the really good news is that with this 20-minute-a-day programme, you will definitely get better results in far less time than you would in a typical hour of exercise.

The Interval Walking part of the programme is designed to give your heart and lungs a really good workout, which is vital for cardiovascular health. The beauty of interval training – in our programme, alternating periods of fast or very fast walking with periods of slower recovery walking – is that it boosts your metabolism so you burn more calories and fat and that translates into *faster weight loss*. It also means that you will continue to burn more fat and calories after you've finished exercising – even while you're going about your daily activities or resting.

The Total Body Workout focuses on exercises that strengthen your core – the vital muscles in your abdomen, back, pelvis and hips. Not only do these exercises help promote balance, stability, good posture and co-ordination, they also tone your arms and legs and increase your flexibility. By the end of the first 20-minute session, you'll *feel* the difference. And it just keeps getting better and better as you continue.

The entire programme is designed so that you can tailor it to your own level of fitness. If you have never exercised before, you can work at a very easy pace until you feel confident moving ahead. If you're very fit, we offer exercise variations that make the programme more challenging.

Like the South Beach Diet itself, the fitness programme is divided into three phases, each with specific goals.

Phase 1 lasts 2 weeks – or longer, depending on your fitness level. It gently eases you into the cardio walking programme and core exercises, providing a firm foundation so you can progress to the more difficult Phase 2 routine without injury.

Phase 2 of the fitness programme lasts 4 weeks – or longer, if you feel you're not ready to move on. During this phase, you'll slim down and become stronger and better co-ordinated.

Phase 3 of the programme is a real workout. This phase provides a fitness blueprint that you can follow for the rest of your life.

The Best Time to Exercise

I've noticed that the people who are most likely to commit to an exercise routine are those who set aside a specific time every day for fitness – and stick to it. For many people, including me, the best time is first thing in the morning, before they're confronted with the demands and distractions of the day. For others, it could be after work or during their lunch hour.

A WORD OF CAUTION

Talk to your doctor before you make a sudden change in your level of activity, especially if you are aged 50 or older, have been inactive, have difficulty keeping your balance, have periods of dizziness or have known heart problems.

Pick the time that works best for you and try to make a commitment to a set schedule.

What If I Can't Work Out?

There will be times when your job or family obligations get in the way of exercising for 20 minutes straight – or at all. On days when you're super-busy, try to get in a 5- or 10-minute walk, or simply incorporate more movement throughout your day. (In Chapter 5, I discuss how even the smallest movements are important.)

When you do miss a day on the programme, just pick up where you left off. Don't fall into the 'I-missed-my-workout-today-so-I-might-as-well-quit' trap. Just as we don't want you to feel that you have 'blown it' if you have a bad day on the South Beach Diet, you shouldn't feel as if all is lost when you must skip a day or even a few days of exercise. And just as you are learning how to make better food choices most of the time on the diet, with our Supercharged Fitness Programme, you are learning a more efficient way to incorporate exercise into your daily life.

If you must stop exercising for an extended period, I do recommend that you start again with the Phase 1 exercises until you are sufficiently conditioned. When you are ready, move on to Phase 2.

Interval Walking Basics

The walking, or cardio, portion of your workout is divided into 'intervals', which, as we noted earlier, means that you will alternate between short bursts of fast walking and periods of walking at a slower pace. It will take around 20 minutes daily, but you can walk for longer if you like (see page 97 for cautions about not overdoing it).

You will begin each cardio session with a short walk at a slow or moderate pace to warm up your muscles. Then you're ready to start doing the intervals. Each interval consists of a higher-intensity burst of activity, followed by an easier recovery period. The recovery period gives your muscles time to recharge before the next period of fast walking. You will do several intervals during each session, ending with a short cool-down at an easy pace.

Why do I favour this kind of interval training? The reason is that you send your metabolism soaring when you work your body at higher intensities, but you have to work hard for only a short time to achieve that result. Before you know it, the hard part is over and you're back to a relaxed pace. And then, when you've recharged, you're ready to intensify your walk again. Studies show that breaking up your walk into fast/slow intervals is not only better for weight loss, but it's a lot more fun and the time seems to go faster.

The Interval Walking portion of the programme is also convenient. You can walk outdoors on nice days or, when the weather doesn't co-operate, do your programme on a treadmill, stationary bike or elliptical trainer at home or at the gym. (See the tips on adapting intervals to exercise equipment on page 92.) If you don't have a home machine or a gym membership, don't worry. You can easily apply the interval concept to other exercises (see page 93 for suggestions) and still get the benefits in the comfort of your own living room.

Wherever you do your walking, it's extremely important that you wear walking shoes, cross-training shoes or running shoes that give you the proper support. If you're buying new exercise shoes, try them on with the socks you plan to walk in. Synthetic athletic socks are better than cotton because they draw away moisture and keep your feet dry and blister-free. I also recommend that you have 240ml (8floz) of water before you start and also carry a small water bottle and sip from it as needed.

Keep in mind that when you're walking, posture counts! Hold your abdominal muscles in tight and consciously try to keep your belly from touching the waistband of your trousers. Keep your chest lifted and your chin parallel to the ground (believe it or not, leading with your chin while walking can result in neck and back pain). With each step, strike the ground from heel to toe and feel your buttocks (glutes) contract. This will help strengthen your buttocks and the backs of your legs as you walk. Remember to relax and enjoy yourself and don't stiffen up.

I love to walk outdoors, especially on the beach, which is easy enough to do in South Beach. But I realize that many people live in communities where walking can be a challenge due to poor weather, lack of pavements or heavy traffic. Be careful! Walk during daylight hours and avoid heavily congested areas. If you use an iPod, keep the volume low enough that you can still hear traffic sounds. If you walk very early in the morning or in the early evening, wear light-coloured clothing with light reflectors so you can be seen by passing cars.

Keeping Track of Time

During all three phases of the Interval Walking programme, you will alternate between walking fast for a brief period – between 15–60 seconds – followed by a slower recovery period. In general, the more intense the work (in other words, the faster you go), the shorter the duration of the work and the longer the recovery period. Conversely, when you're not working as hard, your work period will be longer and your recovery period will be shorter.

You'll need to keep track of time so that you can complete the designated numbers of intervals per session in about 20 minutes. There are several ways you can do this. The simplest is to keep track of the seconds by counting to yourself. You can use the tried-and-true 'a thousand and one, a thousand and two' approach, which measures 1 second. You could wear a watch with a second hand or even carry a stopwatch. You don't have to worry about following the programme down to the second, however; if you run a few seconds over or under for a particular interval, it doesn't matter. Just stay in the 'ballpark' and you'll be fine.

How Hard Are You Working?

The Interval Walking programme is divided into four levels of intensity: Easy, Moderate, Revved Up and Supercharged! You'll work at different levels on different days. How do you know if you're working at the right intensity? We don't prescribe a specified walking speed because what's difficult for one person might be easy for another. Moreover, if you're walking on hilly terrain or in deep sand at the beach, you'll be working harder than you would on flat ground.

To determine whether you are working at the right level, follow the helpful intensity levels described below. When you start the walking programme, you may need to refer to this page for guidance, but as you become more accustomed to how you feel as you walk, shifting back and forth from lower to higher levels of intensity will become second nature.

Easy Pace. When you're working at a low level of intensity, you should feel as if you're walking through a shopping centre (no stopping at the windows!) or strolling through town. Although you're constantly moving, you could easily carry on a conversation with a friend who's walking with you. This is the pace at which you will usually be working when you do your warm-up before beginning the actual intervals.

Moderate Pace. When you're working at a moderate level of intensity, you're walking at a brisk, but not fast pace and breathing faster than when you walk at an easy pace. You can still carry on a conversation, but doing so is more difficult.

Revved Up. When you're Revved Up, you're really moving! You're a bit short of breath and it's difficult – but not impossible – to maintain your pace. You should have difficulty carrying on a conversation at this level of intensity.

Supercharged! When you're working at your absolute top level, you are truly Supercharged! You're walking as fast as you can go and you can't sustain the pace for very long. Not surprisingly, as you get fitter, you will find that the pace that once tired you out is now relatively easy and even your Supercharged! pace will get faster.

INTERVAL TRAINING INDOORS

Stuck indoors? No problem. Do your interval training programme on a treadmill, a stationary bike or an elliptical machine, if you have access to one. Or you can do intervals without a machine (see opposite).

Treadmill. The first step is to determine what Easy Pace, Moderate Pace, Revved Up and Supercharged! feel like on a treadmill. A treadmill is like a moving pavement: walking on one feels very different from when you are walking outdoors. You can pick up your pace very quickly because the belt moves backwards under you rather than you propelling yourself forwards.

When you get on the treadmill, start slowly, gradually increasing the speed as you move from Easy to Moderate Pace. When you reach Revved Up, adjust the gradient so that you're working at a higher resistance. Find a gradient at which you can do the more intense intervals, yet easily go into your slower recovery period. If you don't adjust the gradient and try to walk faster and faster until you get to Supercharged!, you run a greater risk of falling off the back of the machine. It's also very difficult not to break out into a run when the treadmill speed exceeds 6.5kph (4mph).

Start the programme at an Easy Pace, just as you did the walking programme. We suggest this even if you're at a high fitness level, since you need to get a feeling for treadmill walking and become comfortable with the controls. You may have to try a few settings until you hit the right one. You'll find that the nice thing about a treadmill is that both the speed and gradient change gradually, so you can adjust your intensity as you go. Also remember that this gradual change will affect how you shift from the work to recovery cycles, so you may not want to start timing your intervals until the machine has reached the level you've chosen. Once you're used to walking at an Easy Pace and Moderate Pace, you're ready for your Revved Up and Supercharged! intervals. Remember, as your fitness improves, you'll have to adjust your speed and gradient to match your new feelings for each of the paces.

Stationary bike. When using a stationary bike, first adjust the seat so that you're comfortable. This usually means that each leg is only slightly bent at the bottom of the pedal stroke on that side. As you would with a treadmill, you must determine what Easy Pace, Moderate Pace, Revved Up and Supercharged! feel like on the bike. Then you'll begin your workout by cycling slowly to warm up.

You use your muscles on a bike differently from how you do when walking, so it's important to allow your body time to get used to the new interval patterns. You can change your intensity in two ways: either cycle faster or increase the resistance level.

In order to work at the Revved Up or Supercharged! level, you will have to increase both. Experiment with different combinations of speed and resistance to figure out which settings work best for you. Try not to apply so much resistance that you can't turn the pedals at least 60 times per minute. Remember, speed is better than resistance. We only use resistance to add intensity when we have achieved all we can at maximal speed.

Elliptical machine (cross trainer). The workout for an elliptical machine is similar to that for a stationary bike or a treadmill, but the way you use your muscles on this machine is different from either of the others. You'll need to allow time for your muscles to adapt. First, determine what Easy Pace, Moderate Pace, Revved Up and Supercharged! feel like. As with the bike, speed is better than resistance. However, once you've achieved your maximal speed, most brands of ellipticals allow you to adjust the gradient and resistance to increase intensity. Experiment with each to see what combination is most effective for you.

When you don't have an exercise machine. It's easy to create an interval cardio programme that you can do at home without a machine. Since you won't be able to walk fast enough around your living room to get to Moderate, Revved Up or Supercharged!, you'll need to choose other exercises to get a good workout. First, put on some music you like that has a strong beat. Wear a watch so that you know you've completed your goal after about 20 minutes. Start by simply marching in place to warm up your lower body, then mix in some shoulder rolls or swing your arms to get your upper body warmed up. After you've warmed up for 5 minutes, you can begin doing intervals following the time guidelines we've provided for each phase and day. Don't worry about being exact about time; you shouldn't be checking your watch while you're doing jumping jacks! Simple exercises work best in a small space: You can skip (without the rope), do jumping jacks, do side steps or jog in place. You can also add an exercise step if you like. After 15–30 seconds, depending on how hard you're working, return to marching in place to get back to an Easy Pace to recover. When you've done the suggested number of reps, be sure to cool down by walking in place for a couple of minutes before having a shower and moving on with your day. A great tool for helping you do cardio/interval training indoors is a fitness DVD. Look for titles that promise interval training and different levels of intensity.

Total Body Workout Basics

On the days when you're not doing Interval Walking, you will be doing the Total Body Workout for 20 minutes, or longer if you have the time and inclination. These exercises are designed to work several muscle groups simultaneously, which is how we move our bodies in real life. For example, at the same time that you're working your upper arms or raising your legs, you'll also be holding in your abdominal muscles and keeping your buttocks tight. That's why we call it a Total Body Workout.

In the Interval Walking programme, you begin your walk at an Easy or Moderate Pace to warm up. But with the Total Body Workout, the warm-up process is already built into the exercises themselves. In fact, the exercises for each phase are designed to be done in a specific order that gives your body time to warm up.

These exercises also have a built-in stretching component. You shouldn't need to do any additional stretching before or after, which also saves you time.

When doing the workout, wear comfortable clothing that allows for a full range of motion. You can listen to music, but I advise people not to watch television; you need to concentrate on each movement to get the most out of these exercises. If you have a large mirror, work out in front of it to check your positions.

Learning the Jargon

For those of you who are unfamiliar with exercise jargon, let me define a few terms that we'll be using. *Rep* (short for *repetition*) refers to one complete exercise movement. For example, in the first exercise in Phase 1, the Spinal Arch and Curl, one forwards and backwards movement is *1 rep*. If you do 8 reps, we say that you have completed a *set* for this exercise. The goal for many of these exercises is to do 3 *sets* of 8 *reps*. In some cases, depending on the difficulty of the exercise, I will suggest doing fewer reps. At first, you may be able to do only 1 or 2 reps. That's fine. Keep at it and each time you do the workout, you will get stronger. You can rest a minute or two between sets if you want, but it's not necessary.

Buying Equipment Is Optional

Many of the exercises in all three phases do not use any equipment and the equipment that is recommended is optional.

For the Phase 1 exercises, you will need a chair (ideally, one without arms) or exercise bench, plus a mat or a thick towel to protect your back and knees during the floor exercises.

For Phase 2, you'll need a mat or towel along with optional 0.5–2kg (1–3lb) weights and an optional exercise step. You can buy weights and a step, also called an 'aerobic step' or a 'home exercise workout step', from any shop or Internet site that sells fitness equipment. Most exercise steps are adjustable. Simply select the height that's most comfortable for you. If you don't want to purchase a step, you can use the first step of a staircase in your home.

Hand weights are useful if you want to increase the intensity of your workout. They're not essential, however, because you'll be creating your own resistance by tightening your muscles and moving slowly and deliberately through each movement. In fact, if you have neck or shoulder problems, I strongly recommend that you *don't* use weights for the arm exercises. If you haven't exercised before, it's a good idea to learn the exercises first without the weights and then add them to your workout when you become proficient.

Many of the Phase 3 exercises are done on the floor, so you'll need a mat or towel. For the Wall Sit, you'll need to find a clear wall to support you. In addition, a few of the exercises use optional hand weights.

I recommend you do all of the exercises barefoot. This allows you to flex and point your toes more easily and feel the floor and exercise step much better. Don't work out in socks – much too slippery.

PHASE 1

INTERVAL WALKING

Interval Walking on Phase 1 eases your body into working at a higher intensity, but it does this so gradually that you won't even realize it's happening. Your fast intervals are very brief and they're followed by nice long recovery periods.

The programme varies slightly from day to day over 2 weeks in terms of intensity and the number of fast-slow patterns. Depending on what day it is, you will do between 6 and 12 short intervals. For example, on Day 1 of this phase, you will start off with a 5-minute warm-up walk. Once you are warmed up, you'll begin your intervals. You'll walk fast for 15 seconds and then recover by walking slowly for 60 seconds. You'll repeat this fast-slow pattern *six* times and then end with your cool-down. The entire programme for the day takes about 15 minutes. Of that time, you will be working hard for only 1½ minutes.

On your second day of Phase 1 Interval Walking (which is actually Day 3 because you will have done the Total Body Workout on Day 2), your assignment is a bit different. Instead of doing 15 seconds of fast walking and 60 seconds of slow walking, you will do 15 seconds of fast walking followed by 45 seconds of slow walking. This time you will repeat that interval *eight* times before ending with your cool-down. This walk is slightly harder than your first day out, but you still have a generous amount of recovery time between your high-intensity fast-walking intervals.

You may wonder why the walking programme is more difficult on some days than on others, and you may be tempted to try to work at your highest intensity level all the time. Don't! If you worked at your highest intensity level every time you did cardio, you would run the risk of an over-use injury, which I talked about in Chapter 5. Your body needs time to recover with less strenuous days between high-intensity workouts. Furthermore, if your muscles never get a chance to fully recharge and are always tired out, you won't be able to work as hard as you're supposed to on your high-intensity days. If you don't recharge, you'll feel as if you're working harder than you actually are and you'll just be cheating yourself. (For a refresher on why interval training works, reread Chapter 4, 'Supercharge Your Metabolism'.)

As noted above, you will do your cardio interval walking every other day, alternating with the Total Body Workout. Ideally, on days when you are not doing cardio, try to also fit in a 15–20-minute recreational walk when you have the time.

The beauty of the Phase 1 walking programme is that you're making progress every day: Your heart and lungs are getting stronger, your cells are burning more fat and you feel more and more energized. By the end of 2 weeks, you will see an increase in your cardiovascular capacity, which means that everyday tasks, such as walking up a flight of stairs or running for a bus, should feel much easier.

THE TOTAL BODY WORKOUT

Phase 1 of the Total Body Workout will give you a trimmer, leaner, more defined body. After each session, you'll notice that you're standing a bit taller, your mid-section feels tighter and you feel lighter on your feet. The Total Body Workout is not just about strength and toning. It also teaches you how to use your body safely so that you remain free of injury and pain. The focus is on awareness, mobility and movement, not just while you are doing the exercises, but in your everyday life. The simple movements in Phase 1 prepare you for the more complicated exercises in Phase 2. Each exercise builds on the others, helping you to maintain and restore function and mobility in your body. By the end of 2 weeks, you'll feel stronger, more confident and ready to begin Phase 2. If you're pressed for time, you can shorten your workout by doing 2 sets of each exercise instead of 3. Or, if you are physically unable to complete the entire workout, you can do 1 set and gradually work up to 3.

Phase 1 is fairly easy and safe for most people. If, however, during any exercise you feel any pain or discomfort, stop doing it. Make sure that you are using proper form and have followed the instructions correctly. For example, when the directions say 'tighten your abdominal muscles' for an exercise that involves strengthening your shoulders, it's for a good reason. These core muscles provide stability and if you're not engaging them, you're not getting the most out of your workout. Even worse, you may inadvertently be putting strain on your neck or back.

Remember to go slowly and breathe through each exercise. You don't need to rush to finish a rep or a set. You've probably seen people at the gym racing through their exercises without the guidance of a trainer. These men and women are candidates for injury. While I urge you to increase your pace during Interval Walking, I much prefer that you take it slow and easy, concentrating on every movement, when you're performing the Total Body Workout.

For your convenience, the chart on the following pages lays out what you'll be doing every day for the entire 2 weeks of Phase 1 of the South Beach Supercharged Fitness Programme. As you'll see at a glance, you'll alternate Interval Walking days with the Total Body Workout days. You may want to photocopy these pages and keep them handy for quick reference.

PHASE 1 – WEEK 1

DAY 1 – INTERVAL WALKING

Warm-up: start with a 5-minute walk at Easy Pace.
- Walk for 15 seconds at Moderate Pace.
- Walk for 60 seconds at Easy Pace.
- *Repeat 6 times.*

Cool-down: end with a 2-minute walk at Easy Pace.

DAY 2 – TOTAL BODY WORKOUT

Phase 1 exercises: see pages 103–111.

Take a recreational walk at Easy Pace for 15–20 minutes (optional).

DAY 3 – INTERVAL WALKING

Warm-up: start with a 5-minute walk at Easy Pace.
- Walk for 15 seconds at Moderate Pace.
- Walk for 45 seconds at Easy Pace.
- *Repeat 8 times.*

Cool-down: end with a 2-minute walk at Easy Pace.

DAY 4 – TOTAL BODY WORKOUT

Phase 1 exercises: see pages 103–111.

Take a recreational walk at Easy Pace for 15–20 minutes (optional).

DAY 5 – INTERVAL WALKING

Warm-up: start with a 5-minute walk at Easy Pace.
- Walk for 15 seconds at Moderate Pace.
- Walk for 60 seconds at Easy Pace.
- *Repeat 11 times.*

Cool-down: end with a 2-minute walk at Easy Pace.

DAY 6 – TOTAL BODY WORKOUT

Phase 1 exercises: see pages 103–111.

Take a recreational walk at Easy Pace for 15–20 minutes (optional).

DAY 7 – INTERVAL WALKING

Warm-up: start with a 5-minute walk at Easy Pace.
- Walk for 15 seconds at Revved Up.
- Walk for 60 seconds at Easy Pace.
- *Repeat 8 times.*

Cool-down: end with a 2-minute walk at Easy Pace.

PHASE 1 – WEEK 2

DAY 1 – TOTAL BODY WORKOUT

Phase 1 exercises: see pages 103–111.

Take a recreational walk at Easy Pace for 15–20 minutes (optional).

DAY 2 – INTERVAL WALKING

Warm-up: start with a 5-minute walk at Easy Pace.
- Walk for 15 seconds at Revved Up.
- Walk for 45 seconds at Easy Pace.
- *Repeat 10 times.*

Cool-down: end with a 2-minute walk at Easy Pace.

DAY 3 – TOTAL BODY WORKOUT

Phase 1 exercises: see pages 103–111.

Take a recreational walk at Easy Pace for 15–20 minutes (optional).

DAY 4 – INTERVAL WALKING

Warm-up: start with a 5-minute walk at Easy Pace.
- Walk for 15 seconds at Revved Up.
- Walk for 30 seconds at Easy Pace.
- *Repeat 12 times.*

Cool-down: end with a 2-minute walk at Easy Pace.

DAY 5 – TOTAL BODY WORKOUT

Phase 1 exercises: see pages 103–111.

Take a recreational walk at Easy Pace for 15–20 minutes (optional).

DAY 6 – INTERVAL WALKING

Warm-up: start with a 5-minute walk at Easy Pace.
- Walk for 15 seconds at Supercharged!
- Walk for 60 seconds at Easy Pace.
- *Repeat 8 times.*

Cool-down: end with a 2-minute walk at Easy Pace.

DAY 7 – TOTAL BODY WORKOUT

Phase 1 exercises: see pages 103–111.

Take a recreational walk at Easy Pace for 15–20 minutes (optional).

Phase 1
Total Body Workout
Exercises

SPINAL ARCH AND CURL

Increases spinal mobility and function, helps posture, tones the buttocks and relieves stress. It also feels great!

1. Sit up straight on the edge of a chair with your feet hip-width apart and your knees in line with your ankles. Place your palms on your thighs, press your heels into the floor and contract your buttock muscles.

2. Slide your hands up towards your hips as you continue to contract your buttock muscles; you should feel a slight lifting sensation. Gently arch your back and look up, tightening your abdominal muscles. Feel your neck lengthen as you lift your head. Imagine that you are hovering over the chair.

3. Continuing to hold your abdominal muscles in, round your back as you slide your hands towards your knees. Look down to the ground. Return to the starting position (1). Arching and curling is 1 rep.

    Do 3 sets of 8 reps. This exercise should be done in one fluid motion without stopping between repetitions.

SPINAL DIVE

Improves posture by strengthening upper-back muscles and stretching chest muscles.

1. Sit up straight on the edge of a chair with your feet hip-width apart and your knees in line with your ankles. Your feet should be firmly planted on the floor. Place your palms on your thighs.

2. Pull your abdominals in and round your back as you drop your head in between your knees.

3. Arch your spine and tighten your abdominal muscles as you slowly unfurl into the upright starting position. Be sure to keep your shoulders down. Move slowly so you can feel your back muscles working. This is 1 rep.

Do 3 sets of 8 reps.

Caution: *Stop if you become dizzy.*

SPINAL TWIST

Improves back flexibility.

1. Sit up straight on the edge of a chair with your feet hip-width apart and your knees in line with your ankles. Your feet should be firmly planted on the floor. Place your palms on your thighs.

2. Keeping your back straight, pull in your abdominal muscles. Twist from your waist as you turn to the left, sliding your right hand down your right thigh and your left hand up your left thigh. Your feet and legs should remain still.

3. Twist from your waist as you turn to the right, sliding your left hand down your left thigh and your right hand up your right thigh. When you finish 1 twist to the left and 1 twist to the right – this is 1 rep – keep going. This movement should be done in a single fluid motion.

   Do 3 sets of 8 reps.

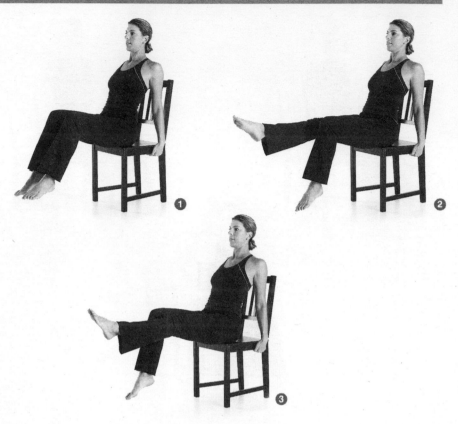

LEG FLUTTER

Tightens the mid-section and improves the muscles that track and support the knees.

1. Sit up straight on a chair, gripping the seat with both hands. Your feet should be hip-width apart and your knees in line with your ankles. Keep your arms straight and your chest lifted as you pull in your abdominal muscles. Lean back slightly and lift both feet about 10–15cm (4–6in) off the floor, keeping your knees close together and your back relaxed. Make sure that you are using your abdominal muscles to lift your legs and are not sinking into your arms or stressing your back. If your back hurts, support it with a cushion.

2–3. Kick out your right leg in a controlled manner, return to the starting position and kick out your left leg (this is 1 rep). This should be a fluid motion; don't stop between reps. Work at a slow, controlled pace and feel the contraction in your upper thighs.

    Do 3 sets of 8 reps. If this is too difficult, do as many reps as you can and gradually increase.

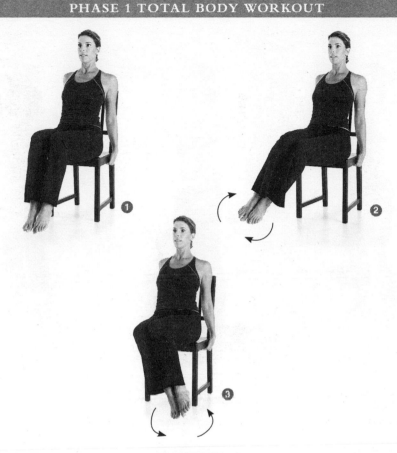

LEG CIRCLE

A beautiful leg-shaper. Excellent for lower abdominal strength, hip- and knee-joint flexibility and mobility.

1. Sit up straight on a chair, gripping the seat with both hands, your feet together and your knees in line with your ankles. Keep your arms straight and your chest lifted as you squeeze in your abdominal muscles. Lean back slightly and lift both feet 10–15cm (4–6 in) off the floor, keeping your knees close together and your back relaxed. Make sure that you are using your abdominal muscles to lift your legs and are not leaning on your arms or stressing your back.

2. Circle both legs to the right 4 times, as though stirring a tall drink.

3. Without lowering your legs, reverse direction and do 4 circles to the left.

    Do 3 sets of 4 circles to the right and 4 circles to the left. Do not stop between sets unless you have to rest.

SALSA SHOULDERS

Increases awareness, flexibility and mobility in the neck, shoulders and ribcage. Great for people with neck pain.

1. Stand with your feet firmly planted on the floor. Press your heels into the floor and contract the muscles in your buttocks (keep them contracted throughout the exercise). Hold your arms up with your elbows bent at a 90-degree angle, palms facing forwards.

2. Circle your shoulders forwards 4 times.

3. Reverse direction and circle your shoulders backwards 4 times.

   Do 3 sets of 4 circles forwards and 4 circles backwards. Do not stop between sets unless you have to rest.

BIKINI SWIRL

Increases flexibility and mobility in the neck and ribcage. Strengthens the back.

1–3. Stand straight and place your hands on top of your head. Pull your elbows back. Press your heels into the floor to contract the muscles in your buttocks (keep them contracted throughout the exercise). Pull in your abdominal muscles and, moving from your waist, circle your ribcage 4 times from left to right without moving your hips (try to draw a circle on the ceiling with the top of your head). It should feel as if you are using a hula hoop with the hoop just under your ribcage. Switch directions and do 4 circles from right to left.

Do 3 sets of 4 circles from left to right and 4 circles from right to left.

ROLL-DOWN

Gives you flat abs and a sexy six-pack!

1. Sit on the floor with your knees bent and your feet hip-width apart. Press your feet firmly into the floor and contract your thigh muscles. Work against your body weight. Imagine that you are trying to squeeze your legs together but they're so heavy, they won't budge.

2–3. Contract your pelvic floor muscles and squeeze your belly button in towards your spine. Roll back one vertebra at a time, resisting gravity as you lower yourself all the way down to the floor. Keeping your abdominal muscles tight, lift your spine one vertebra at a time back to the starting position (1). This is 1 rep.

Do 1 set of 8 reps. Work up to 3 sets.

Variation: When you are strong enough to do Roll-Downs comfortably without losing form, try this variation. Roll down to the point where it's most challenging to hold yourself up. Keeping your abdominal muscles tight, make a complete circle with your entire torso to the right 8 times. Keep your hips and sitting bones stable – don't rock your pelvis. Make a complete circle with your entire torso to the left 8 times.

Do 1 set of 8 circles to the right and 8 circles to the left.

CAT 'N' HAMMOCK BACK STRETCH

Strengthens and lengthens the abdominals and the posture muscles in the back. Feels wonderful, too! A great movement.

1. Get on your hands and knees with your back in a flat tabletop position. Your hands should be in line with your shoulders and your knees in line with your hips.

2. Press your palms into the floor and pull your abdominal muscles in towards your spine. Squeeze your buttock muscles and round your back and neck like a cat. Hold this position for 10 seconds.

3. From the Cat Stretch, flow into the Hammock Back Stretch. Pull your shoulders down and away from your ears and slowly raise your head and chest. Keeping your abdominal muscles tight, allow your back to sway as if you were a human hammock. Hold this position for 10 seconds, then return to the flat back position.

Alternate in a flowing manner between the Cat Stretch and the Hammock Back Stretch 3–5 times. End with the Cat Stretch.

INTERVAL WALKING

Over the next 4 weeks, you're going to teach your body how to become a champion fat burner. In this phase, Interval Walking is stepped up. You will be doing longer periods of fast walking within the 20 minutes, with shorter recovery periods in between. You'll notice that the increase in work levels is very gradual and you will easily rise to the challenge.

By now, you will be seeing the fruits of your labour. As you increase your metabolism, you'll burn more fat and calories, lose more weight and look trimmer. You'll also be surprised at how much more stamina you have, not only during your workout, but as you go about your day-to-day activities.

In fact, you may be so pleased by your progress that you're tempted to push yourself to do even more. Don't! More is *not* better and if you overdo it, you risk injuring yourself. For the best results, please follow the programme. As I explained earlier, your recovery periods are very important for achieving your long-term goals. If you try to work as hard as you can every day, the intensity of your workouts will suffer and intensity is the name of the game in interval training. Your body needs to rest and recover, so don't cut this part out.

If you feel that Phase 2 Interval Walking is too challenging, repeat the Phase 1 walking programme for another week or two and then give Phase 2 another try.

THE TOTAL BODY WORKOUT

The Total Body Workout in Phase 2 builds on what you've learned during Phase 1. These exercises incorporate more co-ordinated and choreographed movements, but you're ready for it. With each workout session, you'll get a bit more proficient at doing the exercises. As you become more aware of how your body moves, your work becomes deeper and more effective. You're learning how to make each workout count. You will notice a steady improvement in how you feel, particularly if you've had stiffness and joint problems in the past. And you'll notice that you look slimmer and sleeker.

If you're having difficulty completing the number of sets, you can do fewer sets or fewer reps per set. Or, if you simply can't keep up with Phase 2, go back to Phase 1 for 2 weeks and then give Phase 2 another try.

You will do Phase 2 for 4 weeks – or longer, if you feel you're not ready to move on. See the plans on the following pages for what to do each day.

PHASE 2 – WEEK 1

DAY 1 – INTERVAL WALKING

Warm-up: start with a 3-minute walk at Easy Pace.
- Walk for 30 seconds at Moderate Pace.
- Walk for 30 seconds at Easy Pace.
- *Repeat 12 times.*

Cool-down: end with a 2-minute walk at Easy Pace.

DAY 2 – TOTAL BODY WORKOUT

Phase 2 exercises: see pages 119–127.

Take a recreational walk at Easy Pace for 15–20 minutes (optional).

DAY 3 – INTERVAL WALKING

Warm-up: start with a 3-minute walk at Moderate Pace.
- Walk for 15 seconds at Supercharged!
- Walk for 45 seconds at Moderate Pace.
- *Repeat 12 times.*

Cool-down: end with a 2-minute walk at Easy Pace.

DAY 4 – TOTAL BODY WORKOUT

Phase 2 exercises: see pages 119–127.

Take a recreational walk at Easy Pace for 15–20 minutes (optional).

DAY 5 – INTERVAL WALKING

Warm-up: start with a 3-minute walk at Easy Pace.
- Walk for 30 seconds at Revved Up.
- Walk for 30 seconds at Easy Pace.
- *Repeat 8 times.*

Cool-down: end with a 2-minute walk at Easy Pace.

DAY 6 – TOTAL BODY WORKOUT

Phase 2 exercises: see pages 119–127.

Take a recreational walk at Moderate Pace for 15–20 minutes (optional).

DAY 7 – INTERVAL WALKING

Warm-up: start with a 2-minute walk at Moderate Pace.
- Walk for 15 seconds at Supercharged!
- Walk for 60 seconds at Moderate Pace.
- *Repeat 8 times.*

Cool-down: end with a 2-minute walk at Easy Pace.

PHASE 2 – WEEK 2

DAY 1 – TOTAL BODY WORKOUT

Phase 2 exercises: see pages 119–127.

Take a recreational walk at Easy Pace for 15–20 minutes (optional).

DAY 2 – INTERVAL WALKING

Warm-up: start with a 3-minute walk at Easy Pace.
- Walk for 30 seconds at Moderate Pace.
- Walk for 30 seconds at Easy Pace.
- *Repeat 10 times.*

Cool-down: end with a 2-minute walk at Easy Pace.

DAY 3 – TOTAL BODY WORKOUT

Phase 2 exercises: see pages 119–127.

Take a recreational walk at Easy Pace for 15–20 minutes (optional).

DAY 4 – INTERVAL WALKING

Warm-up: start with a 2-minute walk at Moderate Pace.
- Walk for 15 seconds at Supercharged!
- Walk for 45 seconds at Moderate Pace.
- *Repeat 15 times.*

Cool-down: end with a 2-minute walk at Easy Pace.

DAY 5 – TOTAL BODY WORKOUT

Phase 2 exercises: see pages 119–127.

Take a recreational walk at Moderate Pace for 15–20 minutes (optional).

DAY 6 – INTERVAL WALKING

Warm-up: start with a 3-minute walk at Easy Pace.
- Walk for 30 seconds at Moderate Pace.
- Walk for 45 seconds at Easy Pace.
- *Repeat 8 times.*

Cool-down: end with a 2-minute walk at Easy Pace.

DAY 7—TOTAL BODY WORKOUT

Phase 2 exercises: see pages 119–127.

Take a recreational walk at Easy Pace for 15–20 minutes (optional).

PHASE 2 – WEEK 3

DAY 1 – INTERVAL WALKING

Warm-up: start with a 2-minute walk at Moderate Pace.
- Walk for 30 seconds at Supercharged!
- Walk for 60 seconds at Moderate Pace.
- *Repeat 10 times.*

Cool-down: end with a 2-minute walk at Easy Pace.

DAY 2 – TOTAL BODY WORKOUT

Phase 2 exercises: see pages 119–127.

Take a recreational walk at Moderate Pace for 15–20 minutes (optional).

DAY 3 – INTERVAL WALKING

Warm-up: start with a 3-minute walk at Easy Pace.
- Walk for 45 seconds at Moderate Pace.
- Walk for 30 seconds at Easy Pace.
- *Repeat 8 times.*

Cool-down: end with a 2-minute walk at Easy Pace.

DAY 4 – TOTAL BODY WORKOUT

Phase 2 exercises: see pages 119–127.

Take a recreational walk at Moderate Pace for 15–20 minutes (optional).

DAY 5 – INTERVAL WALKING

Warm-up: start with a 2-minute walk at Easy Pace.
- Walk for 30 seconds at Supercharged!
- Walk for 45 seconds at Moderate Pace.
- *Repeat 8 times.*

Cool-down: end with a 2-minute walk at Easy Pace.

DAY 6 – TOTAL BODY WORKOUT

Phase 2 exercises: see pages 119–127.

Take a recreational walk at Moderate Pace for 15–20 minutes (optional).

DAY 7 – INTERVAL WALKING

Warm-up: start with a 3-minute walk at Moderate Pace.
- Walk for 45 seconds at Revved Up.
- Walk for 15 seconds at Moderate Pace.
- *Repeat 6 times.*

Cool-down: end with a 2-minute walk at Easy Pace.

PHASE 2 – WEEK 4

DAY 1 – TOTAL BODY WORKOUT

Phase 2 exercises: see pages 119–127.

Take a recreational walk at Easy Pace for 15–20 minutes (optional).

DAY 2 – INTERVAL WALKING

Warm-up: start with a 3-minute walk at Easy Pace.

- Walk for 60 seconds at Moderate Pace.
- Walk for 30 seconds at Easy Pace.
- *Repeat 8 times.*

Cool-down: end with a 2-minute walk at Easy Pace.

DAY 3 – TOTAL BODY WORKOUT

Phase 2 exercises: see pages 119–127.

Take a recreational walk at Moderate Pace for 15–20 minutes (optional).

DAY 4 – INTERVAL WALKING

Warm-up: start with a 2-minute walk at Moderate Pace.

- Walk for 30 seconds at Supercharged!
- Walk for 60 seconds at Moderate Pace.
- *Repeat 10 times.*

Cool-down: end with a 2-minute walk at Easy Pace.

DAY 5 – TOTAL BODY WORKOUT

Phase 2 exercises: see pages 119–127.

Take a recreational walk at Moderate Pace for 15–20 minutes (optional).

DAY 6 – INTERVAL WALKING

Warm-up: start with a 3-minute walk at Easy Pace.

- Walk for 30 seconds at Revved Up.
- Walk for 45 seconds at Easy Pace.
- *Repeat 8 times.*

Cool-down: end with a 2-minute walk at Easy Pace.

DAY 7 – TOTAL BODY WORKOUT

Phase 2 exercises: see pages 119–127.

Take a recreational walk at Easy Pace for 15–20 minutes (optional).

Phase 2
Total Body Workout
Exercises

STAIR STEP-UP

Lifts the buttocks, shapes the legs, improves balance and strengthens upper-thigh muscles.

1. Stand in front of your exercise step. Place your left foot on the step, pressing your heel into the step. Keep your right foot on the floor behind you. (If you have knee problems, do this exercise without using the exercise step. If you have poor balance, hold on to a wall or chair for greater stability.)

2. Straighten your right leg and lift it to the point where you can feel your buttocks contract. Hold that position. Keep your buttocks tight and lifted.

3. Tightening your abdominals and not allowing yourself to wobble, slowly pulse your right leg slightly higher while keeping your buttocks and abdominal muscles tight. Do 8 pulses with your right leg and then return to the starting position.

Switch legs and repeat the exercise.

Do 3 sets of 8 pulses with each leg.

Variation: When you are proficient at doing Stair Step-Ups, add this more difficult variation. Instead of pulsing the extended leg up and down, draw 4 small circles to the right in the air with your toes. Reverse the direction and draw 4 more small circles to the left. Switch leg positions and repeat the exercise.

Do 3 sets of 4 circles to the right and 4 circles to the left with each leg.

Caution: Stop if you have knee or hip pain.

SIDE REACH

Lifts the buttocks, shapes and strengthens the legs and inner thighs and improves balance.

1. Place your left foot on an exercise step, pressing your heel into the step. Lift your right leg up to the point where you can feel your buttock muscles contract, then cross your right leg behind your left leg, reaching through your toes.

2. Holding your abdominal muscles in tight and not allowing yourself to wobble (hold on to a chair if you need to), slowly bend and straighten your *left* leg (this is 1 rep).

Switch legs and repeat the exercise.

Do 3 sets of 8 reps with each leg.

Caution: *Stop if you have knee or hip pain.*

SUPER SQUAT

Lifts the buttocks and strengthens the thigh muscles. A great knee strengthener if done properly.

1. Place your left foot on the exercise step. Keep your right foot flat on the floor. Turn out both feet. (If you have knee problems, you can do this exercise without using the step.)

2. Bend both knees into a comfortable squat position. Your ankle bones should be directly in line with your knees to prevent knee problems.

3. Lower yourself into a deeper squat until you feel your buttock muscles contract. Hold at the lowest point you can manage, then pulse your legs up and down 2.5–5cm (1–2 in) (a single up-and-down movement is 1 rep). Your hamstrings should feel as if they're 'on fire'. This is a small, controlled movement.

Switch legs and repeat the exercise.

Do 8 reps with your left foot on the step and 8 reps with your right foot on the step (this is 1 set). Work up to 3 sets.

Variation: Once you feel strong enough, try this more difficult variation. Lift the heel of the foot that is not on the step while you pulse up and down with both legs (this is 1 rep).

Do 8 reps with your left foot on the step and 8 reps with your right foot on the step (this is 1 set). Work up to 3 sets.

Caution: *Stop if you have any knee or hip pain.*

SINGLE ARM REACH

Great for flexibility and range of motion in the shoulders.

1. Stand up straight with your legs shoulder-width apart. Hold both arms at chest height, with your upper arms parallel to the floor, elbows bent at 90 degrees and palms facing towards you. Keep your chest open and lifted on all movements. Your chin stays parallel to the floor and should not jut forwards.

2. Straighten your right arm as you raise it towards the ceiling, feeling the muscles under your arm contract. When your arm is straight overhead, rotate your hand and arm away from your body.

3. In a fluid motion, keep your right arm straight as you slowly move it behind you and down. This movement should feel as if you are reaching over and behind the passenger seat of your car.

4. Without stopping, continue to move your arm down and around until your elbow is at your hip. Return to the starting position. This is 1 rep.

Do 8 reps with your right arm, then 8 reps with your left arm (this is 1 set). Work up to 3 sets.

Caution: *People with existing shoulder injuries or previous rotator cuff or impingement issues should be careful doing this exercise.*

BEAUTIFUL BICEPS

Enhances upper-arm shape and strength.

You can use 0.5–2kg (1–3lb) hand weights or perform this exercise without weights. Don't use weights if you have shoulder injuries or feel any shoulder pain as you do the exercise.

1. Holding a weight in each hand, stand up straight with your legs shoulder-width apart. With your palms up, bend your arms, keeping your elbows at chest height as though resting them on an imaginary table. If you're not using weights, hold your palms open and facing towards you.

2–3. While keeping your elbows at chest height (try not to lower them), do 4 basketball-size outward circles with your forearms. Without stopping, reverse direction and do 4 inward circles.

   Do 3 sets of 4 circles outward and 4 circles inward.

SHOULDER STROKE

Strengthens shoulders, chest, biceps and triceps. Improves posture and increases shoulder mobility.

You can use 0.5–2kg (1–3lb) hand weights, or perform this exercise without weights. Don't use weights if you have shoulder injuries or feel any pain during the exercise.

1. Holding a weight in each hand, stand with your legs shoulder-width apart. Turn your palms down and hold both arms straight out at chest height, parallel to the floor. If you're not using weights, make fists and turn your palms down.

2–3. Keeping your left arm at shoulder height, lower your right arm to your right thigh, then, without stopping, raise your right arm to shoulder height and lower your left arm to your left thigh (this is 1 rep). Don't stop between reps.

Do 3 sets of 8 reps.

Tip: Your fists should not be raised above your shoulders. The muscles under your arms should contract and you should feel a pulling sensation from your shoulder blades. Make sure your shoulders don't hunch up – it will put a strain on your neck. Watch your posture. Your chin should be parallel to the floor and your chest lifted as you do this exercise.

FAB ABS

Creates a supersexy six-pack and flat abs. Stretches chest muscles. Improves balance and co-ordination.

1. Sit on the floor with your knees bent and your arms straight behind you. Your hands should be flat on the floor with your fingertips pointing away from you. Contract your pelvic-floor muscles and pull your abdominal muscles in tight to keep you balanced as you lift your feet 7.5–10cm (3–4in) off the floor.

2–3. Tightening your abdominals, straighten and bend your legs (this is 1 rep). Repeat 8 times in a fluid manner. If you're not strong enough to extend both legs, extend one leg at a time, alternating legs.

   Do 3 sets of 8 reps.

   Variation: When you have mastered the basic exercise, make it more challenging by doing circles with both legs extended. One outward and 1 inward circle is 1 rep.

   Do 3 sets of 8 reps.

AB CIRCLE

Shapes and flattens lower and upper abdominals.

1. Lie down on your back with your body propped up on your elbows. Press your fore-arms and palms firmly into the floor, fingertips facing forwards. Squeeze your shoulder blades together to keep your chest lifted. Bend your knees out to the side and press the bottoms of your feet firmly together. (The harder you press your feet into one another, the more intense the work.) Lift your feet off the floor about 10cm (4in) keeping your soles pressed together.

2. Circle your feet out, up, around and back towards your body as you circle towards the start position (1). Repeat 4 times.

3. Still keeping the soles of your feet together, reverse the direction of the circle. Repeat 4 times.

   Do 3 sets of 4 circles in each direction.

BEACH KNEEL

Tightens and lifts the buttocks, strengthens the back and improves posture and stretches the chest, hips and thighs.

1. Kneel on the floor with your knees hip-width apart. Tighten your buttock muscles and pull your abdominal muscles in tight.

2. Slowly lean back without bending at the hips. Use your buttock muscles and muscles in the back of your upper thighs (your hamstrings) to support your body weight. Hold this position for 5 seconds, then return to the starting position (this is 1 rep).

Do 3 sets of 8 reps.

Caution: *People with knee injuries or back pain should not do this exercise.*

PHASE 3

INTERVAL WALKING

Congratulations on graduating to the Phase 3 Interval Walking part of our fitness programme! After at least 6 weeks of intervals on Phases 1 and 2, you're sure to be seeing results not only on the scales but also in the way you feel. Your body and heart are stronger, you have more energy, you can breathe more deeply and you're probably a lot happier. You're making the right food choices and you're doing a beneficial new form of exercise – it's an unbeatable combination. Thanks to your revved-up metabolism, you've vastly increased your capacity to burn fat and calories – all the time.

Because Phase 3 Interval Walking offers the blueprint you'll use for exercising long-term, I want to give you some information on how this phase really works, so you can adapt the intervals to any form of cardio you enjoy.

If you study the Phase 3 charts on pages 130–133, you'll see that each week varies a bit in terms of the amount and intensity of work and recovery. Here's how.

Weeks 1 and 2: The Slow Build. During the first 2 weeks of Phase 3, the work becomes a bit more challenging each day as the level of intensity keeps increasing. It's a slow and steady build with a break on Week 2, Day 2 to help you handle the increase in difficulty. In addition, the amounts of work and recovery change over these 2 weeks to further vary the intensity of your workout. This allows you to demand more and more from your body while still providing enough time to recharge between bursts of increased activity.

Week 3: The Supercharged! Week. During the third week of Phase 3, you'll be able to work at your highest intensity as the work periods shorten and the recovery periods lengthen to allow you to replenish more of your energy. The repetitions peak on Day 5, then decrease on Day 7, so you can work even harder. Intensity is the name of the game, but you also need recovery. There's a good reason for this: if you were to continue to increase both the intensity and duration of your workout each day, you could suffer from excessive fatigue, leading to reduced gains and possible over-use injuries (see Chapter 5).

Week 4: The Mellow Week. During the final week of Phase 3, there's a marked *decrease* in work intensity and time. After Week 3, this should feel like a breeze. But don't try to make it harder. Remember, you need this time to refresh yourself for the next 4-week cycle.

The key to interval training is knowing how to pace yourself. Therefore, I can't stress enough the importance of recovery. It is not simply a rest period; recovery serves a critical purpose: it gives your body time to recharge so that it's able to work to its maximum potential when called upon again. If you don't take your recovery periods seriously, you are only cheating yourself because you will never truly achieve your Supercharged! potential.

THE TOTAL BODY WORKOUT

You deserve praise for being ready to move on to the Phase 3 Total Body Workout, particularly if you never exercised before starting this fitness programme. During Phase 3, you'll appreciate the incredible progress you've made over the past weeks. In fact, you may be surprised at how easily you're able to adapt to these new exercises. The individual movements are more challenging, but you're ready for them.

In addition to being stronger, you will have developed a new body awareness. And it shows, not just when you're working out, but in the grace and ease you express as you perform your daily activities. More important, you're steadier on your feet, which will help prevent injury. By now, you feel so good after your workout, you find that you're actually *looking forward* to doing it.

PHASE 3 – WEEK 1

DAY 1 – INTERVAL WALKING

Warm-up: start with a 3-minute walk at Easy Pace.
- Walk for 45 seconds at Moderate Pace.
- Walk for 15 seconds at Easy Pace.
- *Repeat 15 times.*

Cool-down: end with a 2-minute walk at Easy Pace.

DAY 2 – TOTAL BODY WORKOUT

Phase 3 exercises: see pages 135–143.

Take a recreational walk at Easy Pace for 15–20 minutes (optional).

DAY 3 – INTERVAL WALKING

Warm-up: start with a 3-minute walk at Moderate Pace.
- Walk for 30 seconds at Revved Up.
- Walk for 15 seconds at Easy Pace.
- *Repeat 20 times.*

Cool-down: end with a 2-minute walk at Easy Pace.

DAY 4 – TOTAL BODY WORKOUT

Phase 3 exercises: see pages 135–143.

Take a recreational walk at Easy Pace for 15–20 minutes (optional).

DAY 5 – INTERVAL WALKING

Warm-up: start with a 2-minute walk at Moderate Pace.
- Walk for 30 seconds at Revved Up.
- Walk for 30 seconds at Moderate Pace.
- *Repeat 16 times.*

Cool-down: end with a 2-minute walk at Easy Pace.

DAY 6 – TOTAL BODY WORKOUT

Phase 3 exercises: see pages 135–143.

Take a recreational walk at Moderate Pace for 15–20 minutes (optional).

DAY 7 – INTERVAL WALKING

Warm-up: start with a 2-minute walk at Moderate Pace.
- Walk for 30 seconds at Supercharged!
- Walk for 45 seconds at Easy Pace.
- *Repeat 12 times.*

Cool-down: end with a 2-minute walk at Easy Pace.

PHASE 3 – WEEK 2

DAY 1 – TOTAL BODY WORKOUT

Phase 3 exercises: see pages 135–143.

Take a recreational walk at Easy Pace for 15–20 minutes (optional).

DAY 2 – INTERVAL WALKING

Warm-up: start with a 3-minute walk at Easy Pace.
- Walk for 45 seconds at Revved Up.
- Walk for 30 seconds at Easy Pace.
- *Repeat 12 times.*

Cool-down: end with a 2-minute walk at Easy Pace.

DAY 3 – TOTAL BODY WORKOUT

Phase 3 exercises: see pages 135–143.

Take a recreational walk at Easy Pace for 15–20 minutes (optional).

DAY 4 – INTERVAL WALKING

Warm-up: start with a 3-minute walk at Moderate Pace.
- Walk for 60 seconds at Supercharged!
- Walk for 30 seconds at Easy Pace.
- *Repeat 10 times.*

Cool-down: end with a 2-minute walk at Easy Pace.

DAY 5 – TOTAL BODY WORKOUT

Phase 3 exercises: see pages 135–143.

Take a recreational walk at Moderate Pace for 15–20 minutes (optional).

DAY 6 – INTERVAL WALKING

Warm-up: start with a 3-minute walk at Easy Pace.
- Walk for 45 seconds at Supercharged!
- Walk for 15 seconds at Moderate Pace.
- *Repeat 10 times.*

Cool-down: end with a 2-minute walk at Moderate Pace.

DAY 7 – TOTAL BODY WORKOUT

Phase 3 exercises: see pages 135–143.

Take a recreational walk at Easy Pace for 15–20 minutes (optional).

PHASE 3 – WEEK 3

DAY 1 – INTERVAL WALKING

Warm-up: start with a 3-minute walk at Moderate Pace.
- Walk for 60 seconds at Revved Up.
- Walk for 30 seconds at Moderate Pace.
- *Repeat 10 times.*

Cool-down: end with a 2-minute walk at Easy Pace.

DAY 2 – TOTAL BODY WORKOUT

Phase 3 exercises: see pages 135–143.

Take a recreational walk at Easy Pace for 15–20 minutes (optional).

DAY 3 – INTERVAL WALKING

Warm-up: start with a 3-minute walk at Easy Pace.
- Walk for 45 seconds at Revved Up.
- Walk for 30 seconds at Easy Pace.
- *Repeat 10 times.*

Cool-down: end with a 2-minute walk at Easy Pace.

DAY 4 – TOTAL BODY WORKOUT

Phase 3 exercises: see pages 135–143.

Take a recreational walk at Easy Pace for 15–20 minutes (optional).

DAY 5 – INTERVAL WALKING

Warm-up: start with a 2-minute walk at Easy Pace.
- Walk for 30 seconds at Supercharged!
- Walk for 45 seconds at Moderate Pace.
- *Repeat 12 times.*

Cool-down: end with a 2-minute walk at Easy Pace.

DAY 6 –TOTAL BODY WORKOUT

Phase 3 exercises: see pages 135–143.

Take a recreational walk at Moderate Pace for 15–20 minutes (optional).

DAY 7 – INTERVAL WALKING

Warm-up: start with a 2-minute walk at Moderate Pace.
- Walk for 30 seconds at Supercharged!
- Walk for 60 seconds at Moderate Pace.
- *Repeat 9 times.*

Cool-down: end with a 2-minute walk at Easy Pace.

PHASE 3 – WEEK 4

DAY 1 – TOTAL BODY WORKOUT

Phase 3 Exercises: see pages 135–143.

Take a recreational walk at Easy Pace for 15–20 minutes (optional).

DAY 2 – INTERVAL WALKING

Warm-up: start with a 2-minute walk at Easy Pace.
- Walk for 30 seconds at Revved Up.
- Walk for 45 seconds at Moderate Pace.
- *Repeat 12 times.*

Cool-down: end with a 2-minute walk at Easy Pace.

DAY 3 – TOTAL BODY WORKOUT

Phase 3 exercises: see pages 135–143.

Take a recreational walk at Easy Pace for 15–20 minutes (optional).

DAY 4 – INTERVAL WALKING

Warm-up: start with a 3-minute walk at Easy Pace.
- Walk for 30 seconds at Revved Up.
- Walk for 60 seconds at Easy Pace.
- *Repeat 8 times.*

Cool-down: end with a 2-minute walk at Easy Pace.

DAY 5 – TOTAL BODY WORKOUT

Phase 3 Exercises: see pages 135–143.

Take a recreational walk at Moderate Pace for 15–20 minutes (optional).

DAY 6 – INTERVAL WALKING

Warm-up: start with a 2-minute walk at Easy Pace.
- Walk for 30 seconds at Moderate Pace.
- Walk for 60 seconds at Easy Pace.
- *Repeat 6 times.*

Cool-down: end with a 2-minute walk at Moderate Pace.

DAY 7 – TOTAL BODY WORKOUT

Phase 3 exercises: see pages 135–143.

Take a recreational walk at Easy Pace for 15–20 minutes (optional).

Phase 3
Total Body Workout
Exercises

Variation 1   Variation 2

WALL SIT

Strengthens and shapes the buttocks, thighs and calves.

1. Squat against a wall with your palms pressed against the wall, your feet planted firmly on the floor hip-width apart and your knees in line with your ankles. Tighten your abdominals. Pretend you are sitting on an imaginary chair. Try to squeeze your legs together without moving them. Hold the squeeze for 15 seconds (this is 1 rep). Release the squeeze.

   Do 5 (15-second) squeezes.

   Tip: *Make sure your palms stay pressed against the wall – they help to stabilize your back muscles.*

   Caution: *Stop if this exercise causes any knee pain.*

Variation 1: While sitting against the wall, lift your heels and hold for 5 seconds. Return to the starting position. Repeat. Work up to longer holds as you get stronger.

   Do 5 (5-second) holds.

Variation 2: While sitting against the wall, extend your left leg. Do 4 outward circles and then 4 inward circles with that leg. Return to the starting position and repeat with the right leg.

   Do 3 sets of 4 circles outwards and 4 circles inwards with each leg.

CHEST HUG

Shapes and strengthens shoulders, biceps and triceps.

You can use 0.5–2kg (1–3lb) hand weights, or perform this exercise without weights. Don't use weights if you have shoulder injuries or feel any pain.

1. With a weight in each hand or with your hands in fists, stand straight with your feet shoulder-width apart. Hold your arms out in front of you at chest height as though hugging someone (your closed fists are facing you).

2–3. Working from your elbows, open your arms, then, still working from the elbows, bring your arms back to the starting position. Think of your elbows as the hinges of a door that's opening and closing. Each out-and-in movement is 1 rep.

Do 3 sets of 8 reps.

Caution: *People with existing shoulder injuries or previous rotator cuff or impingement issues should not use weights.*

DOUBLE ARM REACH

Strengthens and sculpts the shoulders and arms.

1. Stand up straight with your legs shoulder-width apart. Hold both arms at chest height, with your upper arms parallel to the floor, elbows bent at 90 degrees and palms facing towards you. Keep your chest open and lifted on all movements. Your chin stays parallel to the floor and should not jut forwards.

2. Straighten both arms as you raise them towards the ceiling. Feel the muscles under both arms contract as you do so. When your arms are straight overhead, rotate your hands and arms away from your body.

3–4. In one fluid motion, keep your arms straight as you slowly move both arms behind you and down. Without stopping, continue to move your arms down and around until your elbows are at your hips and bent at 90 degrees, palms facing up. Return to the starting position. This is 1 rep.

Do 3 sets of 8 reps.

Caution: *People with existing shoulder injuries or previous rotator cuff or impingement issues should be careful doing this exercise.*

BREASTSTROKE

Strengthens and sculpts shoulders, biceps and triceps. This is the 'dry dock' version of the breaststroke.

You can use 0.5–2kg (1–3lb) hand weights or perform this exercise without weights. Don't use weights if you have shoulder injuries or feel any pain.

1. With a weight in each hand, stand with your legs shoulder-width apart. Hold your hands in front of you at chest height, with your elbows bent as though hugging some-one but your palms facing away from your chest.

2. In one continuous motion, open your arms and pull your elbows behind your shoulders as though doing the breaststroke. Squeeze in your shoulder blades and contract the backs of your arms to intensify the movement.

3–4. Bring your bent arms down, around and in a circular motion, towards your waist, as you move towards the starting position. This is 1 rep.

Do 3 sets of 8 reps.

Tip: This exercise should be done in a fluid, rhythmic motion in which one movement flows into the other, just like swimming. Do not stop between reps.

Caution: *People with existing shoulder injuries or previous rotator cuff or impingement issues should not use weights.*

HEEL BEAT

Strengthens and flattens upper and lower abdominal muscles, sculpts and strengthens the legs and improves flexibility and function in hip joints.

1. Lie on your back on the floor. Prop yourself up on your elbows and press your forearms and palms firmly into the floor, fingertips facing forwards. Squeeze your shoulder blades together to keep your chest lifted. Your legs are straight, your feet are flexed and your legs are hip-width apart. Lift your legs off the floor about 10cm (4in).

2–3. Opening and closing your legs, slowly beat your heels together without actually letting your heels touch. These movements should be fluid; don't stop between beats (1 beat is 1 rep).

   Do 3 sets of 8 reps.

   Variation: If you have mastered the basic move, try this more difficult variation. When your legs are lifted off the floor, flex your feet and do 1 small circle inwards with both feet, followed by 1 small circle outwards (this is 1 rep).

   Do 3 sets of 8 reps.

SWIMMING FROG

Sculpts and strengthens upper and lower abdominal muscles. Improves flexibility and function of the hip and knee joints.

1. Lie down on your back on the floor. Prop yourself up on your elbows and press your forearms and palms firmly into the floor, fingertips facing forwards. Squeeze your shoulder blades together to keep your chest lifted. Bend your knees and open them to either side. Press the bottoms of your feet together. Tighten your abdominal muscles. Lift your feet off the floor about 10cm (4in).

2. Still pressing the bottoms of your feet together, extend your legs until they are straight, then flex your feet at the point where you can no longer keep the bottoms of your feet pressed together.

3. Separate and extend your straightened legs wider than hip-width apart. Make sure that your tight abdominal muscles are holding you in position so you don't strain your back.

4. Bring your heels back together. Bend your legs and press the bottoms of your feet together as you return to the starting position (1) to complete 1 rep. Your legs will still be hovering about 10cm (4in) off the floor. These movements should be fluid. Don't stop between reps.

   Do 3 sets of 8 reps.

ALTERNATING LEG KICK

Improves hamstring strength and endurance, strengthens the back and abdominals and improves posture.

1. Lie face down on the floor. Prop yourself up on your elbows and press your forearms into the floor. Contract your arm muscles and feel your arms pull towards one another, but don't actually move them. Keep your chest lifted – don't let it sink into the floor.

2. Tighten your abdominal muscles and contract your buttocks as you lift both legs about 10cm (4in) off the floor.

3–4. Bend your right leg at the knee and try to kick your buttocks with your right heel, then, in a continuous motion, switch legs and try to kick your buttocks with your left heel. This is 1 rep.

Do 3 sets of 8 reps.

Caution: *Don't do this exercise if you have low-back pain or disc or knee injuries.*

STRAIGHT LEG TRIANGLE

Great for hamstring strength and endurance.

1. Lie face down on the floor. Prop yourself up on your elbows and press your forearms into the floor. Contract your arm muscles and pull your arms towards one another without actually moving them. Keep your chest lifted – don't let it sink to the floor. Tighten your abdominal muscles and contract your buttocks. Flex both feet and bend your knees.

2. Straighten your legs, then separate them to form a triangle, keeping your feet about 15cm (6in) off the floor.

3. Bring your legs together, lower them and return to the starting position. Repeat 4 times.

Reverse the order: Begin with your legs in the Step 3 position, move to the Step 2 position and end in the Step 1 position. Repeat 4 times.

Do 3 sets of 4 triangles each way.

Caution: *Don't do this exercise if you have low-back pain or disc or knee injuries.*

STRAIGHT LEG CIRCLE

Improves hamstring strength and endurance. Strengthens back and abdominal muscles.

1. Lie face down on the floor. Prop yourself up on your elbows and press your forearms into the floor. Contract your arm muscles and pull your arms towards one another without actually moving them. Keep your chest lifted – don't let it sink to the floor. Tighten your abdominal muscles and contract your buttocks as you lift both legs about 10cm (4in) off the floor.

2–3. While keeping your legs straight, simultaneously circle each leg in an outward direction 4 times. Without stopping, do 4 leg circles in an inward direction. This should be a slow, controlled movement. Rest between sets if you need to.

Do 3 sets of 4 outward and 4 inward circles.

Caution: *Don't do this exercise if you have low-back pain or disc injuries.*

Make Exercise a Lifestyle

You've now finished all three phases of the South Beach Supercharged Fitness Programme, and you deserve a huge round of applause. By now, when you look in the mirror, you should be delighted with your reflection. To maintain your good results, you'll want to incorporate exercise into your daily routine. Here are some tips on how you can go forwards with what you've learned and adapt it to your own lifestyle.

Continuing with Interval Training

Now that you fully understand the principles of interval training, you can apply them to nearly any type of exercise or sport to enhance your results. You can take the Interval Walking programme in this book and use it as a blueprint for an interval cycling or swimming programme, for example, or adapt it for the treadmill, stationary bike or elliptical trainer, as described in 'Interval Training Indoors' on page 92. Better still, mix up different types of exercise on different days to keep your routine fresh.

If you've discovered that you really love walking, simply continue with the Phase 3 programme and repeat it in the 4-week cycles described on pages 130–133. Because we know that most people are pressed for time, we intentionally designed the walking programme to be 20 minutes long. But if you enjoy doing cardio for a longer period, you can adapt the programme to fit your schedule. For example, if you like taking an hour-long walk on weekends, you can certainly do intervals, but don't try to spend the entire hour working at high intensity. Never forget this key concept: the longer you exercise, the lower the overall intensity of your intervals. And be sure to always add in your recovery periods.

Continuing with the Total Body Workout

Now that you've completed all three phases of the Total Body Workout, you're going to notice how great you look. But these changes go even deeper. You're now far more aware of how your body works and your everyday movements are more graceful and purposeful. You stand taller and straighter and you're more flexible. Good posture is now second nature to you. Your shoulders don't slump, your head doesn't jut forwards and your belly doesn't sag. You're using your core muscles to hold you up and keep your body in proper alignment, and you look and feel better for it. You may be surprised that a nagging ache in your knee or pain in your lower back has vastly improved or even disappeared. And you are undoubtedly delighted that your abdominal muscles are flatter and stronger, and your arms and legs are leaner and better defined.

Sticking with our core functional fitness programme and adapting it to your lifestyle will help you maintain a toned body for the rest of your life. Here are some suggestions on how you can keep the Total Body Workout working for you.

Do two phases in succession. You can create your own workout by combining the exercises from any *two* phases. Do all the exercises in Phase 1 and then go right into Phase 2 or 3 or do all the exercises in Phase 2 followed by Phase 3. Keep the workout fresh by doing different exercise combinations on alternate days. Don't work so fast that you're sloppy, but try to do both workouts in under 30 minutes.

Do three phases in succession. For a fun, high-energy workout that's also a real challenge, once a week set aside an hour to do all the exercises in all three phases.

Do Phase 1 anytime. Phase 1 contains basic movements that make you feel great. All of the chair exercises can be done at your desk in the office or while sitting in your living room. Do them whenever you want to give your joints and muscles a treat. Keeping up with these exercises will help you stay flexible and injury free.

Stops and Starts

Of course there will be times when you must take a day or two off from the Interval Walking programme and/or the Total Body Workout. Skipping a few sessions won't make a big difference in your overall fitness level. Just pick up where you left off as soon as you are able. If, however, you miss several weeks of exercise, I recommend that you start again with Phase 1 for both the walking and the core exercises. This will gradually prepare your body for a more intense workout and keep you from injury.

Change It Up

Whatever activity or activities you choose, you do need to continue to do *something*. In fact, now that you're in such good shape, it's a great time to explore new types of exercise. Maybe you used to love riding your bike outdoors but haven't been on it in years. On the next beautiful day, take your bike out of the garage and give it a try – just for the sheer joy of it. If you love the feeling, start doing bicycle intervals. Or maybe you've always wanted to participate in a walk for your favourite charity, but thought that you couldn't keep up with everyone else. Trust me, after you've completed the three phases of the Interval Walking programme, the other participants will have trouble keeping up with *you*. Or maybe you've always wanted to try Pilates, go ballroom dancing or take a Spinning class at the gym. Stop thinking about it – do it! Experiment with different forms of exercise and see what you really enjoy. Doctor's orders!

Staying active will prevent the weight you've lost from creeping back and will keep you fit and healthy for your entire life.

And that's what the South Beach Diet is all about.

PART III

Supercharged
Eating on
The South Beach Diet

Getting Started on the South Beach Diet

If you're new to the South Beach Diet, you're undoubtedly eager to begin losing unwanted weight and improving your health. On the following pages, you will find all the tools you need to get started. The secret to looking and feeling great is literally right at your fingertips.

If you're already a follower of the South Beach Diet, you're probably eager to see what's new. I'm delighted to say that we're providing expanded lists of Foods to Enjoy, as well as helpful new Meal Plans and fresh, delicious, easy-to-prepare recipes for Phases 1 and 2.

I've also been listening to you for 5 years – in my practice, in my daily encounters, and on SouthBeachDiet.com. Some questions about the diet seem to come up time and again. Therefore, I've provided a question and answer section for each phase.

So let's get started.

By now you know that the South Beach Diet is divided into three phases. On pages 165–169, you'll find the Phase 1 Foods to Enjoy list, followed by Phase 1 Foods to Avoid. The Phase 1 Foods to Enjoy include the lean proteins, good fats, good carbohydrates (vegetables and pulses), and low-fat dairy products that you're allowed to eat during this 2-week phase. Bear in mind that even on this, the strictest phase of the diet, the Foods to Enjoy list is much longer than the Foods to Avoid list. Furthermore, it will be only 2 weeks before you start Phase 2 and can resume eating fruits and whole grains again. I guarantee that if you plan your meals and snacks around the Foods to Enjoy list for Phase 1, you will feel satisfied and your cravings for sweets and starchy carbohydrates are likely to disappear.

On page 241, you'll find the list of Foods to Re-introduce on Phase 2. As you move from Phase 1 to Phase 2, you will gradually add these foods back into your diet (page 236 explains how to do this while continuing to lose weight).

If you are starting the diet with Phase 2, you can eat all the foods allowed on Phase 1 (see pages 165 to 169), as well as those allowed on Phase 2, but there are still a few foods to be careful about because they are high in refined starches or sugar. On page 243, you will find the lists of Phase 2 Foods to Avoid or Eat Rarely. Eventually, you'll learn how to make the best food choices most of the time – and the South Beach Diet will become a lifestyle – but while you're still trying to lose weight on Phase 2, it's best to steer clear of the Foods to Avoid. We're not expecting perfection; a little cheat now and then is okay. Once you become familiar with the healthy eating principles of the South Beach Diet, it will be easy for you to put meals together. But at first, you'll probably need to refer to the food lists from time to time. In fact, we've found that many people like to photocopy the lists and carry them around until knowing which foods to eat becomes second nature.

To make it even easier for you to incorporate these enjoyable foods into your daily diet, we have provided 2 weeks of Sample Meal Plans for Phases 1 and 2. These are meant to be guidelines, not absolutes. I've had people walk over to me in airports or shopping centres, clutching their copies of the original South Beach Diet book, and ask, 'Since I don't like hummous, can I eat a different snack on Day 13?', or 'I don't eat pork. Can I substitute smoked salmon for turkey bacon and eat it with my eggs on Day 9?' The answer to both questions is yes. We understand that not everyone has the same tastes in food and some people have dietary restraints. The point is, we want you to eat foods you like. That's why we've provided you with enough choices to give you plenty of options.

What about Portion Size?

The South Beach Diet doesn't require you to weigh, measure or count what you eat in ounces, calories, grams of fat or carbohydrate, or any other way. Weighing, measuring and counting can be a nuisance and it certainly isn't in harmony with turning a diet into a lifestyle. It's also difficult to sustain.

But while we don't count calories, calories do count. It's the quality of those calories that naturally leads to appropriate hunger satisfaction. Generally, if you are making the right food choices, the amount you're eating takes care of itself. By enjoying meals consisting of lean protein and nutrient- and fibre-rich foods, you will naturally feel satisfied and have no desire to overeat.

Another way to avoid those once-automatic second helpings is to savour each bite and eat slowly, so that your brain has time to detect your normal rise in blood sugar. Don't rush your meals. In fact, wait 20 minutes before you even consider going back for seconds. That way, you'll know if you're still truly hungry – or if you're just eating more out of

A DIET FOR THE REAL WORLD

We may have our principles, but we're not doctrinaire. The South Beach Diet is for people living in the *real* world. We don't expect you to be perfect, and you shouldn't expect perfection from yourself, either. Our goal is to teach you how to make good food choices *most of the time*. If, on occasion, you indulge in a few bites of chocolate cake or half a bag of crisps, we don't want you to feel like all is lost. The worst thing you can do is think, *Oh well, I've already blown my diet for today by eating that chocolate cake, so I might as well fill up on junk and start again tomorrow.* When you view the diet as a real lifestyle and not as an interruption to real life, an occasional bad choice won't throw you. You'll simply make better choices the next time.

habit or because you didn't give yourself time for satiety and blood sugar signals to reach your brain.

If you read the Foods to Enjoy lists carefully, you'll see that while I don't recommend weighing and measuring most foods, I do strongly suggest that you eat a minimum of 225g (8oz) of vegetables with lunch and dinner and, ideally, 60g (2oz) with breakfast, so that you get the maximum health benefits they provide, including plenty of heart-protective antioxidants and fibre. As you'll also see, I do make suggestions about amounts of fats, dairy products and certain sauces. Nuts in particular can be a problem because it's so easy to eat more than a handful once you get started, so I do limit them to one serving daily (see page 167).

Preparing Your Kitchen

If you're starting on Phase 1, you should clear your kitchen of foods that you will not be eating and stock up on foods you can enjoy. If you have whole grain products or wine, beer or other alcohol, simply move them to the back of the cupboard; you will be reunited with them in just 2 weeks, when you begin Phase 2. I do recommend that you throw out the junk carbs, however. The crisps and doughnuts have to go – especially if you're prone to cravings. The following list identifies many of the foods that you'll need to eliminate *during Phase 1*.

Baked goods. All baked goods – even healthy breads made from wholemeal or other whole grain flours – must disappear on Phase 1. This includes all breads, cakes, biscuits, fairy cakes, scones, muffins, pastries and waffles, both home-made and packaged.

Cereals. All cereals are off-limits for the first 2 weeks, even porridge and bran cereals. Low-sugar, high-fibre cereals reappear on Phase 2.

Flour. All flour is eliminated on Phase 1, including flours made from soyabeans and nuts. Maize meal and polenta go also.

Packaged snacks. Get rid of cereal bars, cheese puffs, popcorn, crisps, pretzels and the like.

Pasta. All pasta – even wholewheat – is banished during Phase 1. Replace it with spaghetti squash served with marinara sauce.

Rice. All varieties, including brown, are off-limits for 2 weeks.

Instead, serve your main course on a bed of lentils or finely chopped cauliflower (which looks like rice), or on a big bed of kale or spinach.

Starchy vegetables. No beetroot, carrots, sweetcorn, peas, sweet or white potatoes, squash or yams on Phase 1. Instead choose a wide variety of high-fibre, nutrient-dense vegetables from our expanded list of Foods to Enjoy. Remember to go through your freezer and get rid of any packaged foods that contain these vegetables as well.

Drinks. Eliminate all fruit juice, soft drinks and any other drinks containing sugar, fructose or corn syrup. All alcoholic beverages – beer, cocktails and wine – are off-limits during Phase 1. Instead, enjoy vegetable juice cocktail, tomato juice, unsweetened flavoured waters and sugar-free powdered mixes for drinks. Of course, you can always have plain water, soda water and mineral water, as well as herbal teas and the occasional diet soft drink. You can have caffeinated drinks such as coffee, tea or caffeinated diet soft drinks, but don't go overboard. Interestingly, recent research has shown that caffeine may actually improve insulin resistance in people with diabetes.

Cheese and dairy. Clear your refrigerator of all full-fat milk, cheese, yogurt and cream cheese. Toss the ice cream and frozen yogurt as well. Instead, stock up on skimmed milk, reduced-fat cheeses and low-fat or fat-free natural yogurt.

Fruit. No fresh fruits, dried fruits, jellies or jams are permitted during Phase 1. They are re-introduced in 2 weeks, when you get to Phase 2.

Oils and fats. Dispose of all solid vegetable fats, lard, butter and hydrogenated oils. Replace them with extra-virgin olive oil, rapeseed oil and cooking spray, and with margarines and spreads that do not contain trans fatty acids.

Meat and poultry. Eliminate anything processed that includes sugars, such as honey roast ham. Do away with fatty fowl such as duck and goose, pâté, dark-meat chicken and turkey (legs and wings), processed fowl such as packaged chicken nuggets or burgers, beef brisket, liver, rib-eye steaks or other fatty cuts. Instead, eat the white-meat poultry and lean cuts of meat recommended in the Foods to Enjoy list.

Soup mixes. Remove all powdered soup mixes and tinned cream soups. Instead, enjoy clear stock or bouillon soups, gazpacho and lentil and bean soups. Check labels on all tinned soups for hydrogenated oils and other hidden ingredients.

Sweeteners. All sweeteners, except sugar substitutes, are off-limits on Phase 1. These include white sugar, brown sugar, honey, treacle and golden syrup. Instead, use the sugar substitute of your choice.

Sauces. Remove ketchup, mayonnaise, salad cream, cocktail sauce and fat-free salad dressings that contain sugar. Instead, use prepared dressings that contain less than 3 grams of sugar – better yet, make your own healthy salad dressings (see pages 214 to 217 for recipes).

When You're Dining Out

When you're not preparing your own meals, your diet can quickly become derailed. This is true not only during Phases 1 and 2, when you're trying to shed weight, but also during Phase 3, when you're trying to maintain. A few weeks of poorly chosen restaurant meals can cause the resurgence of cravings and pile on weight before you know it. Therefore, it's essential to learn how to follow the principles of the South Beach Diet whether you are eating at home, at a restaurant or on the go.

More than a decade ago, when I first began prescribing the South Beach Diet to my heart patients, dining out was a real challenge. Trans fats were hard to avoid. They were in nearly all fried and most processed foods. Few restaurants offered wholemeal bread or wholewheat pasta and most served up the white, highly refined stuff. If you found yourself in a fast-food restaurant, you had to choose between going hungry or filling up on servings of foods laden with bad fats and refined carbs.

The world has certainly become a friendlier place for people looking for whole grains and other healthy carbohydrates, and I feel wonderful when magazine and newspaper food editors tell me that the South Beach Diet has had a lot to do with that change. It's now not unusual for restaurants and even some fast-food chains to offer many different types of bread, including whole grain and whole-wheat sourdough.

Since we first published the South Beach Diet 5 years ago, it's become easier than ever to follow our healthy eating principles in just about any restaurant, whether it offers fast food, ethnic dishes or gourmet cuisine. Here are some suggestions on how to eat out wisely and well.

Scan the menu first. Before selecting a restaurant, review the menu. If all the selections look like they jumped off your Foods to Avoid list, this place may not be the best choice for you. You can get away with splurges every once in a while when you are on Phase 3 and have achieved your weight loss goal, but to get to Phase 3, you need to be more careful during Phases 1 and 2.

Skip the bread. If you're on Phase 1, just say no to the bread basket. You don't need it. If you're on Phase 2 or 3, you can enjoy a piece of wholegrain bread or a wholegrain bread roll on occasion. Have it with olive oil; the fat slows down the absorption of the carbs by your bloodstream. Even on Phase 3, if you find yourself tempted to empty the bread basket before you get to the main course, ask the waiter to take it away. If you're dining with friends, simply move it away from you on the table.

Consider your drinks. Skip the mixed drink or cocktail and order a non-alcoholic beverage, such as water, soda water with a twist of lemon, diet soft drinks or mineral water. You can have a glass of red or white wine with dinner if you're on Phase 2 or 3, but if you start drinking too early in the evening, you may be tempted to have several drinks and those liquid calories can really add up.

Order soup as a first course. I'm a big fan of soup these days. You should be, too, because it's a filling way to start a meal. If possible order it as soon as you sit down so that when you order your main course you're not feeling ravenous. If you're on Phase 1, stick to clear soup or consommé, a plain bean soup or vegetable soup made with chicken or vegetable stock and thickened with puréed vegetables.

Have a salad next. Another trick for filling up before the main course comes is to order a big salad of mixed greens after your soup. Ask for olive oil and vinegar on the side.

Pretend you're at home. Order your main course the way you would create a healthy meal at home. First, look for lean protein on the menu. Ask for grilled fish or shellfish, white meat chicken or turkey or a lean cut of beef, such as sirloin or fillet. Instead of starchy side dishes, request extra servings of vegetables that have either been steamed or lightly cooked in olive oil or chicken stock.

Enjoy Your Favourite Cuisine

Keep in mind that different cuisines may pose different challenges. Do you love French food but worry about the sauces? Are you crazy about Mexican cuisine but wonder about the cheese and nachos? Here are some tips on how you can eat at your favourite foreign restaurants without compromising the principles of the South Beach Diet.

Indian. Indian cuisine offers some terrific options for South Beach dieters. Thanks to clever cooking techniques and the liberal use of spices, the same lean protein, good carbs and good fats you've been eating every day take on an exciting new flavour in the hands of an Indian chef. Try the tandoori-style dishes, in which fish, poultry, meat and/or vegetables are roasted at very high temperatures in a clay oven. Other good choices include *dhal* (a dish made with lentils or various other kinds of beans), *raitas* (yogurt-based sauces), vegetable salads, curries and masala-style dishes made with sautéed tomatoes and onions. Many Indian restaurants serve the meal with white basmati rice. Ask your waiter not to bring it, or simply don't eat it. You should also avoid Indian breads such as puri, a puffy, deep-fried flat bread or naan, which is baked but still typically high in refined carbs. Indian appetizers such as *samosas* (triangular fried pastries filled with vegetables) are also off-limits. And be sure to steer clear of dishes cooked with butter and cream.

Greek and Middle Eastern. Mediterranean restaurants, such as those offering Greek, Turkish, Israeli or Lebanese cuisine, are great choices. Here you're likely to find grilled seafood, lamb and chicken, along with chickpeas, fresh vegetables and salads with small amounts of feta cheese. Sounds like food right out of the pages of the South Beach Diet, and indeed, much of our plan is modelled on the healthy Mediterranean diet and lifestyle. Even in this South Beach Diet-friendly environment, however, there are some dishes to avoid. If you're still trying to lose weight, pass on casseroles such as *moussaka* (lamb or beef, aubergine/eggplant and potatoes) and *pastitsio* (pasta with meat), which are typically made with a high-fat béchamel sauce. If you're on Phase 3, eat these dishes rarely, as a special treat.

French. French cuisine has an undeserved reputation for being bad for dieters. Just look at the number of slim people in France. Sure, there's the heavy haute cuisine smothered in cream sauce and butter, which is not diet friendly. But there is also the lighter, healthier Mediterranean style of French cooking that uses olive oil instead of butter and is abundant in fresh vegetables, fresh fish and shellfish, poultry and salads. If you're dining in a French restaurant, you can't go wrong by ordering fish sautéed in olive oil with a side of vegetables. Enjoy your repast with a glass of red or white wine. Do as the French do – eat slowly and savour your food. End the meal with a small amount of dessert on occasion – a few strawberries, perhaps or a small piece of dark chocolate. Sounds just like our Phase 3 lifestyle, right?

Japanese. It's a safe bet that a South Beach dieter will find something great in a Japanese restaurant. This cuisine is known for its fresh fish, lightly cooked vegetables and grilled meat and poultry dishes. Sushi, Japanese-style raw fish served with a small amount of rice, has become one of the most popular foods in the world. You can enjoy sushi on Phase 2 if you ask for it with brown rice, a staple in many Japanese restaurants these days, or request a rice-free roll. If you are on Phase 1, stick to the rice-free rolls or sashimi, thin slices of raw fish served without rice. Tofu dishes are usually good choices, but steer clear of tempura or deep-fried foods. And even though teriyaki dishes are grilled, the sauce is often loaded with sugar. If you love teriyaki, you can enjoy it occasionally on Phase 3, but not on Phases 1 or 2. On Phases 2 and 3 you can also enjoy soba noodles in moderation; unlike most Japanese noodles, which are made from wheat and rice flour, soba noodles are made from buckwheat. Most Japanese restaurants also offer edamame, seaweed salads and stir-fried or steamed vegetables, making it easy for you to have your 225g (8oz) of vegetables with your meal.

Italian. To many of us, Italian food means a heaping plate of lasagne, manicotti or some other pasta, or a large pepperoni pizza. To Italians, Italian food means starting the meal with a big salad and having a small (and

I do mean small) starter portion of pasta followed by grilled chicken or seafood with lots of vegetables. By now you know which version of Italian food works better for the South Beach dieter. If you are on Phase 1, skip the bread and pasta and eat just the salad, vegetables and lean fish or chicken. If you're on Phase 2, you can enjoy a piece of wholegrain bread and even order a small portion of wholewheat pasta with tomato sauce for a starter. Don't order anything fried or breaded. If you want to eat dessert like an Italian – and you're on Phase 2 – order some fresh fruit.

If your version of Italian is more pizzeria than trattoria, don't despair. Today many restaurants offer crisp thin-crust pizza. When you have the option, ask for a wholemeal crust. Avoid high-fat toppings such as sausage, meatballs or pepperoni. Instead, request mushrooms, spinach or other vegetables. Only eat a very little bit of the mozzarella cheese, or even better, try it the Neapolitan way by ordering Pizza Marinara – tomato sauce without any mozzarella.

Mexican. For South Beach dieters, Mexican food can be very good or very bad, depending on the choices you make. For starters, pass on the basket of nachos. Skip the fat-laden refried beans and rice. Avoid tacos, tortillas, quesadillas and other refined carbs (like white rice and sweet-corn). On the other hand, fajitas – made with strips of grilled chicken, steak or (better yet) seafood and lots of grilled vegetables – are a great option. If you're on Phase 1, skip the fajita wrapper and just enjoy the delicious contents. If you're on Phase 2, try to find a restaurant that offers wholemeal tortillas or eat just a bite or two of a regular one.

Chinese. Chinese food is very popular in the West. Authentic Chinese cuisine is very healthy. Westernized Chinese cuisine is quite different from the real thing. People who visit China for the first time are often surprised that the vegetables are served *al dente* with little or no sauce, and rice is usually served at the end of the meal, after diners have eaten their fill of other foods. So be smart and choose your options in proper *Chinese* style: no heavy sauces; no deep-fried, breaded food; no fried noodles on the table to get you into trouble; no sweet-and-sour sauce or sugary hoisin sauce. Pass on the rice if you're on Phase 1. If you're on Phase 2 or 3, choose brown rice instead of white if it is available. Avoid lo mein noodles and other noodles made from wheat and rice flour. Clear soups with vegetables or any combination of steamed fresh vegetables with small amounts of meat, poultry or seafood, are always good options. Lightly sautéed chicken, beef or pork with vegetables are also healthy choices. Ask if the restaurant cooks with MSG, a food additive that can give some people flushing or headaches. If it does, just don't go there.

Fast-food tips. Many fast-food restaurants now offer healthy alternatives to their normal fare, including meal-size salads (skip the croûtons and dressings), grilled or rotisserie chicken and vegetarian burgers that are lower in fat than the usual burger and chips. Drink diet soft drinks, mineral water or water instead of sugary soft drinks.

· · · · · · · · · · · ·

The beauty of the South Beach Diet is that it doesn't require special foods and is adaptable to virtually any cuisine. If you follow the guidelines suggested above, you'll be able to find a healthy, satisfying and delicious meal in most restaurants around the world.

When You're Travelling

As someone who travels often for work, I understand that staying on any diet can be a challenge when you're on the road. Work-related stress, time-zone changes and shifts in your eating and sleeping schedule can be very disruptive, not to mention the sheer frustration that modern travel entails. All is not lost! With a little advance planning, most people find that they can follow the South Beach Diet on the road almost as easily as if they were at home.

The first step is anticipating where you're likely to run into trouble. And for many people, that could be in the first few hours after leaving home! In my experience, airport terminals and airplanes can be dangerous territory for dieters. With the combination of long security queues and more frequent delays, air travel has become very stressful. Add to that the fact that many airlines have cut back on food choices and instead of offering meals or even a sandwich, now hand out (and charge for) crisps, chocolate bars and biscuits. If you're not careful, you could be headed for big trouble before you've even reached your destination. Depending on the airport, you may be able to buy an acceptable meal, such as a salad, low-fat yogurt or a sandwich on wholemeal bread before boarding the plane. Also be on the lookout for healthy snacks, like a small packet of dry-roasted nuts or some low-fat cheese.

If you're not sure that you'll be able to find healthy foods, bring your own. (Security will confiscate drinks before you get through the scanners, but they won't take your food.) Having healthy food on hand is critical if you are on Phase 1 and need to be eating primarily lean protein, vegetables, pulses and low-fat dairy. So, before you leave home, put some washed, cut-up vegetables in a plastic bag and throw in a few pieces of low-fat cheese, a handful of nuts and some lean ham or turkey slices. Eat your snacks before you get ravenous so you're not tempted to grab the first thing that comes your way.

If you're on Phase 2 or 3, you can pack a white-meat turkey, lean ham or natural peanut butter sandwich on wholemeal bread and a piece of fruit or two, along with some reduced-fat cheese and chopped vegetables. Or buy a low-fat plain or artificially sweetened yogurt before boarding.

Hotel rooms with mini bars stuffed with sweets and crisps can also spell big trouble. Don't even open the mini bar – not even just to look. If you're hungry, check out the room-service menu or go down to the hotel restaurant, where you will definitely find something better to eat. Pretend you're at home and order something that closely resembles what you would normally eat for dinner. My favourite on-the-road meals include Caesar salad with grilled chicken (ask the kitchen to omit those fried white bread croûtons) and dressing on the side, grilled salmon with vegetables or a turkey burger with a big salad and olive oil and vinegar on the side. My point is, you don't have to order the cheeseburger and chips. If you do, you won't respect yourself in the morning.

It's also important to try to keep up with your fitness routine when you're travelling. Besides burning calories, it will help motivate you to stick with your diet and it's a great stress reliever. Fortunately, you can do our Total Body Workout in your hotel room. Interval Walking may be a bit trickier to accomplish. Depending on where you're staying, you may not be able to walk outdoors, but many hotels have gyms with cardio equipment such as treadmills, stationary bikes or elliptical trainers. If you can, try to stay in a hotel that has a gym. I give a few suggestions for doing interval cardio with and without a machine in 'Interval Training Indoors' on page 92.

Remember that even if you miss a few workout sessions, it's not the end of the world. When you get back home, you'll pick up where you left off.

PHASE 1

Losing the Cravings

Do you have 4.5kg (10lb) or more to lose? Do you have food cravings for refined starches and sugar? If you replied yes to either question, Phase 1 is for you. If you answered no to both questions, you can begin the diet with Phase 2.

Phase 1 is the most restrictive phase of the diet, but it's also the shortest, lasting only 2 weeks. During Phase 1, you will not eat any starches or sugary foods. No refined white bread, pasta or rice. No cakes, biscuits or pastries. No beer or alcohol of any kind. Not even any whole grains or whole fruits, two 'good' carbohydrates that I reintroduce on Phase 2. Fruits (and especially fruit juices) can be high in natural sugars, and even whole grains can be a problem when you're trying to stabilize your blood sugar and eliminate the cravings that caused you trouble in the past. By eliminating problem foods, Phase 1 allows you to gain control over your food choices. Although this may seem hard at first, remember that this phase is only 2 weeks long, after which you'll be adding many of these foods back into your diet.

In fact, Phase 1 may not be as difficult as you expect because you're not going to be hungry. After the first couple of days, most dieters find it fairly easy. During Phase 1 you'll eat plenty of healthy food, including lean protein (fish and shellfish, skinless white-meat poultry and lean cuts of meat), high-fibre vegetables, nuts, reduced-fat cheeses, eggs, low-fat dairy and good unsaturated fats, such as extra-virgin olive oil and rapeseed oil. (No, you won't have to eat your salads dry.) You'll enjoy three satisfying meals a day, plus two snacks, and you'll even have some high-protein, low-sugar desserts, such as the Ricotta Cheesecake with Lemon Drizzle and Pine Nuts on page 226.

Snacks are *required* on Phase 1 and should be eaten 1–2 hours after a meal, or an hour before your cravings typically strike. The goal is to fight hunger before it hits because if you let yourself get too famished, you'll have a greater tendency to overeat. The best snack is one that combines some protein and some high-fibre vegetables – for example, you might have some lean white-meat turkey, reduced-fat cheese, plain fat-free or low-fat yogurt with a handful of nuts, or some hummous with some celery sticks or green or red pepper slices.

By the end of 2 short weeks, there will be a real difference in how you look and feel. Most people lose weight fairly quickly on Phase 1, especially from their bellies. While quick weight loss is a strong motivator, it's not the primary goal of Phase 1. This phase is designed to banish your food cravings so that you can start Phase 2 with a clean slate. You'll be well on the way to making good food choices most of the time, which is what the South Beach Diet is all about. For the most part, by the end of Phase 1, your cravings will be gone, you'll feel lighter and your clothes will fit a lot better.

On the following pages, we provide a list of Foods to Enjoy and Foods to Avoid during this phase, as well as 14 days of Sample Meal Plans for Phase 1. To support the meal plans, we've developed plenty of delicious, new, quick-and-easy recipes, many of them time-saving one-dish meals and we've included some of your all-time favourite recipes as well. In addition, there are a number of recipes developed for the Phase 2 Meal Plans that you can enjoy. We have provided a note at the end of the Phase 2 recipes where this pertains.

The wide variety on the Foods to Enjoy list allows you to mix and match foods to fit your taste preferences. For example, if you don't like ham in your omelette, which I recommend on Day 1, substitute salmon or vegetables. Not a fan of cod on Day 6? Substitute another firm white-fleshed fish, like halibut. These Sample Meal Plans really are meant to be guidelines, and you should adjust them to suit your personal tastes.

In addition, on pages 231–235, you'll find answers to some of the questions our nutritionists and I are most commonly asked about Phase 1. If you have additional questions, it's likely you'll find the answers on our website, www.SouthBeachDiet.com.

As I explained in Part II, adding daily exercise to Phase 1 of the diet will certainly help move your weight loss along faster. Successful South Beach dieters tell us that when they start to lose weight on Phase 1, they feel so much lighter and have so much more energy that they're inspired to become even more active. They not only walk more, but are more motivated to pursue other forms of regular exercise as well.

Therefore, as you embark on Phase 1 of the diet, I urge you to also embark on Phase 1 of our new three-phase South Beach Supercharged Fitness Programme (page 83). You will certainly lose more weight faster if you're active on a regular basis.

Phase 1 of the diet may be the hardest for you, but you'll find that the Phase 1 fitness programme is the easiest. What they have in common is that both help you become leaner and healthier.

BEEF

Lean* cuts, such as:
    Thick flank (top rump)

Minced beef:
    Extra lean
    Lean sirloin

Pastrami, lean

Rump steak

Sirloin steak

T-bone

Tenderloin (fillet steak)

Lean meat has 10g or less total fat and 4.5g or less saturated fat per 100g portion.

POULTRY (SKINLESS)

Minced chicken breast

Minced turkey breast

Poussin

Low-fat turkey sausage (3–6g fat per 60g serving)

Turkey rashers

Turkey or chicken breast

SEAFOOD

All types of fish and shellfish (limit those high in mercury and other contaminants, such as swordfish, tilefish, albacore tuna – use yellowfin tuna instead – and shark)

Salmon roe

Sashimi

PORK

Boiled ham

Loin, chop or roast

Tenderloin

VEAL

Chop

Escalope

Steak

LAMB (REMOVE ALL VISIBLE FAT)

Leg, centre cut

Loin, chop or roast

GAME MEATS

Ostrich

Venison

DELI MEATS (FAT-FREE OR LOW-FAT ONLY)

Boiled ham

Deli-sliced turkey breast

Lean deli roast beef

Smoked ham

Smoked turkey breast

SOYA-BASED MEAT SUBSTITUTES

Unless otherwise stated, look for products that have 6g (¼oz) or less fat per 60–90g (2–3oz) serving.

Seitan

Soya burger

Tempeh – 60g (2oz) suggested serving size

Tofu (all varieties) – 115g (4oz) suggested serving size

TVP

(continued)

CHEESE (FAT-FREE OR REDUCED-FAT)

For hard cheese, look for varieties with 6g or less fat per 28g (1oz).

Blue cheese (does not come as reduced fat, so use in moderation)

Cheddar

Cottage cheese (low-fat)

Emmenthal

Feta

Fromage frais (fat-free)

Mozzarella

Parmesan

Provolone

Ricotta, reduced-fat

EGGS

The use of whole eggs is not limited unless otherwise directed by your doctor. Egg whites and egg substitutes are okay.

DAIRY

480ml (16floz) allowed daily, including fat-free or low-fat natural yogurt.

Buttermilk, low-fat

Evaporated milk, fat-free

Greek yogurt, fat-free

Milk, skimmed

Soya milk, low-fat plain, vanilla or artificially sweetened (4g or less fat per 240ml (8floz) serving). Be sure that the product does not contain high-fructose corn syrup.

Yogurt, fat-free or low-fat

DRIED PEAS, LENTILS AND BEANS

Fresh, frozen or tinned (without added sugar). Start with a 60g–115g (2–4oz) serving size.

Aduki beans

Black beans

Black-eyed beans

Borlotto beans

Broad beans

Butter beans

Cannellini beans

Chickpeas

Edamame

Haricot beans

Kidney beans

Lentils

Mung beans

Pigeon peas

Pinto beans

Soya beans

Split peas

VEGETABLES

May use fresh, frozen or tinned without added sugar. Eat a minimum of 225g (8oz) with lunch and dinner.

Artichoke hearts

Artichokes

Asparagus

Aubergine (eggplant)

Broccoli

Brussels sprouts

Cabbage (red, Savoy, white)

Capers

Cauliflower

Celeriac

Celery

Chinese greens

Courgettes (zucchini)

Cucumbers

Daikon radish

Endive

Escarole

Fennel

French beans

Garlic

Green beans

Hearts of palm

Kale

Kohlrabi

Leeks

Lettuce (all varieties)

Mangetout

Mushrooms (all varieties)

Mustard greens

Okra

Onions

Pak choi (bok choy)

Parsley

Peppers (all varieties)

Purple sprouting broccoli

Pickles (dill or artificially sweetened)

Pimentos

Radicchio

Radishes

Rocket

Rhubarb

Runner beans

Sea vegetables (seaweed, nori)

Shallots

Spinach

Spring greens

Spring onions

Sprouts (alfalfa, bean, broccoli, lentil, radish, sunflower)

Sugar snap peas

Swiss chard

Tomatoes (all varieties)

Tomato juice

Turnip greens

Vegetable juice cocktail

Vine leaves

Water chestnuts

Watercress

NUTS AND SEEDS

Limit to one serving per day as specified. Dry roasted recommended.

Almonds 15

Brazil nuts 4

Cashews 15

Chestnuts 6

Edamame, dry roasted 30g (1oz)

Flaxseed 30g (1oz.)

Hazelnuts 25

Macadamia nuts 8

Peanut butter, natural, and other nut butters 30g (1oz)

Peanuts, dry roasted 20 small

Pecans 15

Pine nuts 30g (1oz)

Pistachio nuts 30

Pumpkin seeds 30g (1oz)

(continued)

NUTS AND SEEDS (*cont.*)

Sesame seeds 30g (1oz)

Sunflower seeds 30g (1oz)

Walnuts 15

FATS AND OILS

Up to 30ml (2tbsp) of the following fats or oils are allowed daily. Monounsaturated oils are particularly recommended.

Monounsaturated Oils

Olive (particularly extra-virgin)

Rapeseed

Polyunsaturated Oils or a Blend of Monounsaturated and Polyunsaturated

Corn

Flaxseed

Grapeseed

Peanut

Sesame

Sunflower

Other Fat Choices

Avocado – ⅓ whole = 15ml (1tbsp) oil

Guacamole – 30g (1oz) = 15ml (1bsp) oil

Margarine, trans-fat-free – 30g (1oz)

Mayonnaise, low-fat – 30g (1oz) (avoid varieties made with high-fructose corn syrup)

Mayonnaise, regular – 15g (½oz)

Olives (green or black) – 15 = 7.5ml (½tbsp) oil

Salad dressing – 30ml (2tbsp) Use those that contain 3g sugar or less per 30ml (2tbsp) Best choices contain olive or rapeseed oil; dressings labeled 'low-carb' may only be used if they meet these guidelines.

Trans-fat-free spreads – 30g (1oz)

SEASONINGS AND SAUCES

All spices that contain no added sugar

Bouillon

Coconut milk, low-fat

Espresso powder

Essences (almond, vanilla or others)

Horseradish and horseradish sauce

Lemon juice

Lime juice

Pepper (black, cayenne, red, white)

Salsa (check label for added sugar)

Stock

Trans-fat-free cooking spray

Use the following toppings and sauces sparingly; check label for added sugar or monosodium glutamate (MSG).

Cream cheese, fat-free or light – 30g (1oz)

Hot pepper sauce

'Low-carb' seasonings and sauces may only be used if they are trans-fat-free and contain no added sugar.

Miso – 7.5ml (½tbsp)

Shoyu – 7.5ml (½tbsp)

Soured cream, light or reduced-fat 30ml (2tbsp)

Soy sauce – 7.5ml (½tbsp)

Steak sauce – 7.5ml (½tbsp)

Taco sauce – 15ml (1tbsp)

Tamari – 15ml (1tbsp)

Whipped topping, light or fat-free – 30ml (2tbsp)

Worcestershire sauce – 15ml (1tbsp)

SWEET TREATS

Limit to 75–100 calories per day.

Boiled sweets, sugar-free

Chewing gum, sugar-free

Chocolate powder, no sugar added

Chocolate syrup, sugar-free

Cocoa powder, unsweetened (also for cocoa)

Drink mix, sugar-free and nutrient-enhanced

Gelatine, sugar-free

Ice lollies, sugar-free

Jam, sugar-free

Jelly, sugar-free

Syrups, sugar-free

Some sugar-free products may be made with sugar alcohols (isomalt, lactitol, mannitol, sorbitol or xylitol) and are permitted on the South Beach Diet. They may have associated side effects of gastrointestinal distress if consumed in excessive amounts.

SUGAR SUBSTITUTES

Acesulfame K

Aspartame

Fructose (count as Sweet Treats, 75–100 calorie limit)

Saccharine

Sucralose (Splenda)

Some sugar substitutes may be made with sugar alcohols (isomalt, lactitol, mannitol, sorbitol or xylitol)

and are permitted on the South Beach Diet. They may have associated side effects of gastrointestinal distress if consumed in large amounts.

DRINKS

Caffeinated and decaffeinated coffee and tea (drink caffeinated in moderation)

Diet, caffeinated and decaffeinated, sugar-free soft drinks (drink caffeinated in moderation)

Herbal teas (such as peppermint and chamomile)

Milk, skimmed

Soya milk, low-fat plain, vanilla or sucralose-containing (4g or less fat per 240ml (8floz) serving). Be sure that the product does not contain high-fructose corn syrup.

Sugar-free powdered drink mixes

Tomato juice

Vegetable juice cocktail

BEEF

Brisket

Jerky, unless homemade without sugar

Liver

Rib roast

Rib-eye steak

Skirt steak

POULTRY

Chicken, wings and legs

Duck

Goose

Turkey, dark meat (including wings and thighs)

PORK

Bacon

Honey-roast ham

Pork crackling

VEAL

Breast

DAIRY

Ice cream

Milk, semi-skimmed or full-fat

Soya milk, whole

Yogurt, full-fat, fruit and frozen

CHEESE

Full-fat

FRUITS

Avoid all fruits and fruit juices on Phase 1.

VEGETABLES

Beetroot

Carrots

Green peas

Potatoes, sweet

Potatoes, white

Pumpkin

Squash, winter (acorn, butternut, etc.)

Swedes

Sweetcorn

Turnips

Yams

STARCHES

Avoid all starchy food on Phase 1, including:

Bread, all types

Cereal, all types

Croutons, all types

Pasta, all types

Porridge

Pastries and baked goods, all types

Rice, all types

Savoury and sweet biscuits

SAUCES

Cocktail sauce

Ketchup

DRINKS

Alcohol of any kind, including beer and wine

Fruit juice, all types

Milk, full-fat and semi-skimmed

Powdered drink mixes containing sugar

Soft drinks containing sugar

Soya milk with more than 4g fat per 240ml (8floz) serving

DAY 1

BREAKFAST

180ml (6floz) vegetable juice

Ham and cheese omelette with chives

Coffee or tea with skimmed milk and sugar substitute

MID-MORNING SNACK

Raw vegetable sticks with avocado-coriander guacamole (⅓ avocado mashed with 75g (2½oz) fat-free cottage cheese, chopped onion, finely chopped garlic, finely chopped coriander and dried chilli flakes)

LUNCH

Chock-Full-of-Vegetables Chilli (see page 212)

Large mixed green salad

30ml (2tbsp) Ranch Dressing (page 217) or reduced-sugar prepared dressing of your choice

MID-AFTERNOON SNACK

Chilled prawn cocktail with spicy red pepper sauce (for the sauce, in a blender, combine 1 diced red pepper (capsicum) with 2tbsp reduced-fat soured cream or crème fraiche, 1 clove garlic and hot pepper sauce to taste)

DINNER

Grilled sirloin steak (grill extra for Day 2 lunch)

Hearts of Palm 'Potato' Salad (page 213)

Grilled peppers (capsicum) and onions with finely chopped garlic and balsamic vinegar (grill in advance and let marinate in the dressing for best flavour)

DESSERT

Maple-Almond Flan (page 225)

DAY 2

BREAKFAST

180ml (6floz) vegetable juice

Vegetable Quiche Cups (page 189)

Coffee or tea with skimmed milk and sugar substitute

MID-MORNING SNACK

30g (1oz) reduced-fat cheddar cheese cubes with cherry tomatoes

LUNCH

Clear mushroom soup (chicken stock and reconstituted dried mushrooms)

Sliced steak on a bed of mixed greens (use leftover steak from Day 1 dinner)

30ml (2tbsp) Lemon Vinaigrette (page 216) or reduced-sugar prepared dressing of your choice

MID-AFTERNOON SNACK

Grilled Chicken and Roasted Red Pepper (Capsicum) Roll-Up (page 196)

DINNER

South Beach Diet Shepherd's Pie (page 208)

Radicchio and endive salad

30ml (2tbsp) Dijon Vinaigrette (page 215) or reduced-sugar prepared dressing of your choice

DESSERT

Peanut butter delight (stir together 115g (4oz) ricotta cheese (reduced fat if available), 1tbsp wholenut peanut butter, 2.5ml (½tsp) vanilla essence and 1 sachet sugar substitute; chill and serve)

DAY 3

BREAKFAST

180ml (6floz) tomato juice

Poached egg and salmon Florentine (1 poached egg with smoked salmon served on 20g (¾oz) spinach cooked in olive oil)

MID-MORNING SNACK

Tex-Mex Smoked Turkey Roll-Up (page 197)

LUNCH

Phase 1 soup of your choice, optional (page 192)

Chopped salad with tuna and white beans (on a bed of chopped cos lettuce, layer 170g (6oz) yellowfin tuna with chopped cucumber, tomato, celery and radishes; 115g (4oz) tinned cannellini beans; and 75g/2½oz diced avocado)

MID-AFTERNOON SNACK

Reduced-fat cottage cheese with sliced tomatoes

DINNER

Roasted rotisserie chicken on a bed of mixed greens with toasted pistachios (buy supermarket rotisserie chicken breast and get extra for Day 4 lunch)

30ml (2tbsp) Green Goddess Dressing (page 216) or reduced-sugar prepared dressing of your choice

Roasted artichoke hearts (toss drained artichoke hearts with a little olive oil, sea salt and freshly ground black pepper and bake at 180°C/350°F/Gas 4 until crisped)

DESSERT

Lime Rind Ricotta Crème (page 220)

DAY 4

BREAKFAST

180ml (6floz) vegetable juice

2 eggs scrambled with chopped onion and roasted red peppers (from a jar)

2 turkey sausages

Coffee or tea with skimmed milk and sugar substitute

MID-MORNING SNACK

Roast Beef and Horseradish Roll-Up (page 197)

LUNCH

Green Gazpacho (page 190)

Texan chicken salad (toss leftover chicken from Day 3 dinner with up to 115g (4oz) tinned black eyed beans, ⅓ diced small avocado, chopped spring onions and shop-bought salsa; serve on a bed of greens)

MID-AFTERNOON SNACK

Celery sticks stuffed with 1 triangle reduced-fat soft cheese

DINNER

Grilled Salmon with Tomatoes, Spinach and Capers (page 203; make extra for Day 5 lunch)

Rocket and red onion salad

30ml (2tbsp) Blue Cheese Dressing (page 214) or reduced-sugar prepared dressing of your choice

DESSERT

Chilled Espresso Custard (page 223)

DAY 5

BREAKFAST

180ml (6floz) vegetable juice

Asparagus and mushroom omelette (sauté asparagus and mushrooms in olive oil before filling)

Coffee or tea with skimmed milk and sugar substitute

MID-MORNING SNACK

Caprese bites (break 1 slice reduced-fat mozzarella cheese into 4 pieces; place each piece in a hollowed-out cherry tomato and microwave to melt cheese, if desired)

LUNCH

Phase 1 soup of your choice, optional (page 192)

Easy salmon salad (toss leftover salmon from Day 4 dinner with cucumber, watercress, 2tbsp reduced-fat soured cream or crème fraiche and chopped dill)

MID-AFTERNOON SNACK

Raw vegetable sticks with Indian-style yogurt dip (mix fat-free or low-fat yogurt with a little ground cumin, coriander and turmeric)

DINNER

Home-style Turkey Meatloaf with Mushrooms and White Beans (page 200)

Mixed baby lettuces with 30g (1oz) toasted pine nuts

30ml (2tbsp) Dijon Vinaigrette (page 215) or reduced-sugar prepared dressing of your choice

DESSERT

Cocoa-Nut Mousse (page 224)

DAY 6

BREAKFAST

180ml (6floz) vegetable juice

Portobello breakfast stack (top a Portobello mushroom with a slice of tomato and grill 3 minutes; top mushroom with scrambled eggs and chopped chives)

Coffee or tea with skimmed milk and sugar substitute

MID-MORNING SNACK

1 reduced-fat soft cheese triangle with cucumber sticks

LUNCH

Cobb salad (top chopped cos lettuce with diced smoked chicken, ⅓ diced small avocado, 2 crumbled cooked turkey rashers and chopped fresh tomatoes and red onion)

30ml (2tbsp) Lime Vinaigrette (page 216) or reduced-sugar prepared dressing of your choice

MID-AFTERNOON SNACK

4 Labne Balls (page 195) with raw vegetable sticks

DINNER

Mediterranean Cod (page 202)

Oven-roasted asparagus with lemon rind and black pepper

Julienned vegetable salad with crumbled reduced-fat feta cheese

30ml (2tbsp) Balsamic Vinaigrette (page 214) or reduced-sugar prepared dressing of your choice

DESSERT

No sugar-added fat-free chocolate-milk ice-lolly, with 240ml (8floz) glass of skimmed milk

DAY 7

BREAKFAST

180ml (6floz) tomato juice

Spanish Artichoke 'Tortilla' (page 188)

Coffee or tea with skimmed milk and sugar substitute

MID-MORNING SNACK

30g (1oz) assorted reduced-fat cheese cubes with raw vegetable sticks

LUNCH

Crab meat salad in a tomato bowl (mix 115g/4oz crab meat, 4tbsp finely diced peppers/capsicum and 1 finely chopped spring onion with 1tbsp low-fat mayonnaise and 1tbsp fat-free natural yogurt; serve in a hollowed-out tomato)

Sugar-free ice-lolly

MID-AFTERNOON SNACK

Grande latte with skimmed milk (sweetened with sugar substitute, if desired)

30 pistachio nuts

DINNER

Ginger-Dijon Glazed Pork Tenderloin (page 206; make extra for Day 8 lunch)

Surprise South Beach Diet Mashed 'Potatoes' (page 219)

Assorted grilled vegetables, such as asparagus, courgettes (zucchini) and peppers (capsicum)

DESSERT

Baked Ricotta Custard (page 222)

DAY 8

BREAKFAST

180ml (6floz) vegetable juice

Chunky Vegetable Hash (page 187)

1 or 2 eggs, cooked in any way

Coffee or tea with skimmed milk and sugar substitute

MID-MORNING SNACK

115g (4oz) fat-free Greek yogurt with a dash of almond essence

LUNCH

Tomato Soup with Vegetables (page 191)

Sliced pork tenderloin (use leftovers from Day 7 dinner) on a bed of baby greens

30ml (2tbsp) Lemon-Dill Dressing (page 216) or reduced-sugar prepared dressing of your choice

MID-AFTERNOON SNACK

Curried Turkey Roll-Up (page 196)

DINNER

Pecan-Crusted Trout (page 204)

Kale (or other greens) cooked with garlic and olive oil

Red Bean Mash (page 218)

DESSERT

Vanilla Ricotta Crème (page 220)

DAY 9

BREAKFAST

180ml (6floz) vegetable juice

2 scrambled eggs with turkey rashers

Sliced tomatoes

Coffee or tea with skimmed milk and sugar substitute

MID-MORNING SNACK

Smoked salmon with 30g (1oz) fat-free or light cream cheese and capers on endive leaves

LUNCH

Lean beef burger with 60g (2oz) melted reduced-fat Emmental cheese, Dijon mustard and tomato on a bed of lettuce

Three-bean salad (combine 75g/2½oz each black eyed beans, kidney beans and chickpeas with chopped red onion; toss with a reduced-sugar prepared dressing of your choice, page 214)

MID-AFTERNOON SNACK

115g (4oz) reduced-fat cottage cheese with pepper (capsicum) strips

DINNER

Vegetable Moussaka (page 210)

Radish, cucumber and spring onion salad

30ml (2tbsp) Ranch Dressing (page 217) or reduced-sugar prepared dressing of your choice

DESSERT

Fat-free Greek yogurt topped with 1tbsp South Beach Diet Nutty Granola (page 228)

DAY 10

BREAKFAST

Wake-up energy shake (blend 120ml/4floz low-fat, reduced-sugar artificially sweetened vanilla soya milk, 115g/4oz fat-free natural yogurt, 90g/3oz firm silken tofu and 4tbsp dry-roasted almonds until frothy)

Coffee or tea with skimmed milk and sugar substitute

MID-MORNING SNACK

California Roll-Up (page 196)

LUNCH

South Beach Diet Phase 1 soup of your choice (page 192)

Grilled tuna steak (marinate 1 hour in ginger- and garlic-flavoured olive oil; use for basting)

Steamed green and yellow beans with grated lemon rind

MID-AFTERNOON SNACK

15 almonds and 240ml (8floz) glass of skimmed milk

DINNER

Moroccan Lemon Chicken with Courgettes (Zucchini) and Green Olives (page 198)

Fennel and red onion salad with chopped kalamata olives

30ml (2tbsp) Spicy Lemon-Cumin Vinaigrette (page 217) or reduced-sugar prepared dressing of your choice

DESSERT

Vanilla chill (blend 225g/8oz) fat-free yogurt, 150ml/5floz low-fat plain or artificially sweetened soya milk, 5ml/1tsp vanilla essence, ice cubes and a sprinkling of cinnamon until frothy

DAY 11

BREAKFAST

180ml (6floz) vegetable juice

Red Bean Cakes (page 218) topped with scrambled eggs and shop-bought salsa

Coffee or tea with skimmed milk and sugar substitute

MID-MORNING SNACK

Celery sticks with 2tbsp wholenut peanut butter

LUNCH

Grilled turkey burger with tomato and onion on a bed of watercress

30ml (2tbsp) Thousand Island Dressing (page 217) or reduced-sugar prepared dressing of your choice

MID-AFTERNOON SNACK

115g (4oz) shelled edamame (young podded soybeans) with sea salt

DINNER

Spicy Prawn and Pak Choi (Bok Choy) Stir-Fry (page 205)

Julienned courgette (zucchini) tossed with black pepper and 30ml (2tbsp) Lemon Vinaigrette (page 216)

DESSERT

Ricotta crème of your choice (page 220)

DAY 12

BREAKFAST

180ml (6floz) vegetable juice

Cheddar cheese omelette

Sliced tomatoes

Coffee or tea with skimmed milk and sugar substitute

MID-MORNING SNACK

Smoked salmon on cucumber rounds

LUNCH

Provençal White Bean Soup (page 194)

Endive salad with toasted walnuts and reduced-fat goat's cheese

30ml (2tbsp) Dijon Vinaigrette (page 215) or reduced-sugar prepared dressing of your choice

MID-AFTERNOON SNACK

Spiced aubergine (eggplant) purée (Baba ghanoush) with raw vegetable sticks

DINNER

Pan-Fried Pork Chops with Sautéed Swiss Chard (page 207)

Red-leaf lettuce salad

30ml (2tbsp) Blue Cheese Dressing (page 214) or reduced-sugar prepared dressing of your choice

DESSERT

Creamy Lemon-Vanilla Ricotta Soufflé (page 221)

DAY 13

BREAKFAST

180ml (6floz) vegetable juice

Vegetable scrambled eggs (sauté chopped mushrooms, courgettes/zucchini and onions in extra-virgin olive oil before scrambling with 2 eggs)

Coffee or tea with skimmed milk and sugar substitute

MID-MORNING SNACK

Hummous with red peppers (capsicum), celery and cucumber sticks

LUNCH

Yellowfin tuna in spring water with tomato and onion slices on a bed of greens

30ml (2tbsp) Creamy Coriander Dressing (page 215) or reduced-sugar prepared dressing of your choice

MID-AFTERNOON SNACK

4tbsp dry-roasted soya nuts

240ml (8floz) skimmed milk

DINNER

Sautéed Lamb with Spinach and Chickpeas (page 209)

Baked aubergine (eggplant) rounds with Parmesan cheese

DESSERT

Lemon-Thyme Ice (page 229)

DAY 14

BREAKFAST

Morning mocha smoothie (blend 120ml/4floz skimmed milk, 225g/8oz fat-free natural yogurt, instant coffee powder to taste, 30ml/2tbsp sugar-free chocolate syrup and 6 ice cubes until frothy)

Coffee or tea with skimmed milk and sugar substitute

MID-MORNING SNACK

Hollowed out red pepper (capsicum) stuffed with reduced-fat cottage cheese and chives, with chopped green pepper (capsicum)

LUNCH

Phase 1 soup of your choice (page 192)

Chef's salad (at least 30g/1oz each ham, turkey and low-fat cheese on mixed greens)

30ml (2tbsp) Creamy Dijon-Thyme Dressing (page 215) or reduced-sugar prepared dressing of your choice

MID-AFTERNOON SNACK

2 sliced hard-boiled eggs with chilled asparagus spears and sea salt

DINNER

Grilled chicken, peppers (capsicum) and red onion kebabs

Greek salad (diced cucumbers and tomatoes, kalamata olives and 30g/1oz reduced-fat feta cheese on a bed of cos lettuce)

30ml (2tbsp) Balsamic Vinaigrette (page 214) or reduced-sugar prepared dressing of your choice

DESSERT

Ricotta Cheesecake with Lemon Drizzle and Pine Nuts (page 226)

Recipes
for Phase 1 Meal Plans

(continued)

Chunky Vegetable Hash

Prep time: 10 minutes • Cook time: 15 minutes

This bright, crisp hash is delicious served with eggs cooked in any way, and it can also be turned into an omelette filling. Use any dried herb you prefer, or add a combination of chopped fresh herbs.

15ml (1tbsp)	extra-virgin olive oil
1	small onion, chopped
	pinch of dried thyme
	pinch of paprika
	pinch of salt
1	small red pepper (capsicum), diced
4	large button mushrooms, roughly chopped
2	small courgettes (zucchini), diced
1	small garlic clove, finely chopped

In a large frying pan, heat oil over a medium-high heat. Add onion, thyme and paprika, reduce heat to medium-low and cook, stirring occasionally, 7 minutes, or until onion is softened. Stir in salt, red pepper, mushrooms, courgettes (zucchini) and garlic. Cover and cook, stirring occasionally, 4 minutes longer. Remove from the heat and serve hash on its own or with a poached egg.

Makes 4 generous servings

Nutrition at a Glance

Per serving (without egg): 59 calories, 4g fat, 0.5g saturated fat, 2g protein, 6g carbohydrate, 2g fibre, 81mg sodium

Per serving (with 1 egg): 77 calories, 5g fat, 1g saturated fat, 3g protein, 6g carbohydrate, 2g fibre, 99mg sodium

Spanish Artichoke 'Tortilla'

Prep time: 10 minutes • Cook time: 50 minutes

In Spain and parts of South America, tortillas are omelette-like dishes typically made with potatoes. They're a café staple and often served as tapas. In this Phase 1 variation, we've replaced the potatoes with tasty artichoke hearts. Make the tortilla for breakfast, or serve it with your favourite salad for a light lunch or dinner.

15ml (1tbsp)	extra-virgin olive oil
2	medium onions, thinly sliced
2	garlic cloves, finely chopped
¼	teaspoon salt
250g (9oz)	tinned artichoke hearts, drained and quartered
½	teaspoon paprika
	pinch of cayenne pepper
3	large eggs plus 180ml (6floz) very low-fat egg substitute, lightly beaten

In a medium non-stick frying pan, heat oil over a medium heat. Add onions, garlic and salt. Cook, stirring occasionally, 5 minutes, or until onions begin to soften. Cover, reduce heat to medium-low and cook until onions are very tender, 15 minutes longer.

Add artichoke hearts, paprika and cayenne pepper; cook, uncovered, until artichokes are heated through, about 5 minutes. Pour eggs over vegetables, cover and cook over a low heat until set, about 20 minutes.

Uncover the pan and place a large plate over the frying pan. Carefully invert the pan and release tortilla onto the plate. Slide inverted tortilla back into the frying pan and continue cooking until bottom is golden brown, 5 to 7 minutes. Transfer to a serving plate and cut into quarters. Serve warm.

Makes 4 servings

Nutrition at a Glance

Per serving: 163 calories, 8g fat, 2g saturated fat, 11g protein, 12g carbohydrate, 5g fibre, 336mg sodium

Vegetable Quiche Cups

Prep time: 15 minutes • Cook time: 25 minutes

This crustless quiche recipe can be used as a base for any combination of vegetables and low-fat cheese. If you don't have a muffin tin, follow the variation below. Once prepared, the quiches can be frozen individually and reheated in the microwave.

280g (10oz)	frozen chopped spinach
90g (3oz)	grated low-fat cheddar cheese
180ml (6floz)	very low-fat egg substitute
45g (1½oz)	finely diced green pepper (capsicum)
45g (1½oz)	finely diced onion
3 drops	hot pepper sauce (optional)

Preheat the oven to 180°C/350°F/Gas 4. Line a 12-muffin tin with paper cases, if desired. Spray the pan or paper cases with cooking spray.

Place spinach in a microwavable container and cook in the microwave on high power for 2½ minutes. Drain excess liquid.

In a large bowl, combine spinach, cheese, egg substitute, green pepper and onion. Mix well. Divide mixture evenly among the muffin moulds.

Bake for 20 minutes, or until a toothpick or cake tester inserted in the centre comes out clean.

Serves 6

Nutrition at a Glance

Per serving: 77 calories, 9g protein, 3g carbohydrate, 3g fat, 2g saturated fat, 2g fibre, 160mg sodium

Breakfast Quiche: If you don't have a muffin tin, pour the mixture into a 20cm (8in) square baking dish or a 23cm (9in) round pie dish. Bake at 180°C/350°F/Gas 4 for 20 to 25 minutes, or until a toothpick or cake tester comes out clean. Cut into 6 pieces.

Green Gazpacho

Prep time: 30 minutes • Chill time: 2 hours or overnight

Bursting with fresh vegetable flavour, this refreshing cold soup gets its good monounsaturated fat from the avocado garnish, which also lends fantastic texture and taste. Any type of lettuce (for example, cos, iceberg, little gem) or even spinach can be used, so choose whatever looks best at the greengrocer or supermarket.

1kg (2½lb) cucumbers (3 to 4 medium), peeled, seeded and roughly chopped	1 garlic clove, peeled
	30ml (2tbsp) water
	30ml (2tbsp) fresh lime juice
60g (2oz) roughly chopped lettuce of your choice	15ml (1tbsp) extra-virgin olive oil
	¼tsp salt
1 small green pepper (capsicum), seeded and roughly chopped	pinch of ground cumin
	cayenne pepper
2 spring onions, trimmed and roughly chopped	1 small ripe avocado, diced

In a blender, purée cucumbers, lettuce, green pepper, spring onions, garlic, water, lime juice, oil, salt and cumin in batches until smooth. Season with additional salt and add cayenne pepper to taste.

Transfer to a large bowl. Cover and chill gazpacho at least 2 hours or overnight. When ready to serve, peel and dice avocado. Divide soup among 4 bowls, sprinkle avocado over and serve.

Makes 4 servings

Nutrition at a Glance

Per serving: 138 calories, 11g fat, 1g saturated fat, 2g protein, 11g carbohydrate, 5g fibre, 156mg sodium

Variations: Try jalapeño or Serrano chillies in place of cayenne pepper, or top with a swirl of your favourite hot sauce (try a green one!). Add chopped coriander or rocket.

Tomato Soup with Vegetables

Prep time: 15 minutes • Cook time: 15 minutes

Prepared with basic staples and store cupboard items, this hearty vegetable soup is rich in protein and cooks quickly, making it a good choice for weeknight meals or other busy times.

15ml (1tbsp)	extra-virgin olive oil
1	small onion, finely chopped
2	sticks celery, finely chopped
4	garlic cloves, finely chopped
¼tsp	dried basil
¼tsp	dried oregano
¼tsp	dried chilli flakes
140g (5oz)	button mushrooms, trimmed and quartered
1	medium yellow or green courgette (zucchini), diced
400g (14oz)	tin butter beans, rinsed and drained
400g (14oz)	tin chopped tomatoes, with juice
225g (8oz)	passata
180ml (6floz)	water

In a medium saucepan, heat oil over a medium heat. Add onion, celery, garlic, basil, oregano and chilli flakes; cook, stirring occasionally, 5 minutes. Add mushrooms and courgette (zucchini); cook, stirring occasionally, 5 minutes longer. Stir in beans, chopped tomatoes and their juice, passata and water; bring to the boil and simmer briefly just to heat through. Serve warm.

Makes 4 servings

Nutrition at a Glance

Per serving: 146 calories, 4g fat, 0.5g saturated fat, 6g protein, 22g carbohydrate, 6g fibre, 594mg sodium

EASY SOUTH BEACH DIET SOUPS
FOR PHASE 1 – OR ANY PHASE

Soup is a great way to fill up at the start of a Phase 1 meal, or, if you prefer, you can prepare a higher-protein soup like the Fish Chowder, opposite, as the main course. If you're on Phase 2 or 3, you can prepare these soups or those on pages 265 to 267.

Black Bean Soup: In a medium saucepan, heat 15ml (1tbsp) extra-virgin olive oil over a medium heat. Add 4 thinly sliced spring onions, 1 thinly sliced celery stick, 4 finely chopped garlic cloves, 2tsp ground cumin, pinch of cayenne pepper and a pinch of salt and freshly ground black pepper. Cook, stirring occasionally, until vegetables soften. Add 800g (28oz) tinned black beans and their liquid, 400g (14oz) tin chopped tomatoes with juice and 360ml (12floz) low-sodium chicken stock. Bring to the boil and simmer for 10 minutes. Transfer 450ml (15floz) soup to a blender and process until smooth. Return soup to the pan and stir to combine. Return to the simmer and cook for 10 minutes longer. Season with 15ml (1tbsp) fresh lime juice and adjust seasoning. Serve hot with hot pepper sauce and extra sliced spring onions on the side.

Creamy Cauliflower Soup: In a medium saucepan, heat 15ml (1tbsp) extra-virgin olive oil over a medium heat. Add 1 thinly sliced small onion and cook, stirring occasionally, until softened, about 5 minutes. Add 1 (900g) head cauliflower, cut into florets, along with the finely chopped stems. Add 960ml (32floz) low-sodium chicken stock, bring to the boil and simmer until cauliflower is tender, about 15 minutes. Transfer soup in batches to a blender and puree until smooth. Return to the saucepan and whisk in 60ml (2floz) reduced-fat soured cream and ¼ teaspoon nutmeg. Season with salt and pepper to taste and serve hot. Or chill in the refrigerator and serve cold.

Chicken Soup with Kale: In a medium saucepan, heat 15ml (1tbsp) extra-virgin olive oil over a medium heat. Add 1 thinly sliced small sweet onion, 2 thinly sliced celery sticks, 2 finely chopped garlic cloves and a pinch of salt and freshly ground black pepper. Cook, stirring occasionally, until onion softens, about 7 minutes. Add 1 large bunch chopped kale leaves; stir and cook for 1 minute. Add 225g (8oz) cubed boneless, skinless chicken breast; stir and cook for 1 minute longer. Add 960ml (32floz) low-sodium chicken stock, bring to the boil and simmer until chicken is cooked through, about 7 minutes. Stir in 3tbsp finely chopped parsley. Serve hot.

Chilled Tomato Bisque: In a medium saucepan, heat 15ml (1tbsp) extra-virgin olive oil over a medium heat. Add 1 thinly sliced small red onion, 2 finely chopped garlic cloves, ¼tsp dried chilli flakes and a pinch of salt and freshly ground black pepper. Cook, stirring occasionally, until onion softens, about 7 minutes. Add 800g (28oz) tinned chopped tomatoes with juice and 330ml (11floz) low-sodium vegetable juice. Bring to the boil and simmer for 15 minutes. Remove from the heat and cool to room temperature. Transfer to a covered container and refrigerate until chilled. Just before serving, transfer half of the soup to a blender and purée until smooth. Place puréed soup in a large serving bowl and stir in remaining soup. Whisk in 2tbsp low-fat soured cream or crème fraiche and serve cold.

Creamy Broccoli Soup: In a large saucepan, heat 15ml (1tbsp) extra-virgin olive oil over a medium heat. Add 1 finely chopped large onion and 1 finely chopped garlic clove; cook, stirring occasionally, until onion softens, about 7 minutes. Add 450g (1lb) roughly chopped broccoli stems and florets and a pinch of salt and freshly ground black pepper; stir well. Add 500ml (16floz) vegetable stock and 120ml (4floz) skimmed milk. Bring to the boil and simmer, partially cover and reduce heat to low; cook until broccoli is very tender, about 25 minutes. Transfer soup in batches to a blender and purée until smooth. Return soup to the pan and stir in 30ml (2tbsp) fresh lemon juice. Heat through and serve hot.

Cucumber and Mint Soup: In a blender, combine 2 large peeled and chopped cucumbers, 225g (8oz) low-fat or fat-free natural yogurt, 180ml (6floz) cold water, 15ml (1tbsp) fresh lime juice, ¼tsp salt and ¼tsp freshly ground black pepper; purée until smooth. Stir in 4tbsp chopped fresh mint and serve.

Fish Chowder: In a large saucepan, heat 15ml (1tbsp) extra-virgin olive oil over a medium heat. Add 1 chopped medium onion, 3 chopped celery sticks, 90g (3oz) chopped lean back bacon and ¼tsp dried thyme. Cook, stirring occasionally, until vegetables soften and bacon is lightly browned, about 7 minutes. Stir in 500ml (16floz) fish stock, 300ml (10floz) water and 240ml (8floz) skimmed milk. Add 675g (1½lb) fresh cod or hake, cut into 1cm (½in) wide strips and 1 diced medium courgette (zucchini); bring to the boil and simmer until fish is opaque, about 10 minutes. Break up any large fish chunks with a wooden spoon. Season with freshly ground black pepper and serve hot.

Provençal White Bean Soup

Prep time: 10 minutes • Cook time: 20 minutes

The addition of basil, rosemary and thyme turns a simple blended soup into heady French-style fare. Add a little extra stock if you prefer a thinner version. Low-sodium chicken stock can be used in place of the vegetable stock, if desired.

15ml (1tbsp)	extra-virgin olive oil
1	small onion, chopped
1	celery stalk, finely chopped
2	garlic cloves, smashed and peeled
½tsp	dried basil
½tsp	dried rosemary
¼tsp	dried thyme
¼tsp	salt
400g (14oz)	tin cannellini beans, drained and rinsed
360ml (12floz)	low-sodium vegetable stock
	freshly ground black pepper

In a large saucepan, heat oil over a medium–high heat. Add onion, celery, garlic, basil, rosemary, thyme and salt; reduce heat to medium-low and cook, stirring occasionally, 15 minutes, or until vegetables are softened.

Add beans and stir to combine. Using a large metal spoon, transfer about ¾ of the bean mixture to a blender. Add stock and purée until smooth. Return mixture to the saucepan, stir to combine and simmer just to heat through. Season with additional salt and pepper to taste. Serve warm.

Makes 4 servings

Nutrition at a Glance

Per serving: 103 calories, 4g fat, 1g saturated fat, 4g protein, 16g carbohydrate, 6g fibre, 500mg sodium

Labne Balls

Draining time: 48 hours • Prep time: 10 minutes

Also known as kefir cheese or yogurt cheese, labne is a thick, drained yogurt popular in the Middle East. When rolled into balls, as here, labne has a texture similar to fresh mozzarella and is a fine alternative to low-fat mozzarella slices for Phase 1 snacks. Look for imported Greek yogurt, which is thicker than regular yogurt; it's sold in the dairy section of most supermarkets.

600g (21oz) fat-free Greek yogurt, drained

1tsp salt

2tbsp dried Italian seasoning

extra-virgin olive oil

Line a sieve with muslin and place over a large bowl. In a small bowl, combine yogurt and salt. Spoon yogurt into the sieve. Cover lightly with clingfilm and refrigerate until thick, about 48 hours. You should have about 360ml (12floz) of drained yogurt. Discard liquid.

Place Italian herb seasoning in a shallow dish. On a large piece of greaseproof paper, roll yogurt by tablespoons into 2cm (¾in) balls. Roll balls in seasoning to coat.

Serve labne balls immediately or store in a covered container in the refrigerator for up to 1 week. For longer storage, cover with extra-virgin olive oil and enjoy as desired.

Makes 24 balls (4 per serving)

Nutrition at a Glance

Per ball: 13 calories, 0g fat, 0g saturated fat, 2g protein, 1g carbohydrate, 0g fibre, 106mg sodium

Herb Variations: Roll the balls in chopped mint, chives, or parsley (or a combination of all three). Or sprinkle with dried chilli flakes just before serving.

Yogurt Cheese Dip: Don't roll the labne into balls. Instead, flavour it with cumin or a seasoning mix of your choice and serve as a dip with raw vegetable sticks.

SOUTH BEACH DIET ROLL-UPS

A lettuce roll-up makes a great snack for Phase 1 (or 2 and 3). The combination of high-fibre vegetables and protein helps stave off hunger mid-morning or mid-afternoon. Each recipe makes 4 or 8 roll-ups, but you can roll up just one at a time if you prefer. Roll-ups are a great take-along snack for trips or when running errands. Make the filling for the Yucatan Prawn Roll-Up or Curried Turkey Roll-Up in advance, if you like, and refrigerate until ready to use.

California Roll-Up: Top each of 4 large red- or green-lettuce leaves with 1 slice each turkey breast and boiled ham, 1 thin slice tomato, 1 thin slice avocado, 5ml (1tsp) fresh lime juice, a few sprigs watercress or rocket and 15ml (1tbsp) Ranch Dressing (page 217). Roll up leaves, secure with toothpicks and serve.

Curried Turkey Roll-Up: Combine 225g (8oz) fat-free or low-fat natural yogurt, 115g (4oz) low-fat mayonnaise, 1tbsp curry powder and ½tsp ground ginger. Fold in 600g (21oz) cubed thickly sliced cooked turkey breast, 2 diced celery sticks, 1 diced small cucumber, 3tbsp finely chopped red onion and 4tbsp chopped fresh parsley. Season with salt and freshly ground black pepper to taste. Divide mixture among 8 large green lettuce leaves. Roll up leaves, secure with toothpicks and serve.

Grilled Chicken and Roasted Red Pepper (Capsicum) Roll-Up: Thinly slice 500g (18oz) grilled skinless, boneless chicken breasts and 3 large roasted red peppers (bottled). Top 4 large red- or green-lettuce leaves with chicken and peppers. Sprinkle with 30g (1oz) low-fat cheddar cheese and 2 thinly sliced spring onions. Roll up leaves, secure with toothpicks and serve.

Roast Beef and Horseradish Roll-Up: Combine 2tbsp prepared horseradish and 2tbsp low-fat mayonnaise; spread mixture on 4 large red- or green-lettuce leaves. Top each with 2 slices roast beef and a few sprigs watercress. Roll up leaves, secure with toothpicks and serve.

Spicy Hummous-Vegetable Roll-Up: Combine 115g (4oz) rocket, 1 thinly sliced and chopped fennel bulb, 1 thinly sliced large cucumber, 1 chopped large tomato, 45ml (3tbsp) fresh lemon juice, 15ml (1tbsp) extra-virgin olive oil and salt and freshly ground black pepper to taste. Divide among 8 large red-lettuce leaves. Dollop 2tbsp shop-bought hummous on top of vegetables on each leaf and spread to cover. Drizzle with hot pepper sauce to taste. Roll up leaves, secure with toothpicks and serve.

Tex-Mex Smoked Turkey Roll-Up: Combine 8 slices chopped smoked turkey breast, 1 diced avocado, 30g (1oz) diced low-fat cheddar cheese, 3tbsp shop-bought salsa and 15ml (1tbsp) fresh lime juice. Divide filling among 4 large red- or green-lettuce leaves. Roll up leaves, secure with toothpicks and serve.

Yucatan Prawn Roll-Up: Toss 450g (1lb) raw prawns with ¼tsp cayenne pepper and a generous pinch of salt. Grill until pink. Roughly chop prawns, then toss with 1 chopped large tomato, 1 diced small avocado, 2tbsp low-fat mayonnaise and 15ml (1tbsp) fresh lime juice. Divide mixture among 8 large red- or green-lettuce leaves. Season lightly with salt. Roll up leaves, secure with toothpicks and serve.

Moroccan Lemon Chicken
with Courgettes (Zucchini) and Green Olives

Prep time: 20 minutes • Cook time: 25 minutes

While the ingredient list for this recipe may seem long, it largely features common store-cupboard spices. When combined, these spices make up a version of *ras al-hanut*, an intriguing blend that is widely used on Moroccan-style meats and fish. If you prefer, look for prepared *ras al-hanut* or another Moroccan blend in the spice section of your supermarket. Mixed with a little extra-virgin olive oil, these spices make a wet rub that blackens while cooking, giving the chicken a rich, exotic taste.

4 x 170g (6oz)	boneless, skinless chicken breasts			pinch of cayenne pepper
1	small onion, thinly sliced		1	lemon
1tsp	ground cumin		20ml (4tsp)	extra-virgin olive oil
1tsp	ground ginger		350g (12oz)	courgettes (zucchini), thinly sliced crossways
½tsp	cinnamon			
½tsp	freshly ground black pepper		65g (2¼oz)	stoned green olives
			30ml (2tbsp)	water
¼tsp	allspice		2tbsp	chopped fresh parsley
¼tsp	salt			

Pound chicken breasts between two sheets of greaseproof paper to 5mm (¼in) thickness. Thinly slice half of the onion and finely chop the remaining half. Set aside.

In a small bowl, mix together cumin, ginger, cinnamon, pepper, allspice, salt and cayenne pepper. Finely grate rind from lemon into spice mixture. Squeeze 15ml (1tbsp) juice from lemon and add to bowl. Add

15ml (1tbsp) of the oil and stir to combine. Spread mixture on both sides of chicken.

Heat a large non-stick frying pan over a medium-high heat. Add chicken, in batches if necessary and cook, turning, until blackened on the outside and cooked through, 3 to 4 minutes per side. Transfer to a plate and loosely cover with foil to keep warm.

Add remaining 5ml (1tsp) oil to the frying pan and return to a medium-high heat. Add reserved onion slices and cook, stirring constantly with a wooden spoon and scraping up any browned bits, 3 minutes. Add courgettes (zucchini), olives and 30ml (2tbsp) water. Season lightly with additional salt and pepper; stir well. Cover and cook until courgettes are tender, 4 to 5 minutes. Remove the pan from the heat. Squeeze a little more lemon juice over chicken and vegetables, sprinkle with parsley and serve warm.

Makes 4 servings

Nutrition at a Glance

Per serving: 264 calories, 8g fat, 1g saturated fat, 41g protein, 6g carbohydrate, 2g fibre, 314mg sodium

Cooking Tip: Use turkey escalopes in place of chicken breasts if you want to avoid the pounding step.

Home-Style Turkey Meatloaf with Mushrooms and White Beans

Prep time: 15 minutes • Cook time: 1 hour 15 minutes

This healthy alternative to typical meatloaf adds haricot beans for a delicious high-fibre twist. Serve extra Dijon mustard on the side; it lends a satisfying, piquant flavour element

10ml (2tsp) extra-virgin olive oil

250g (9oz) chopped onion

½tsp dried thyme

½tsp cayenne pepper

½tsp paprika

½tsp salt

½tsp freshly ground black pepper

350g (12oz) mushrooms, trimmed and chopped

4 large garlic cloves, minced

400g (14oz) tin haricot beans, rinsed and drained

570g (1¼lb) extra-lean turkey, minced

2 large eggs

20g (¾oz) chopped parsley

20ml (4tsp) Worcestershire sauce

2tsp Dijon mustard plus extra for serving

Preheat the oven to 190°C/375°F/Gas 5. Lightly coat a 900g (2lb) metal or glass loaf tin with cooking spray.

In a large frying pan, heat oil over a medium–high heat. Add onion, thyme, cayenne pepper, paprika, salt and pepper. Reduce heat to medium–low and cook, stirring occasionally, 5 minutes. Add mushrooms and garlic; cook, stirring occasionally, until onion is softened and mushrooms are incorporated, about 5 minutes longer. Add beans and stir to combine. Transfer mixture to a plate and let cool, about 5 minutes.

In a large bowl, combine cooled bean mixture, turkey, eggs, parsley and 10ml (2tsp) of the Worcestershire sauce. Mix well with wet hands to combine. Form into a loaf and place into the prepared tin.

Stir together mustard and remaining 10ml (2tsp) Worcestershire sauce and set aside.

Bake meatloaf in the centre of the oven for 50 minutes. Remove from the oven and brush with the reserved Worcestershire mixture. Return to the oven and continue baking 10 to 15 minutes longer, or until a thermometer inserted into meatloaf registers 75°C/170°F. Let meatloaf stand 5 minutes before serving. Serve with additional Dijon mustard.

Makes 6 servings

Nutrition at a Glance

Per serving: 205 calories, 5g fat, 1g saturated fat, 30g protein, 15g carbohydrate, 4g fibre, 549mg sodium

Make in Advance: Cooked meatloaf freezes well for up to 3 months. Cut it into individual portions before freezing and thaw in the microwave when ready to eat.

Mediterranean Cod

Prep time: 15 minutes • Cook time: 30 minutes

Serve this dish in shallow bowls with soup spoons so you don't waste any of the rich sauce. The recipe is best made with red, full-flavoured Spanish piquillo peppers, which you can usually find among the other bottled peppers in your supermarket, or you could substitute 75g (2½oz) thinly sliced roasted red peppers (capsicum) instead.

15ml (1tbsp)	extra-virgin olive oil
1	medium courgette (zucchini), cut into 5mm (¼in) thick slices
1	small onion, thinly sliced
3	garlic cloves, finely chopped
	salt
	freshly ground black pepper
400g (14oz)	tin chopped tomatoes, drained
2	piquillo peppers (bottled), thinly sliced
675g (1½lb)	cod fillets
2tbsp	chopped parsley

In a large frying pan, heat oil over a medium heat. Add courgettes (zucchini), onion, garlic and a pinch of salt and black pepper; cook, stirring occasionally, 10 minutes. Stir in tomatoes and peppers; simmer over a medium heat for 10 minutes longer.

Add fish fillets to the sauce, spooning some of the mixture over the fillets. Cover the pan and continue to simmer until fish is opaque and cooked through, about 10 minutes. Sprinkle with parsley and serve warm.

Makes 4 servings

Nutrition at a Glance

Per serving: 216 calories, 5g fat, 1g saturated fat, 32g protein, 8g carbohydrate, 2g fibre, 489mg sodium

Grilled Salmon with Tomatoes, Spinach and Capers

Prep time: 15 minutes • Cook time: 10 minutes

This simple, elegant and delicious dish gives you a healthy dose of heart-protective omega-3 from the salmon. The tomatoes provide the carotenoid lycopene and the spinach delivers plenty of beta-carotene and folate. Grill extra and use for a salmon salad the next day.

675g (1½lb)	salmon fillets, skin-on	2	garlic cloves, finely chopped
	salt	450g (1lb)	plum tomatoes, chopped
	freshly ground black pepper	90g (3 oz)	baby spinach
15ml (1tbsp)	extra-virgin olive oil	1tbsp	rinsed and drained capers
1	medium onion	4	lemon wedges

Preheat the oven to grill. Lightly coat a large ovenproof baking dish with cooking spray.

Place salmon, flesh side up, in the baking dish, lightly season with salt and pepper and grill without turning until salmon is cooked through, 8 to 10 minutes.

Meanwhile, in a large saucepan, heat oil over a medium heat. Add onion and garlic; cook, stirring occasionally, until softened, about 7 minutes. Stir in tomatoes, spinach and capers; cook for 2 minutes longer. Remove the pan from the heat.

Remove salmon from oven, portion and transfer to 4 serving plates. Spoon tomato mixture over salmon, squeeze lemon wedges over the top and serve warm.

Makes 4 servings

Nutrition at a Glance

Per serving: 386 calories, 22g fat, 4g saturated fat, 36g protein, 10g carbohydrate, 3g fibre, 273mg sodium

Pecan-Crusted Trout

Prep time: 10 minutes • Cook time: 20 minutes

Pecans add even more protein, good monounsaturated fat and tremendous taste to this easy baked trout dish. Serve the fish with asparagus tossed with a little garlic and extra-virgin olive oil and roasted until golden and tender.

60g (2oz)	pecans
1tsp	dried rosemary
1	garlic clove
	pinch of cayenne pepper
4	whole trout (about 350g/12oz each), cleaned, with bones removed
¼tsp	salt
1	large egg white, lightly beaten
10ml (2tsp)	extra-virgin olive oil

Preheat the oven to 200°C/400°F/Gas 6. Line a baking tray with greaseproof paper.

In a food processor, pulse pecans, rosemary, garlic and cayenne pepper until finely chopped. Transfer mixture to a shallow dish.

Place each trout, opened and flesh-side up, on the baking tray.

Season flesh of trout with salt and brush with egg white. Sprinkle nut mixture over and press to adhere. Drizzle evenly with oil and bake until trout is opaque and tender inside, about 20 minutes.

Makes 4 servings

Nutrition at a Glance

Per serving: 382 calories, 24g fat, 3g saturated fat, 38g protein, 3g carbohydrate, 2g fibre, 248mg sodium

Spicy Prawn and Pak Choi (Bok Choy) Stir-Fry

Prep time: 20 minutes • Cook time: 10 minutes

Chilli–garlic sauce is a common Asian ingredient that brings a tangy–hot flavour to any dish. It can be used both for cooking and as a dipping sauce when you want a little extra heat. Look for brands with no sugar added in the Asian section of most large supermarkets.

675g (1½lb)	large raw prawns, peeled and de-veined
4	spring onions, white and green parts thinly sliced and kept separate
2	garlic cloves, finely chopped
10ml (2tsp)	vegetable oil
900g (2lb)	pak choi (bok choy), sliced crossways
30ml (2tbsp)	low-sodium soy sauce
10ml (2tsp)	chilli-garlic sauce

In a large bowl, combine prawns, spring onion whites and garlic.

In a wok or a large non-stick frying pan, heat oil over a medium–high heat. Add prawn mixture and cook, stirring occasionally, until prawns turn pink and are cooked through, 3 to 4 minutes. Transfer to a large clean bowl.

Return the pan to a medium–high heat. Add pak choi, cover and cook, stirring occasionally, until crisp-tender, 3 to 4 minutes. Drain any liquid from the frying pan and add pak choi to bowl with prawns.

Return the pan to a medium–high heat. Add soy sauce and chilli-garlic sauce; stir to combine and bring to a boil. Add prawn mixture and toss until coated. Cook briefly, just to reheat. Stir in spring onion greens and serve warm.

Makes 4 servings

Nutrition at a Glance

Per serving: 225 calories, 6g fat, 1g saturated fat, 35g protein, 9g carbohydrate, 3g fibre, 525mg sodium

Ginger-Dijon Glazed Pork Tenderloin

Prep time: 10 minutes • Cook time: 35 minutes

Dijon mustard, low-fat soured cream and fresh ginger create a flavourful coating for this tender pork roast. Buy an extra pork tenderloin and slice for lunch the next day.

2tbsp	Dijon mustard	675g (1½lb)	pork tenderloin
1tbsp	low-fat soured cream or crème fraiche	1	large garlic clove, thinly sliced
1tsp	grated fresh ginger	7.5ml (1½tsp)	extra-virgin olive oil
¼tsp	dried thyme		freshly ground black pepper
	salt		

Preheat the oven to 230°C/450°F/Gas 8.

In a small bowl, stir together mustard, soured cream or crème fraiche, ginger, thyme and a pinch of salt; set aside.

Make several 5mm (¼in) slits in pork tenderloin. Slip garlic into slits. Brush tenderloin with oil and season with salt and pepper.

Heat a large cast-iron or other ovenproof frying pan over a high heat. Add tenderloin and brown on all sides, about 5 minutes. Remove the pan from the heat.

Spread mustard mixture over pork, then transfer the frying pan to the oven and cook until a meat thermometer inserted into centre of pork registers 65°C/150°F, about 30 minutes. Remove the pan from the oven and transfer pork to a cutting board; loosely cover with foil and let rest for 5 minutes before slicing. Serve warm or at room temperature.

Makes 4 servings

Nutrition at a Glance

Per serving: 267 calories, 11g fat, 3g saturated fat, 38g protein, 2g carbohydrate, 0g fibre, 327mg sodium

Cooking Tip: Studding the meat with garlic before cooking is an easy flavour technique that can be used for any cut of pork or beef.

Pan-Fried Pork Chops with Sautéed Swiss Chard

Prep time: 10 minutes • Cook time: 15 minutes

A member of the beetroot family, Swiss chard is a cruciferous leafy winter green that delivers a good dose of beta-carotene, potassium and fibre. When preparing chard, cut off the thicker bottom 2.5cm (1in) or so of each stem, then thinly slice the rest of the stem (it's tender) and add to the leaves when cooking. Spinach and kale make good substitutes for Swiss chard when you want a bit of variety.

900g (2lb)	Swiss chard	4 x 170–225g (6–8oz)	centre-cut loin pork chops
20ml (4tsp)	extra-virgin olive oil		salt
2	large garlic cloves, finely chopped		freshly ground black pepper
	finely grated rind of 1 lemon	15ml (1tbsp)	water
½tsp	dried rosemary, crumbled		lemon juice

Trim tough ends off Swiss chard stems, tear leaves from stems, roughly chop leaves and thinly slice stems.

In a medium bowl, combine 10ml (2tsp) of the oil, half the garlic, the lemon rind and rosemary. Add the pork chops and turn to coat. Season lightly with salt and pepper.

Spray a large non-stick frying pan with cooking spray and heat over a medium–high heat. Add pork chops and cook for 3 to 4 minutes per side, or until just cooked through (do not overcook). Transfer pork chops to a plate and cover loosely with foil to keep warm.

Wipe the frying pan with kitchen paper; add remaining 10ml (2tsp) oil and heat over a medium heat. Add remaining garlic and cook, stirring, 30 seconds. Add Swiss chard stems and cook, stirring, 1 to 2 minutes. Add leaves and water; stir to coat. Cover and cook until leaves are wilted, 3 to 4 minutes longer. Season with salt and pepper and a squeeze of lemon juice. Serve pork chops with their juice, accompanied by the chard.

Makes 4 servings

Nutrition at a Glance

Per serving: 295 calories, 14g fat, 4g saturated fat, 35g protein, 8g carbohydrate, 3g fibre, 560mg sodium

South Beach Diet Shepherd's Pie

Prep time: 10 minutes • Cook time: 50 minutes

Love shepherd's pie? Then you'll love this Phase 1 twist on the classic. Edamame (young podded soybeans) replace the usual peas and add texture and protein, and mashed cauliflower topped with low-fat cheddar creates the rich, potato–like crust.

450g (1lb)	fresh or frozen cauliflower florets		120ml (4floz)	low-sodium beef stock
15ml (1tbsp)	extra-virgin olive oil		10ml (2tsp)	Worcestershire sauce
1	large onion, chopped		½tsp	freshly ground black pepper
2	garlic cloves, finely chopped			salt
450g (1lb)	extra-lean beef mince		2tbsp	low-fat soured cream or crème fraiche
280g (10oz)	fresh or thawed frozen shelled edamame		1	large egg yolk
			60g (2oz)	low-fat cheddar cheese

Preheat the oven to 180°C/350°F/Gas 4. Spray a 2-litre (3½–pint) casserole with cooking spray.

Bring a medium saucepan of water to the boil. Add cauliflower and cook until tender, about 10 minutes. Drain and transfer to a large bowl.

Meanwhile, in a large frying pan, heat oil over a medium heat. Add onion and garlic; cook, stirring occasionally, until translucent, about 5 minutes. Add beef and brown for 10 minutes, stirring to break up lumps. Add edamame and cook, stirring occasionally, 3 minutes longer. Stir in stock and Worcestershire sauce. Season with pepper and a pinch of salt. Transfer meat mixture to the casserole.

With an electric mixer at medium speed, whisk the cooked cauliflower with soured cream or crème fraiche, egg yolk and another pinch of salt. Spoon cauliflower evenly over meat. Top with cheese and bake for 20 to 25 minutes, or until golden on top. Serve warm.

Makes 4 servings

Nutrition at a Glance

Per serving: 367 calories, 16g fat, 5g saturated fat, 37g protein, 18g carbohydrate, 4g fibre, 324mg sodium

Sautéed Lamb with Spinach and Chickpeas

Prep time: 10 minutes • Cook time: 12 minutes

This rustic, filling dish is perfect for cold winter nights. To save time, have your butcher trim and cut the lamb for you.

675g (1½lb)	leg of lamb, trimmed and cut into 2.5cm (1in) pieces
1	small onion, finely chopped
2	garlic cloves, finely chopped
½tsp	cayenne pepper
½tsp	ground cinnamon
½tsp	ground cumin
¼tsp	freshly ground black pepper
1	lemon, rind finely grated and fruit cut in half
10ml (2tsp)	extra-virgin olive oil
400g (14oz)	tin chickpeas, rinsed and drained
350g (12oz)	baby spinach
¼tsp	salt

In a large bowl, combine lamb, onion, garlic, cayenne pepper, cinnamon, cumin, pepper, lemon rind and oil.

Spray a large non-stick frying pan with cooking spray and heat over a medium-high heat. Add lamb mixture and cook, stirring, 5 to 6 minutes, or until lamb is browned on the outside and still slightly pink on the inside. Transfer lamb to a plate, cover loosely with foil and keep warm.

Return the pan to a medium–high heat. Add chickpeas and spinach, in batches if necessary and cook until spinach is wilted and mixture is warm, 3 to 5 minutes. Return lamb to the pan and stir to combine and just reheat. Remove pan from the heat and stir in salt and a generous squeeze of lemon. Serve warm.

Makes 4 servings

Nutrition at a Glance

Per serving: 389 calories, 12g fat, 4g saturated fat, 41g protein, 30g carbohydrate, 8g fibre, 642mg sodium

Vegetable Moussaka

Prep time: 15 minutes • Cook time: 60 minutes • Stand time: 15 minutes

This moussaka is so filling and flavourful, you won't even miss the lamb.
Lentils provide protein, fibre and a rich meaty taste.

1	large aubergine (eggplant) (about 560g/1¼lb), ends trimmed, cut crossways into 5mm (¼in) thick rounds	1tsp	dried oregano
		¼tsp	ground cinnamon
10ml (2tsp)	extra-virgin olive oil	¼tsp	salt
1	large onion, chopped		freshly ground black pepper
4	garlic cloves, finely chopped	120ml (4floz)	fat-free evaporated milk
400g (14oz)	tin lentils, drained	2	large eggs
400g (14oz)	tin chopped tomatoes, with juice	30g (1oz)	freshly grated Parmesan cheese
4tbsp	chopped parsley		pinch of freshly grated nutmeg

Preheat the oven to 220°C/425°F/Gas 7.

Lightly coat aubergine (eggplant) slices with cooking spray and
arrange on a baking tray. Bake until softened and golden, 20 to 25
minutes. Reduce oven to 180°C/350°F/Gas 4.

Meanwhile, in a large saucepan, heat oil over a medium heat. Add
onion and garlic; cook, stirring occasionally, until onion is translucent,
about 5 minutes. Add lentils, tomatoes and their juice, parsley, oregano,
cinnamon, salt and a pinch of pepper. Bring to the boil and simmer
until thickened, about 20 minutes.

While aubergine and lentils are cooking, in a medium bowl, whisk
together evaporated milk, eggs, 2tbsp of the cheese and nutmeg.

Lightly coat a 20 x 20cm (8 x 8in) baking dish with cooking spray. Arrange one-third of the aubergine slices in a single layer in the dish. Spread half of the lentil mixture over the top. Repeat with remaining aubergine and lentil mixture, ending with a layer of aubergine. Pour evaporated milk mixture over vegetables and sprinkle with remaining 2tbsp cheese. Cover with foil.

Bake moussaka, covered, 20 minutes, then remove foil and bake for 10 to 15 minutes longer, or until heated through and golden on top. Let stand for 15 minutes before cutting. Serve warm.

Makes 4 servings

Nutrition at a Glance

Per serving: 236 calories, 7g fat, 2g saturated fat, 15g protein, 31g carbohydrate, 12g fibre, 290mg sodium

Make in Advance: Moussaka is a great dish to make in advance and freeze – just double or triple the recipe. Cut the moussaka into portions before freezing for up to 3 months. When ready to eat, thaw at room temperature, then reheat in the microwave.

Chock-Full-of-Vegetables Chilli

Prep time: 15 minutes • Cook time: 40 minutes

This basic vegetarian chilli is thick and hearty. Garnish with a dollop of low-fat or fat-free natural yogurt if you like. In later phases, brush wholemeal pitta triangles with olive oil, sprinkle with a mixture of dried Italian herb seasoning and cayenne pepper, lightly toast and serve with the chilli or crumble and serve on top.

15ml (1tbsp)	extra-virgin olive oil
2	peppers (capsicum), any colour, chopped
225g (8oz)	mushrooms, chopped
1	large onion, chopped
2	celery sticks, chopped
3	garlic cloves, finely chopped
1tbsp	chilli powder
1tbsp	dried oregano
1tsp	ground cumin
¼tsp	salt
800g (28oz)	tinned pinto beans
400g (14oz)	tin chopped tomatoes, with juice

In a large saucepan, heat oil over a medium heat. Add peppers, mushrooms, onion, celery and garlic; cook, stirring, until vegetables begin to soften, about 7 minutes. Add chilli powder, oregano, cumin and salt; cook, stirring occasionally, 5 minutes more.

Add beans and tomatoes with their juice. Gently simmer, stirring occasionally, until chilli is fragrant and slightly thickened, 25 to 30 minutes. Serve warm.

Makes 4 servings

Nutrition at a Glance

Per serving: 229 calories, 5g fat, 0.5g saturated fat, 11g protein, 35g carbohydrate, 12g fibre, 501mg sodium

Hearts of Palm 'Potato' Salad

Prep time: 10 minutes

Hearts of palm stand in for potatoes in this summery salad. The vinegary dressing makes it a perfect flavour match for grilled burgers, chicken or fish. Try fresh coriander, tarragon, basil or parsley in place of or along with the chives.

10ml (2tsp)	fresh lemon juice
1tsp	Dijon mustard
1	small garlic clove, finely chopped
15ml (1tbsp)	extra-virgin olive oil
800g (28oz)	tinned hearts of palm, drained and cut into ½-inch slices
2tbsp	chopped chives or parsley
	freshly ground black pepper

In a large bowl, whisk together lemon juice, mustard and garlic. Continuing to whisk, add oil in a slow and steady stream. Add hearts of palm, chives and salt; toss to combine. Season with pepper to taste and serve.

Makes 4 servings

Nutrition at a Glance

Per serving: 77 calories, 4g fat, 0.5g saturated fat, 4g protein, 8g carbohydrate, 4g fibre, 665mg sodium

QUICK AND EASY SOUTH BEACH DIET SALAD DRESSINGS

Home-made salad dressings, made with monounsaturated extra-virgin olive or rapeseed oil and other healthy ingredients, can turn a so-so salad into a vibrant part of any meal. With the exception of Orange-Cumin Vinaigrette and Carrot-Ginger Dressing (just like what is served in a Japanese restaurant), which are Phase 2 or 3 dressings, all of these work for Phase 1 (as well as 2 and 3). Each recipe makes between 120–180ml (8–12tbsp) dressing so you can make a batch one day and have enough left over to use throughout the week. We recommend using no more than 30ml (2tbsp) per serving. For convenience, make and store the dressing in a small plastic container or glass jar with a lid and shake well before using. We've made specific suggestions for using many of these dressings in the Meal Plans for Phases 1 and 2, but feel free to use any dressing you prefer.

Aioli Dressing: Finely chop and mash 3 garlic cloves to a paste with a pinch of salt. Stir garlic mash into 115g (4oz) low-fat mayonnaise. Whisk in 60ml (2floz) fat-free evaporated milk, 10ml (2tsp) fresh lemon juice and ½tsp Dijon mustard. Season with salt and freshly ground black pepper to taste.

Balsamic Vinaigrette: Combine 45ml (3tbsp) balsamic vinegar, 1tbsp Dijon mustard, 1 small finely chopped garlic clove, 1tsp finely chopped shallot or red onion and a pinch of dried thyme. Whisk in 120ml (4floz) extra-virgin olive oil. Season with salt and freshly ground black pepper to taste.

Blue Cheese Dressing: Whisk together 115g (4oz) low-fat mayonnaise, 2tbsp crumbled blue cheese, 15ml (1tbsp) fresh lemon juice and 2.5ml (½tsp) hot pepper sauce. Whisk in 60g (2oz) virtually fat-free yogurt and season with salt and freshly ground black pepper to taste.

Caesar Dressing: Whisk together 30ml (2tbsp) fresh lemon juice, 3 finely chopped anchovy fillets, 1 finely chopped garlic clove and 1tsp Dijon mustard. Slowly whisk in 120ml (4floz) extra-virgin olive oil. Stir in 2tbsp freshly grated Parmesan cheese and season with salt and freshly ground black pepper taste.

Carrot-Ginger Dressing (Phases 2 and 3): In a blender, combine 60g (2oz) grated carrot, 3tbsp thinly sliced spring onion, 30ml (2tbsp) fresh lemon juice, 30ml (2tbsp) mirin (Japanese rice wine), 30ml (2tbsp) rice vinegar, 15ml (1tbsp) low-sodium soy sauce, 2tsp freshly grated ginger and 5ml (1tsp) sesame oil. Purée until smooth.

Champagne Vinaigrette: Whisk together 45ml (3tbsp) Champagne vinegar and 1tbsp Dijon mustard. Slowly whisk in 90ml (3floz) extra-virgin olive oil, then whisk in 15ml (1tbsp) warm water and 1 small finely chopped shallot. Season with salt and freshly ground black pepper to taste.

Creamy Coriander Dressing: Whisk together 115g (4oz) fat-free or low-fat natural yogurt, 4tbsp chopped fresh coriander, 45ml (3tbsp) fresh lime juice and 30ml (2tbsp) extra-virgin olive oil. Season with salt and freshly ground black pepper to taste.

Creamy Dijon-Thyme Dressing: Whisk together 60g (2oz) fat-free or low-fat natural yogurt, 3tbsp low-fat mayonnaise, 2tbsp Dijon mustard, 15ml (1tbsp) skimmed milk and a pinch of dried thyme. Season with salt and freshly ground black pepper to taste.

Creamy Lemon-Dill Dressing: Whisk together 60g (2oz) fat-free or low-fat natural yogurt, 3tbsp low-fat mayonnaise, 15ml (1tbsp) skimmed milk, 1tbsp chopped fresh dill, 1tsp freshly grated lemon rind and 1tsp finely chopped red onion. Season with salt and freshly ground black pepper to taste.

Dijon Vinaigrette: Whisk together 45ml (3tbsp) red wine vinegar, 2tbsp finely chopped red onion, 1tbsp Dijon mustard and 1 finely chopped garlic clove. Slowly whisk in 75ml (2½floz) extra-virgin olive oil. Season with salt and freshly ground black pepper to taste.

Fresh Herb Vinaigrette: Whisk together 45ml (3tbsp) red wine vinegar, 2tbsp finely chopped red onion, 1tbsp Dijon mustard, 1 finely chopped garlic clove, 1tbsp finely chopped parsley and 1tbsp finely chopped fresh basil, marjoram, oregano or thyme. Slowly whisk in 75ml (2½floz) extra-virgin olive oil. Season with salt and freshly ground black pepper to taste.

(continued)

QUICK AND EASY SOUTH BEACH DIET
SALAD DRESSINGS (*cont.*)

Green Goddess Dressing: In a blender, combine ½ medium avocado, 3tbsp low-fat mayonnaise, 3tbsp fat-free or low-fat natural yogurt, 15ml (1tbsp) water, 2 roughly chopped spring onions and 1 small clove garlic; purée until smooth. Add 2tbsp chopped fresh basil, 1tbsp chopped fresh parsley, 1tbsp chopped fresh tarragon and 10ml (2tsp) fresh lemon juice; blend just until combined. Season with salt and freshly ground black pepper to taste.

Lemon Vinaigrette: Whisk together 45ml (3tbsp) fresh lemon juice, ½tsp Dijon mustard, 1 finely chopped garlic clove and 1tsp dried oregano. Slowly whisk in 120ml (4floz) extra-virgin olive oil. Season with salt and freshly ground black pepper to taste. Add a pinch of sugar substitute, if desired.

Lemon-Dill Dressing: Whisk together 45ml (3tbsp) fresh lemon juice, 1tbsp finely chopped dill, ½tsp Dijon mustard and 1 finely chopped garlic clove. Slowly whisk in 120ml (4floz) extra-virgin olive oil. Season with salt and freshly ground black pepper to taste.

Lime Vinaigrette: Whisk together 45ml (3tbsp) fresh lime juice, 1 finely chopped garlic clove, a pinch of ground cumin and a pinch of sugar substitute. Slowly whisk in 75ml (2½floz) extra-virgin olive oil. Season with salt and freshly ground black pepper to taste.

Mint Vinaigrette: Whisk together 5tbsp finely chopped fresh mint leaves, 75ml (2½floz) white wine vinegar and 2tbsp finely chopped red onion. Slowly whisk in 60ml (2floz) extra-virgin olive oil. Season with salt and freshly ground black pepper to taste.

Orange-Cumin Vinaigrette (Phases 2 and 3): Whisk together 75ml (2½floz) fresh orange juice, 45ml (3tbsp) fresh lime juice, 1tbsp finely chopped red onion, 1 finely chopped garlic clove, 2tsp Dijon mustard, 1tsp freshly grated orange rind and a generous pinch of ground cumin. Slowly whisk in 120ml (4floz) extra-virgin olive oil. Season with salt and freshly ground black pepper to taste.

Ranch Dressing: Whisk together 60g (2oz) virtually fat-free natural yogurt, 2tbsp low-fat mayonnaise, 2tbsp low-fat soured cream or crème fraiche, 15ml (1tbsp) red wine vinegar, 1tbsp finely chopped fresh chives, 1tsp crumbled dried basil, 1tsp mustard powder, ¼tsp dried thyme and a pinch of sugar substitute. Season with salt and freshly ground black pepper to taste.

Soy-Ginger Dressing: Whisk together 30ml (2tbsp) low-sodium soy sauce, 30ml (2tbsp) rice wine vinegar, ½tsp grated fresh ginger and 1 finely chopped garlic clove. Slowly whisk in 60ml (2floz) rapeseed oil.

Spicy Lemon-Cumin Vinaigrette: Whisk together 45ml (3tbsp) fresh lemon juice, ½tsp Dijon mustard, 5ml (1tsp) hot pepper sauce, 1 finely chopped garlic clove and ¼tsp ground cumin. Slowly whisk in 120ml (4floz) extra-virgin olive oil. Season with salt and freshly ground black pepper to taste. Add a pinch of sugar substitute, if desired.

Spicy Tomato Vinaigrette: In a blender, combine 1 medium tomato, skinned and chopped, 45ml (3tbsp) white wine vinegar, ½tsp Dijon mustard and 5ml (1tsp) hot pepper sauce; blend until smooth. Season with salt and freshly ground black pepper to taste; adjust hot pepper sauce to your taste.

Thousand Island Dressing: Whisk together 115g (4oz) low-fat mayonnaise, 30ml (2tbsp) chilli-garlic sauce, 2tbsp finely chopped roasted red peppers (bottled), 2tbsp finely chopped dill pickle, 1tbsp Dijon mustard, 1tbsp drained and roughly chopped capers and 1tbsp chopped spring onion. Season with hot pepper sauce to taste.

Tomato-Basil Vinaigrette: In a blender, combine 1 medium tomato, skinned and chopped, 45ml (3tbsp) white wine vinegar, ½tsp chopped fresh basil, ½tsp chopped fresh thyme and ½tsp Dijon mustard; blend until smooth. Season with salt and freshly ground black pepper to taste.

Red Bean Mash

Prep time: 10 minutes • Cook time: 12 minutes

Double this recipe and turn the extra quantity into Red Bean Cakes (see below) for a satisfying and healthy high-fibre breakfast or lunch. Red Bean Mash will keep in a covered container in the refrigerator for up to 3 days. If you prefer, use cannellini beans.

15ml (1tbsp)	extra-virgin olive oil
1	large onion, finely chopped
3	garlic cloves, finely chopped
535g (19oz)	tinned red kidney beans, rinsed and drained
120ml (4floz)	vegetable stock
¼tsp	salt
3tbsp	chopped fresh coriander or parsley (optional)
	Freshly ground black pepper

In a medium saucepan, heat oil over a medium heat. Add onion and garlic; cook, stirring frequently, until softened and fragrant, about 7 minutes. Add beans, stock and salt; bring to the boil and simmer for 5 minutes. Remove the pan from the heat; stir in coriander, if using; and mash with a potato masher to a coarse purée. Add pepper to taste. Serve warm.

Makes 4 servings

Nutrition at a Glance

Per serving: 132 calories, 4g fat, 0.5g saturated fat, 6g protein, 19g carbohydrate, 7g fibre, 368mg sodium

Red Bean Cakes: Form the bean mixture into 4 cakes. In a large frying pan, heat 30ml (2tbsp) extra-virgin olive oil over a medium heat. Add bean cakes and cook until heated through, about 3 minutes per side.

Surprise South Beach Diet Mashed 'Potatoes'

Prep Time: 15 minutes • Cook Time: 20 minutes

Over the years we've made many delicious versions of this South Beach Diet classic. This one is our favourite. Try the variations below, or invent your own!

675g (1½lb)	cauliflower, cut into large florets
3	garlic cloves, peeled
850ml (28floz)	low-sodium chicken stock
	salt
	freshly ground black pepper
2tbsp	chopped fresh chives

In a large saucepan, combine cauliflower, garlic and stock. If cauliflower is not completely covered by stock, add water to just cover. Bring to the boil, reduce heat to medium–low and simmer until cauliflower is tender, about 12 minutes.

Reserve 30ml (2tbsp) of the cooking liquid, then drain cauliflower and garlic. Transfer to the bowl of a food processor and process until smooth, pulsing in some or all of the reserved stock, if necessary, to moisten mixture. Season with salt and pepper to taste. Just before serving, stir in chives. Serve warm.

Makes 4 servings

Nutrition at a Glance

Per serving: 80 calories, 1g fat, 0g saturated fat, 8g protein, 12g carbohydrate, 4g fibre, 183mg sodium

Variations: Fold in low-fat cheddar cheese or a small amount of freshly grated Parmesan cheese after puréeing; mix in cooked, chopped turkey rashers; or use chopped fresh parsley or basil in addition to or in place of the chives.

Vanilla Ricotta Crème

Prep time: 5 minutes • Chill time (optional): 2 hours or overnight

This recipe makes 1 serving but can easily be doubled, tripled or quadrupled. For larger batches, use an electric mixer for a creamier texture.

115g (4oz) ricotta cheese, reduced fat if available

1.25ml (¼tsp) vanilla essence

1tbsp granulated sugar substitute

In a dessert bowl, whisk together the ricotta, vanilla essence and sugar substitute. Serve immediately or chill for 2 hours or overnight.

Serves 1

Nutrition at a Glance

Per serving: 178 calories, 14g protein, 7g carbohydrate, 10g fat, 6g saturated fat, 0g fibre, 155mg sodium

Your Favourite Flavour Ricotta Crème: Use 1.25ml (¼tsp) of your favourite essence, such as almond, rosewater or rum, instead of the vanilla in the recipe above. If desired, sprinkle with 1tsp flaked toasted almonds just before serving.

Mocha Ricotta Crème: Add ½tsp unsweetened cocoa powder to the Vanilla Ricotta Crème recipe above. Dust with a sprinkling of espresso powder.

Lime Rind Ricotta Crème: Add ¼tsp grated lime rind to the Vanilla Ricotta Crème recipe above.

Lemon Rind Ricotta Crème: Add ¼tsp lemon rind to the Vanilla Ricotta Crème recipe above.

Creamy Lemon-Vanilla Ricotta Soufflés

Prep time: 15 minutes • Cook time: 15 minutes

These beautifully puffed desserts are an elegant twist on our classic Phase 1 ricotta crème and are just as easy to make. Prepare and bake them just before serving.

225g (8oz)	ricotta cheese, reduced fat if available
2	large eggs, separated
3tbsp	granulated sugar substitute
2tsp	grated lemon rind
2.5ml (½tsp)	lemon essence
2.5ml (½tsp)	vanilla essence
	pinch of salt

Preheat the oven to 190°C/375°F/Gas 5. Lightly coat 4 (120ml/4floz) ramekins with cooking spray.

In a large bowl, whisk together ricotta, egg yolks, 1tbsp of the sugar substitute, lemon rind and lemon and vanilla essences until well combined.

In another large bowl, with an electric mixer at high speed, whisk egg whites and salt until soft peaks form, 2 to 3 minutes. Add remaining 2tbsp sugar substitute and continue whisking until stiff peaks form. Gently fold one-third of the egg whites into ricotta mixture just until combined. Repeat with remaining egg whites.

Spoon ricotta mixture into ramekins. Bake until soufflés have risen and are set and lightly browned, about 15 minutes. Serve immediately.

Makes 4 servings

Nutrition at a Glance

Per serving: 130 calories, 7g fat, 4g saturated fat, 10g protein, 5g carbohydrate, 0g fibre, 180mg sodium

Baked Ricotta Custard

Prep time: 10 minutes • Cook time: 45 minutes •
Chill time (optional): 2 hours or overnight

A simple sprinkle of cinnamon makes these creamy custards taste just like rice pudding – without the rice!

70g (6oz)	ricotta cheese, reduced fat if available
115g (4oz)	fat-free cream cheese, at room temperature
4tbsp	granulated sugar substitute
1	large egg
1	large egg white
60ml (2floz)	fat-free evaporated milk
1.25ml (¼tsp)	vanilla essence
	ground cinnamon, for garnish

Preheat the oven to 120°C/250°F/Gas 1/2.

In a large bowl, with an electric mixer at medium speed, whisk ricotta and cream cheese until creamy. Add sugar substitute and whisk until well combined. Add egg, egg white, evaporated milk and vanilla essence; whisk until well blended.

Transfer mixture to 4 (240ml/8floz) ramekins. Place ramekins in a baking dish. Add hot water to baking dish to a depth of 2.5cm (1in). Bake until custards are set, about 45 minutes. Remove from water bath and cool on a wire rack. Serve chilled or at room temperature, sprinkled with cinnamon.

Makes 4 servings

Nutrition at a Glance

Per serving: 134 calories, 5g fat, 3g saturated fat, 13g protein, 8g carbohydrate, 0g fibre, 280mg sodium

Chilled Espresso Custard

Prep Time: 10 minutes • Cook Time: 12 minutes • Chill time: 3 hours or overnight

Coffee lovers won't be able to resist this lovely custard flavoured with espresso powder. If you prefer, use decaf espresso powder or instant coffee.

360ml (12floz)	skimmed milk
2	large eggs, beaten
3tbsp	granulated sugar substitute
2tsp	espresso powder
5ml (1tsp)	vanilla essence
	ground cinnamon, to garnish
	lemon twists, to garnish

In a medium bowl, whisk together milk, eggs, sugar substitute, espresso powder and vanilla essence until well blended. Pour into 4 (180ml/6floz) ramekins and place ramekins in a 25cm (10in) frying pan.

Fill the frying pan with water to 1cm (½in) from the tops of the ramekins. Bring water to the simmer over a high heat. Reduce heat to low, cover pan with foil and continue to simmer for 10 minutes. Carefully remove the ramekins from the pan, cover custards with clingfilm (it can touch) and refrigerate for at least 3 hours or overnight. When ready to serve, garnish with cinnamon and lemon twists.

Makes 4 servings

Nutrition at a Glance

Per serving: 110 calories, 3.5g fat, 1.5g saturated fat, 6g protein, 13g carbohydrate, 0g fibre, 80mg sodium

Cocoa-Nut Mousse

Prep Time: 20 minutes • Cook Time: 20 minutes • Chill Time: 2 hours or overnight

Toasted coconut, cocoa and almonds – a familiar (and favourite!) confectionery combination – come together in this creamy, decadent mousse. And as if that isn't enough, the nuts and ricotta cheese offer a dose of healthy protein, making a dessert that is both filling and satisfying to your sweet tooth.

60g (2oz)	flaked almonds	10ml (2tsp)	almond essence
20g (¾oz)	desiccated coconut	10ml (2tsp)	vanilla essence
900g (2lb)	ricotta cheese, reduced fat if available	225g (8oz)	light or fat-free aerosol cream
3tbsp	unsweetened cocoa powder		a few flaked almonds and a pinch of coconut to garnish (optional)
1tbsp + 1tsp	granulated sugar substitute		

Preheat the oven to 140°C/275°F/Gas 1. Spread almonds on a baking tray and toast until golden and fragrant, stirring occasionally, 8 to 10 minutes. Transfer to a plate to cool. Spread coconut on the baking tray and toast until golden, 2 to 3 minutes. Transfer to a plate to cool.

In a large bowl, whisk ricotta with an electric mixer at high speed until light and airy, about 4 minutes. Add cocoa powder, sugar substitute and almond and vanilla essences; whisk just until blended. Fold in aerosol cream, almonds and coconut.

Spoon mousse into 8 dessert bowls or dishes; cover and chill for at least 2 hours or overnight. To serve, remove mousse from refrigerator and garnish with a few almonds and a little coconut, if desired.

Makes 8 servings

Nutrition at a Glance

Per serving: 260 calories, 16g fat, 8g saturated fat, 16g protein, 12g carbohydrate, 2g fibre, 160mg sodium

Make in Advance: Mousse can be prepared up to 1 day in advance; chill in dessert dishes covered with clingfilm until ready to serve. Top with almonds and coconut, if using, just before serving.

Maple-Almond Flan

Prep time: 10 minutes • Cook time: 45 minutes • Chill time: 4 hours or overnight

A traditional Spanish dessert, flan is creamy custard baked with a sugar-based caramel, which imparts a nice toasted flavour. In this version, sugar-free maple syrup is drizzled on top to create a similar effect. The maple taste is the perfect complement to toasted flaked almonds.

3tbsp	flaked almonds	2tbsp	granulated sugar substitute
225g (8oz)	light evaporated milk	1.25ml (¼tsp)	almond essence
90ml (3floz)	skimmed milk	1.25ml (¼tsp)	vanilla essence
120ml (4floz)	very low-fat egg substitute	60ml (2floz)	sugar-free maple-flavoured syrup

Preheat the oven to 160°C/325°F/Gas 3. Spread almonds on a baking tray and toast, stirring once, until lightly golden, about 10 minutes. Transfer almonds to a cutting board to cool, roughly chop and set aside.

Meanwhile, in a small saucepan, combine evaporated milk and skimmed milk and heat over a medium-low heat until scalded but not boiling. Remove the pan from the heat and set aside.

In a large bowl, whisk together egg substitute, sugar substitute and almond and vanilla essences. Whisk in 120ml (4floz) of heated milk mixture, then whisk in remaining milk mixture.

Divide flan among 4 (180ml/6floz) ramekins. Place in a baking dish and add hot water to come halfway up sides of ramekins. Bake until flans are set, about 25 minutes. Remove from the oven, cool in the dish, cover ramekins with clingfilm and chill in the refrigerator for at least 4 hours or overnight.

Half an hour before serving, remove ramekins from refrigerator. Just before serving, run a knife around edges and invert flans onto individual plates. Drizzle each with 15ml (1tbsp) maple syrup and sprinkle evenly with reserved almonds.

Makes 4 servings

Nutrition at a Glance

Per serving: 108 calories, 3g fat, 0g saturated fat, 9g protein, 13g carbohydrate, 1g fibre, 161mg sodium

Ricotta Cheesecake
with Lemon Drizzle and Pine Nuts

Prep time: 10 minutes • Cook time: 1 hour 20 minutes • Chill time: 4 hours or overnight

This traditional Italian dessert is refreshingly light and delicately citrus-flavoured. You'll find it's quite unlike dense, creamy American cheese-cake, but no less delicious.

3tbsp	pine nuts	900g (2lb)	quark or other low-fat soft cheese
6	large eggs, separated		
¾tsp	cream of tartar	1tsp	finely grated lemon rind
5tbsp	granulated sugar substitute	30ml (2tbsp)	fresh lemon juice
10ml (2tsp)	vanilla essence	1tsp	granulated sugar substitute

Position a rack in the centre of the oven and preheat the oven to 140°C/275°F/Gas 1. Lightly coat a 23cm (9in) springform tin with cooking spray. Spread nuts on a baking tray and toast until lightly golden, about 10 minutes. Transfer nuts to a plate to cool. Increase the oven to 160°C/325°F/Gas 3.

In a large metal bowl, with an electric mixer at high speed, whisk egg whites until frothy, about 1 minute. Add cream of tartar and continue to whisk until stiff peaks form, about 3 minutes longer. Set aside.

In a separate large bowl, with an electric mixer at medium speed, whisk egg yolks, 5tbsp sugar substitute and vanilla essence for 1 minute. Add quark and lemon rind and whisk until smooth.

Gently fold one-third of the egg whites into the yolk mixture, then add the rest of the whites and gently fold in until well combined. Pour batter into the prepared tin, place the tin on a baking tray and bake until cake is golden and mostly set, about 1 hour 10 minutes. Remove cake from oven and cool on a wire rack for 20 minutes.

In a small saucepan, combine lemon juice and 1tsp sugar substitute; simmer over a low heat. Remove from the heat and gently brush the surface of the cooled cake with two-thirds of the warm lemon mixture; drizzle remaining mixture into the cracks. Sprinkle the top with pine nuts.

Cool cake completely, then run a knife around the edge before releasing from tin. Chill, loosely covered, for 4 hours or overnight. Serve chilled.

In a small saucepan, combine lemon juice and remaining 1 teaspoon sugar substitute; bring to a simmer over low heat. Remove from the heat and gently brush the surface of the cooled cake with two-thirds of the warm lemon mixture; drizzle remaining mixture into the cracks. Sprinkle the top with pine nuts.

Cool cake completely, then run a knife around the edge before releasing from pan. Chill, loosely covered, for 4 hours or overnight. Serve chilled.

Makes 12 servings

Nutrition at a Glance

Per serving: 140 calories, 9g fat, 4.5g saturated fat, 11g protein, 5g carbohydrate, 0g fibre, 140mg sodium

Make in Advance: You can make the cheesecake a day in advance and refrigerate.

South Beach Diet Nutty Granola Topping

Prep time: 10 minutes • Cook time: 25 minutes

This tasty topping is meant to be enjoyed in 1tbsp-size servings on top of low-fat or fat-free natural yogurt, fat-free or low-fat cottage cheese or ricotta cheese. Made in a large batch, it can be stored in an airtight container in the refrigerator for up to 1 month. Or place in a zip-lock freezer bag, press out the air, seal tightly and freeze for up to 3 months – no thawing necessary, just scoop out and use!

60g (2oz)	flaked almonds	60g (2oz)	walnuts, chopped
50g (1¾oz)	desiccated coconut	2tbsp	trans-fat-free margarine
70g (2½oz)	flaxseed	2tsp	ground cinnamon
60g (2oz)	pecans, chopped	10ml (2tsp)	vanilla essence
70g (2½oz)	pumpkin seeds	2tsp	sugar substitute
70g (2½oz)	sunflower seeds		

Preheat the oven to 160°C/325°F/Gas 3.

In a large bowl, combine almonds, coconut, flaxseed, pecans, pumpkin seeds, sunflower seeds and walnuts.

In a small saucepan, melt margarine over a low heat. Remove the pan from the heat and whisk in cinnamon and vanilla essence. Pour over nut mixture and toss to combine. Sprinkle with sugar substitute and toss again.

Spread mixture on a baking tray and bake, tossing every 5 minutes, for 20 to 25 minutes, or until lightly golden. Cool on a wire rack. Store in an airtight container in the refrigerator for up to 1 month, or freeze for up to 3 months.

Makes about 40tbsp (350g/12.5oz)

Nutrition at a Glance

Per tbsp: 65 calories, 6g fat, 1g saturated fat, 2g protein, 2g carbohydrate, 1g fibre, 6mg sodium

Lemon-Thyme Ices

Prep time: 15 minutes • Freezing time: 2 hours

This pretty dessert makes a lovely ending to any meal. Reminiscent of an Italian lemon ice, it is updated here with a hint of fresh thyme. If you prefer a less tart version, add a little more sugar substitute.

3	fresh thyme sprigs plus 4 extra sprigs to garnish
1½tbsp	granulated sugar substitute
500ml (16floz)	boiling water
240ml (8floz)	fresh lemon juice (from 5 to 6 lemons)
1tbsp	grated lemon rind
	salt

In a medium metal bowl, combine thyme and sugar substitute. Pour boiling water over and stir to dissolve sugar substitute. Steep for 3 minutes, then remove and discard thyme.

Place bowl in freezer until mixture is cool, about 10 minutes. Remove from freezer and whisk in lemon juice, rind and a pinch of salt. Pour into 2 ice cube trays, filling each ice cube compartment to just below the top (you will fill 1 tray and half of a second one).

Freeze until mostly frozen through, 1½ to 2 hours. Place cubes in a food processor or blender and pulse very briefly, just until ice crystals form. (Don't overprocess, or the dessert will be liquid.)

Transfer ice to dessert bowls, garnish with extra thyme sprigs and serve immediately.

Makes 4 generous servings

Nutrition at a Glance

Per serving: 30 calories, 0g fat, 0g saturated fat, 0g protein, 9g carbohydrate, 0g fibre, 0mg sodium

EASY PHASE 1 SUBSTITUTIONS

Avoid This	Use This Instead
Breadcrumbs	Whole or crushed pine nuts (¼ cup/serving)
Chips	Oven-baked courgette (zucchini) fries or roasted whole fresh green beans
Cocktail sauce for prawns	Red pepper sauce with horseradish
Crackers or pitta crisps	Cucumber or courgette (zucchini) rounds
'Creamy' white sauce	Evaporated skim milk, fat-free soured cream, or fat-free Greek yogurt
Croutons	Roasted mushroom 'croutons'
English muffin	Portobello mushroom caps
Green peas	Edamame or mangetout
Meatloaf breadcrumbs	White beans or lentils
Pasta	Julienned courgette (zucchini), or aubergine (eggplant) ribbons (for lasagna)
Pizza crust (individual)	Portobello mushroom caps or courgette (zucchini) boats
Rice	Bed of lentils or finely chopped cauliflower
Popcorn	Roasted cauliflower florets or roasted kale with popcorn salt
Potato chips	Baked courgette (zucchini) chips, celery root (celeriac chips)
Diced potatoes	Diced artichoke hearts, aubergine (eggplant), or hearts of palm
Hash brown potatoes	Shredded courgette (zucchini)
Mashed potatoes	Mashed cauliflower or puréed haricot beans

Dr Agatston Answers Your Questions about Phase 1

Here are the answers to some of the questions that our nutritionists and I are most often asked by dieters who are on Phase 1.

I'm finding the first few days of Phase 1 very difficult. What can I do to make things easier?

When you say you're having difficulty with Phase 1, I presume you're missing the briefly energizing surge in blood sugar caused by eating refined and sugary carbs. You may be feeling a bit sluggish and out of sorts as you stabilize your blood sugar. It can take your body a few days to adjust to this new and healthier way of eating. But, if you follow the Phase 1 guidelines correctly, you can make it easier on yourself.

Make sure that you are adequately satisfying your hunger with the right foods – including lean protein and plenty of vegetables – at every meal, including breakfast (and be sure you're hydrated). I'm not talking about overstuffing yourself, but do eat until you are comfortably full. If you're still craving that doughnut you used to eat mid-morning, be sure to have a mid-morning snack that includes some fibre and protein *before* the cravings for the doughnut set in. Ditto for the timing on your mid-afternoon snack. Strategic snacking is especially important when starting the diet. Studies show that it takes relatively few calories to prevent cravings, but many more to satisfy them once they occur. The quality of calories in your satisfying meals and snacks, along with a dessert that contains protein, should help keep your hunger at bay. But if you find you need something else to satisfy your cravings, try one of the 75–100-calorie sweet treats listed on page 169. Many of our dieters have said that having an occasional sweet treat satisfied their need for more of an indulgence.

Also remember that exercise is a dieter's best friend. It can help stabilize your blood sugar, plus it releases brain chemicals called endorphins that regulate your stress hormones so you feel happier. If your cravings are starting to get the best of you, go out and do your fast-walking cardio intervals for the day (see pages 100–101). You'll burn fat and calories faster and see quicker weight loss. These positive results will get you all the more motivated to keep going. Your cravings will subside within a few days, and in just 2 weeks, you're on Phase 2.

I'm doing so well on Phase 1; why can't I stay on it indefinitely?

There are two types of people on the South Beach Diet: those who cannot wait to start Phase 2 (see above) and those who never want to see Phase 1 end.

Why are some people so enamoured with Phase 1? The reason is that it's simple and to the point. You don't have to do a lot of thinking about food choices. You're basically eating lean protein, high-fibre pulses, low-fat dairy, good fats (including some nuts) and plenty of vegetables. Those highly processed refined carbs that were your downfall are out of sight and, within a few days, out of mind (at least for most people). You're encouraged to eat until you're full and snack before you get hungry. And every time you step on the scales, you get a big grin on your face because those unwanted pounds and fat are just melting away. So it's not surprising to me that Phase 1 fans often ask, 'If I'm doing so well on Phase 1, why do I have to move on to Phase 2?'

Phase 1 is not meant to be a long-term eating plan. Its dual goals are to jump-start weight loss for people who have 4.5kg (10lb) or more to lose (thus providing immediate positive reinforcement) and to control swings in blood sugar and eliminate cravings for sugar and refined starches. Phase 1 can also have a positive effect on sugar in people with prediabetes. In just 2 weeks, you should have achieved these two goals and be ready to move on.

Once your sugar and cravings are under control, there's a key reason to go on to Phase 2: We don't want you to miss out on the myriad vitamins, minerals and other nutrients that come from re-introducing whole fruits and whole grains to your diet, not to mention the added fibre. As I discussed in Chapter 7, these foods contain thousands of phytochemicals that protect your body against a host of diseases, including heart disease and cancer. If you were to continue indefinitely on Phase 1 and deny yourself these foods, you would not be learning how to make good food choices in the real world. More important, you'd be missing out on some of the best medicine nature has to offer.

In addition, if you were to continue with the smaller palette of foods recommended on Phase 1, your diet would get dull over the long haul. And once you're bored, you're much more likely to revert to your old eating habits. For the diet to truly become a lifestyle – one that allows you to sustain weight loss and garner all the related health benefits – there has to be variety and satisfaction in your eating plan. That's another reason why we move you on to Phase 2 so quickly.

Remember, it may take you longer to lose weight by following the three phases of our diet. But the chances of keeping that weight off are far better.

Should I be taking a fibre supplement?

You may be asking this question because on many diets – especially the very high-protein diets – dieters become constipated and often require fibre supplements. This is so common that fibre supplements are actually recommended on many of these diets. This is not the case with the South Beach Diet. Even on Phase 1, when you aren't eating whole grains, you're still eating lots of high-fibre vegetables and pulses, so you should be fine. Some people do, however, find that without grains, they suffer from constipation. In that case, a fibre supplement could help restore normal bowel function. Fibre supplements such as plant-derived psyllium or synthetic methylcellulose or polycarbophil are safe and effective. Just be sure to take them with plenty of water.

I'm on Phase 1 and having really bad headaches. Is this common and do you have any recommendations?

Although it's not common, some people do experience headaches on Phase 1. There are a few possible causes. First, are you eating all your meals and snacks when you're supposed to? Skipping meals or snacks could cause your blood sugar to dip too low, triggering headaches – which leads to my second question: Are you eating enough? Many new dieters mistakenly believe that the only way to succeed on Phase 1 is to starve themselves. Nothing could be further from the truth! If you're famished and headachy, you're not likely to stick with the programme. We want you to eat normal portions and not leave the table hungry. Also, if you've severely limited your caffeine intake (you can have caffeine, just don't go overboard), you may be experiencing caffeine-withdrawal headaches. Try adding a cup or two of caffeinated coffee back into your diet in the morning and see if your headaches subside.

With two kids in university, my partner and I are on a tight budget for a few years. I am thinking of going on the diet but wonder if it's going to be expensive.

Like many people, you may assume that a diet rich in fruits and vegetables is a lot more expensive than eating processed food, fast food or junk food. There's no question that some fruits and vegetables will cost more than the bargain price fast-food special, but you need to consider the cost to your health in *not* eating these healthy foods.

You can adapt the South Beach Diet to most budgets with very little effort. Our Phase 1 Foods to Enjoy list offers a wide range of choices, from pricier cuts of meat and speciality produce to more economical options. For example, you can pass on fillet steak and satisfy your protein needs with less-expensive topside of beef, rump steak, extra-lean minced beef or white-meat chicken or turkey. Instead of fresh tuna, choose tinned yellowfin tuna in spring water. As far as fresh vegetables go, they are actually *less* expensive than many packaged and processed foods. To keep things interesting, we do recommend that you occasionally try different types of vegetables, such as hearts of palm or purple sprouting broccoli or interesting salad greens such as endive, radicchio, rocket or frisée. But if you find that these items are too costly, you can substitute any type of comparable vegetable.

Adding whole grains once you're on Phase 2 won't be appreciably more expensive, either. Most major supermarkets, wholesale members' clubs and health-food shops now offer an array of whole grain products at very reasonable prices. And, of course, high-fibre dried beans, chickpeas, lentils and other pulses, which we recommend on all phases of the diet, are among the most reasonably priced products in the supermarket today. Cook a big pot of bean or lentil soup; it will cost very little.

PHASE 2

Achieving Your Health and Weight Loss Goals

If you have fewer than 4.5kg (10lb) to lose and don't have food cravings, you can begin the diet on Phase 2. If you've been on Phase 1 for 2 weeks and your cravings have resolved, you should now begin Phase 2. Your weight loss will be slower than it was on Phase 1, but most people continue losing 0.5–1kg (1–2lb) a week if they follow the plan correctly. This gradual weight loss is not only expected, it's healthy and it's the transition of turning the diet into a lifestyle. If you were to continue to lose weight rapidly on Phase 2, you could be losing lean muscle mass, which can ultimately slow your metabolism. Plus, if you lose weight gradually, it's more likely to stay off over the long term.

On Phase 2, you can eat everything on the Phase 1 Foods to Enjoy list (see pages 166–169) as well as some new foods (pages 241–243). If you're starting on Phase 2 rather than Phase 1, you'll be eliminating bad fats and highly processed refined carbohydrates from your diet and eating good fats and the nutrient-dense, high-fibre carbs from wholesome fruits and vegetables and whole grains instead. You'll also be eating lean protein and low-fat dairy. You'll soon find that this is a healthy, satisfying way to eat and you will steadily lose weight.

Yes, on Phase 2, you'll be able to have bread . . . and fruit . . . within reason. You'll gradually re-introduce many of the foods that you were advised to avoid on Phase 1, including wholemeal breads, wholewheat pasta and brown rice, as well as most whole fruits and selected root vegetables (such as sweet potatoes), all of which are loaded with beneficial nutrients. You'll notice that a few fruits and vegetables are still off-limits until Phase 3; even then, we recommend that you have them only occasionally. These include fruits that are high in natural sugar, such as watermelon, pineapple, dates and figs, as well as certain vegetables, such as white potatoes, beetroot and sweetcorn. In our experience, these foods are likely to trigger cravings in susceptible people.

While you may be excited to be on Phase 2, don't go wild over the additional choices. One of the biggest mistakes people make is adding too many whole grains, starchy vegetables and fruits too soon. Even though these are 'good carbs', they are still higher in sugar than the lean protein and vegetables that form the mainstay of the Phase 1 menus. And if, after spending 2 weeks eating a very low-sugar diet, you suddenly flood your system with carbohydrates, even good ones, it can sometimes trigger the same cravings that got you into trouble in the first place.

That's why I recommend gradually re-introducing good carbs into your diet. Some people can do it over a 2-week period, others — especially those who find that they're still getting cravings – need to add carbs even more slowly, ultimately sticking with two good starches and two fruits indefinitely, or three fruits and fewer starches if starchy carbs really stimulate cravings. In addition, if you ever find that you're regaining weight on Phase 2, cut back a bit on the total servings of good carbs, or just eat a few bites of these foods and see how it goes.

Let me walk you through how to introduce the good carbs gradually. This mirrors the way more carbs are introduced during the 2 weeks of our Phase 2 Sample Meal Plans on pages 244–257. For purposes of example, we've compressed the carb introduction into 2 weeks. Of course, you can introduce carbs more slowly if you find your weight loss isn't proceeding slowly and steadily.

Phase 2 – Week 1

Days 1–7: 1 good starch, 1 piece of fruit each day. Have one starchy carb and a piece of fruit daily the first week. Although the fruits can vary and be added at any meal, we've found that to keep cravings at bay, it's best not to have fruit at breakfast for the first week. Instead, we generally recommend eating a slice of wholemeal bread or a serving of high-fibre cereal with your egg in the morning. This will help keep your blood sugar levels stable for the rest of the day.

Start with one piece of whole fruit, such as an apple or a serving of berries with lunch, or eat some fruit with a piece of reduced-fat cheese for your snack. Once again, eating fruit along with protein helps prevent the sugar-induced insulin spike that can trigger food cravings.

The gradual introduction of these carbohydrates gives your body the opportunity to adjust to the increase in sugar and you can monitor your reaction to particular foods. If you find that you're hungry an hour after eating a particular good carb, the next day try eating a different good carb – preferably, one with more fibre. And if you're still hungry during the day, add a little more protein to the mix.

Phase 2 – Week 2

Day 8: 2 good starches, 1 piece of fruit. If you've done well on Phase 2, Week 1 – you are losing weight and have no cravings – start the second week by adding one more good starch to your diet. Stick with one piece of whole fruit.

If your cravings are there but minimal, keep trying different good starches and fruits. When you are finally rid of cravings, you can begin to add more good carbs as directed below.

Day 9: 2 good starches, 2 pieces of fruit. If you are fine on Day 8 and have no cravings, add a second piece of fruit today, so you are now up to two pieces of fruit and two servings of good starches daily.

Days 10–11: 3 good starches, 2 pieces of fruit each day. If you're continuing to do fine with the added carbs, you can now add an additional good starch, so you are now eating two pieces of whole fruit and three servings of good starches daily.

Days 12–14: 3 good starches, 3 pieces of fruit each day. By now, your body should have adjusted to the additional good carbs. We don't limit the amount of good carbs you can eat on Phase 2, but most people will continue to lose weight by sticking with three fruits and three starches daily.

• • • • • • • • • • •

Now that you understand the re-introduction of additional carbohydrates, here's something to put cheer in your heart: You'll also be able to enjoy a glass of wine or two with or after a meal or a light beer on occasion, and you'll have more options for dessert, including the occasional piece of dark chocolate!

Keep in mind that Phase 2 is a period of slower but steady weight loss. You're not dropping pounds as quickly as you did on Phase 1, but the trade-off is that you're eating a much more varied diet, one that's full of nutrient-dense, fibre-rich foods; plenty of vitamins, minerals and phyto-nutrients; and plenty of delicious flavour combinations. Short-term success is not what the South Beach Diet is about. It's about learning to eat well for life. If you stick with Phase 2, there's no question that you will eventually reach your desired weight. Millions of South Beach dieters have already proven that.

The really exciting news is that if you adopt the South Beach Super-charged Fitness Programme, starting with either the Phase 1 or Phase 2 exercises (depending on your level of fitness), your weight loss will continue to move along steadily, as you're eating a wider variety of healthy foods.

It's well known that people who don't increase their activity levels while dieting often have more difficulty keeping the weight off long-term. Even if you're already exercising, you may need to kick it up a notch to get your metabolism back in high gear. The Interval Walking programme presented in this book, which gradually gets harder as you get fitter, is the perfect way to boost your metabolism so that you burn more fat and calories, not only while exercising, but also when going about your daily activities, and even when you're sitting at your desk or watching TV. And by doing the Total Body Workout exercises on alternate days, you'll keep your core muscles toned and your body fit and trim.

Keep in mind that you will be following the healthy eating principles of Phase 2 until you reach your optimal weight.

On pages 241–243, you'll find a list of Foods to Re-Introduce on Phase 2 as well as Foods to Avoid or Eat Rarely. With this expanded list of healthy choices, plus all of the Phase 1 foods, you should have no trouble finding foods that fit your taste preferences. And on pages 244–257, we've provided 2 weeks of Phase 2 Meal Plans, which are then followed by delicious recipes for these meal plans. As with the Phase 1 Meal Plans, these are meant to be suggestions for the types of meals and snacks you might enjoy throughout a day. You are of course free to create your own menus as you desire from the allowable foods.

You'll notice that some of the new main-course recipes we've developed for Phase 2 don't include carbohydrates. That's because you'll be getting your good carbs in the form of the fruits or whole grains you eat for breakfast or snacks, in side dishes or even for dessert. This means you'll be able to prepare and enjoy these recipes on Phase 1 (look for a note at the end of the recipes where this pertains).

Finally, on pages 298–302, you'll find answers to some of the most common questions asked by people who are on Phase 2.

You can enjoy all the foods on Phase 1 as well as those listed here.

BEEF

All hot dogs (beef, pork, poultry, soya) can be enjoyed occasionally (once a week) if they are at least 97% fat-free (3–6g fat per serving).

FRUIT

Start with one serving daily, gradually increasing to up to three servings daily. For more on introducing fruits on Phase 2, see page 238.

Apple – 1 small or 5 dried rings

Apricots – 4 fresh or 7 dried

Banana – 1 medium (115g/4oz)

Blackberries – 115g (4oz)

Blueberries – 115g (4oz)

Cantaloupe – ¼ melon or 140g (5oz) diced

Cherries – 12

Clementine – 1

Cranberries – 85g (3oz)

Elderberries – 85g (3oz)

Gooseberries – 85g (3oz)

Grapefruit – one-half

Grapes – 15

Honeydew—⅛ melon or 140g (5oz) diced

Kiwi fruit – 1

Mandarin oranges – 2

Mango – ½ medium (115g/4oz)

Mulberries – 85g (3oz)

Nectarine – 1 small

Orange – 1 medium

Papaya – 1 small (115g/4 oz)

Peach – 1 medium

Pear – 1 medium

Plums – 2

Pomegranate seeds – from 1 medium pomegranate

Pomelo – ½

Prunes – 4

Raspberries – 115g (4oz)

Strawberries – 115g (4oz)

Tangerines – 2

VEGETABLES

Carrots – 115g (4oz)

Peas, green – 115g (4oz)

DAIRY

360–500ml (16–20floz) allowed daily plus yogurt

Yogurt – 115g (4oz) per day (artificially sweetened low-fat flavoured yogurt; avoid varieties that contain high-fructose corn syrup)

WHOLE GRAINS AND STARCHY VEGETABLES

Start with one serving daily, gradually increasing to up to three or four servings daily. For more on introducing starches on Phase 2, see page 238. Unless otherwise stated, choose whole grain products that have 3g or more fibre per serving.

Bagel, wholewheat – ½ small (30g/1oz)

Barley – 55g (2oz) cooked

Bread – 1 slice (30g/1oz)

    Home-made breads made with whole grains (buckwheat, wholemeal, spelt, whole oats, bran, rye)

    Multigrain

    Oat and bran

    Rye

    Sprouted-grain

(continued)

WHOLE GRAINS AND STARCHY VEGETABLES (*cont.*)

Cereal, cold (choose low-sugar with 5g or more fibre per serving; serving sizes vary, so be sure to check the label to determine recommended amount)

Cereal, hot (choose whole grain and slow-cooking varieties or instant plain porridge with at least 3g fibre and no more than 2g sugar; serving sizes vary, so be sure to check the label to determine recommended amount)

Couscous, wholewheat or Israeli – 45g (1½oz)

English muffin, wholemeal – ½ muffin (30g/1 oz) (most contain 2.5g fibre per half a muffin; varieties with 3g fibre are the best choice)

Filo dough and shells, wholewheat – 2 sheets or 4 mini shells

Flour
  Soya
  Spelt
  Wholemeal

Muffin, bran – 1 small, home-made sugar-free, no raisins

Pasta
  Soya – 30g (1oz) (3g or more fibre per serving)
  Wholewheat – 30g (1oz) (3g or more fibre per serving)

Peas, green – 115g (4oz) considered a starchy vegetable; count as a starch/grain serving

Pitta bread – ½ pitta (30g/1oz) (most contain 2.5g fibre per half; varieties with 3g fibre are the best choice, such as stone-ground wholewheat)

Popcorn – 30g (1oz)
  Air-popped
  Home-made, cooked with rapeseed oil
  Microwave, plain, no trans fats

Potato, sweet, 1 small (considered a starchy vegetable; count as a starch/grain serving)

Pumpkin – 30g (1oz) (considered a starchy vegetable; count as a starch/grain serving)

Quinoa – 45g (1½oz)

Rice – 55g (2 oz)
  Basmati
  Brown, regular, converted or parboiled
  Wild

Rice noodles – 30g (1oz)

Savoury biscuits (crackers) – whole grain (3g or more fibre per 30g/1oz, no trans fats)

Soba noodles – 55g (2oz)

Squash, acorn, butternut, etc. – 30g (1oz) (considered a starchy vegetable; count as a starch/grain serving)

Tortilla, whole grain – 1 small (3g or more fibre per 30g (1oz), no trans fats)

Yam – 1 small (considered a starchy vegetable; count as a starch/grain serving)

OCCASIONAL TREATS

Chocolate, dark 30g (1oz)

Mousse, fat-free, sugar-free (one serving per day permitted)

DRINKS

Light beer (1), on occasion (360ml/12 floz.)

Wine, red or white (1–2 glasses, 120ml /4oz each, permitted daily with or after meals)

STARCHES

Bagel, refined wheat flour

Biscuits, sweet and cookies

Bread
  Bread rolls (white)
  Refined wheat flour
  White

Cornflakes

Flavoured porridge

Matzo (except whole grain varieties,
which are allowed)

Pasta, white flour

Potatoes
  Instant
  White

Rice
  Glutinous
  Jasmine
  White

Rice cakes

FRUIT

Tinned fruit, in heavy syrup

Dates

Figs

Fruit juice

Lychee

Pineapple

Raisins

Watermelon

VEGETABLES

Beetroot

Potatoes, white

Sweetcorn

MISCELLANEOUS

Honey

Ice cream

Jam and jelly

DAY 1

BREAKFAST

180ml (6floz) tomato juice

115g (4oz) artificially sweetened fat-free or low-fat vanilla yogurt

Porridge oats with cinnamon and chopped walnuts

Coffee or tea with skimmed milk and sugar substitute

MID-MORNING SNACK

90g (3oz) strawberries and a grande latte with skimmed milk (sweeten with sugar substitute, if desired)

LUNCH

Thai Prawn Soup (page 263)

Tossed salad (mixed greens, chopped cucumber, peppers and cherry tomatoes)

30ml (2tbsp) Lemon-Dill Dressing (page 214) or reduced-sugar prepared dressing of your choice

MID-AFTERNOON SNACK

1 hard-boiled egg with celery sticks

DINNER

Sliced skirt steak with fresh mushroom 'gravy' (cook mushrooms in beef stock with herbs of your choice)

Roasted asparagus with finely chopped shallots

Cannellini Bean Mash (page 218)

DESSERT

Chocolate mousse (115g/4oz sugar-free chocolate pudding mixed with 2tbsp light aerosol cream)

DAY 2

BREAKFAST

180ml (6floz) vegetable juice

Open-face turkey breakfast sandwich (top ½ wholemeal English muffin with 1 slice cooked turkey, 1 slice tomato, 1 cooked turkey rasher/turkey sausage or lean ham, and 1 poached egg)

Coffee or tea with skimmed milk and sugar substitute

MID-MORNING SNACK

1 small Granny Smith apple with 30g (1oz) reduced-fat cheddar cheese cubes

LUNCH

Chilled clear soup

Spinach salad with diced tofu, chickpeas, sliced button mushrooms and onions

30ml (2tbsp) Spicy Tomato Vinaigrette (page 217) or reduced-sugar prepared dressing of your choice

MID-AFTERNOON SNACK

Spicy Hummous-Vegetable Roll-Up (page 196)

DINNER

Chicken and Lentil Stew (page 272)

Curly endive salad with chopped black olives and a sprinkling of blue cheese

30ml (2tbsp) Champagne Vinaigrette (page 215) or reduced-sugar prepared dressing of your choice

DESSERT

Coffee Panna Cotta (page 288)

DAY 3

BREAKFAST

180ml (6floz) tomato juice

2 hard-boiled eggs

Wholesome Oat Muffin (page 261)

Coffee or tea with skimmed milk and sugar substitute

MID-MORNING SNACK

1 sliced kiwi fruit topped with 115g (4oz) fat-free Greek yogurt

LUNCH

Tomato stuffed with tuna salad (90g/3oz tinned yellowfin tuna, chopped celery and onion and 1tbsp low-fat mayonnaise)

MID-AFTERNOON SNACK

1 slice reduced-fat ham with a few slices part-skimmed mozzarella

5 olives of your choice

DINNER

Roasted turkey breast topped with sautéed mushrooms; roast extra turkey for Day 4 lunch

Steamed green beans with lemon and sea salt

Little gem lettuce salad with chopped toasted walnuts

30ml (2tbsp) Thousand Island Dressing (page 214) or reduced-sugar dressing of your choice

DESSERT

115g (4oz) sugar-free vanilla pudding

DAY 4

BREAKFAST

180ml (6floz) vegetable juice

Half a wholemeal bagel topped with 30g (1oz) light cream cheese, smoked salmon, cucumber and tomato slices, chopped red onion and capers

Coffee or tea with skimmed milk and sugar substitute

MID-MORNING SNACK

15 grapes with 30g (1oz) reduced-fat cheddar cheese

LUNCH

Roasted Tomato Soup (page 264)

Sliced roast turkey on a bed of greens with diced avocado (use leftover turkey from Day 3 dinner)

30ml (2tbsp) Green Goddess Dressing (page 214) or reduced-sugar prepared dressing of your choice

MID-AFTERNOON SNACK

Coco-raspberry shake (blend 120ml/4floz skimmed milk, 115g/4oz artificially sweetened fat-free or low-fat raspberry yogurt, 1tbsp granulated sugar substitute and 1tsp unsweetened cocoa powder until frothy)

DINNER

Herbed pork tenderloin (spray pork with olive oil cooking spray and coat with 4tbsp mixed herbs, such as rosemary, thyme, sage and/or parsley; roast an extra pork tenderloin for Day 5 lunch)

Kale and Turkey Rasher Gratin (page 284)

Julienned courgette (zucchini); toss strands with lemon rind

DESSERT

2 Peanut Butter and Jam Cookies (page 285) and 240ml (8floz) skimmed milk

DAY 5

BREAKFAST

180ml (6floz) tomato juice

Cheddar cheese toast (melt reduced-fat cheddar cheese on 1 slice wholemeal bread)

1 slice lean ham

Coffee or tea with skimmed milk and sugar substitute

MID-MORNING SNACK

90g (3oz) fresh blueberries with 115g (4oz) fat-free Greek yogurt

LUNCH

Phase 2 soup of your choice (page 265)

Thinly sliced pork tenderloin over assorted salad greens (use leftovers from Day 4 dinner)

30ml (2tbsp) Spicy Lemon-Cumin Vinaigrette (page 214)

MID-AFTERNOON SNACK

1 reduced-fat mozzarella cheese slice

Red pepper strips and cucumber slices

DINNER

Sun-Dried Tomato and Feta–Stuffed Chicken Breasts (page 270)

Vegetable Napoleon (stack slices of steamed aubergine (eggplant) with slices of tomato and thin slices of reduced-fat mozzarella cheese; bake at 180°C/350°F/Gas 4 until cheese is melted)

Salad leaves

30ml (2tbsp) Balsamic Vinaigrette (page 214) or reduced-sugar prepared dressing of your choice

DESSERT

115g (4oz) sugar-free chocolate pudding

DAY 6

BREAKFAST

180ml (6floz) vegetable juice

Eggs Frijoles (page 260)

Coffee or tea with skimmed milk and sugar substitute

MID-MORNING SNACK

115g (4oz) artificially sweetened fat-free or low-fat yogurt in a flavour of your choice

LUNCH

Creamy Chicken Florentine Soup (page 269)

Tossed salad (mixed greens with cucumber, peppers/capsicum and cherry tomatoes)

30ml (2tbsp) Tomato-Basil Vinaigrette (page 214) or reduced-sugar prepared dressing of your choice

MID-AFTERNOON SNACK

Reuben Wrap (page 278)

DINNER

Quick Lamb Stew (page 280)

Cos lettuce salad (no croutons)

30ml (2tbsp) Caesar Dressing (page 214) or reduced-sugar prepared dressing of your choice

DESSERT

Nectarine or clementine segments sprinkled with 30g (1oz) crumbled blue cheese and toasted almonds

DAY 7

BREAKFAST

180ml (6floz) tomato juice

2 hard-boiled eggs

2 slices lean ham or turkey rashers

Coffee or tea with skimmed milk and sugar substitute

MID-MORNING SNACK

1 small red apple with a wedge of reduced-fat soft cheese

LUNCH

Grilled turkey burger in a wholemeal pitta half with Dijon mustard, sliced tomato and red onion

Mixed greens sprinkled with reduced-fat feta cheese

30ml (2tbsp) Creamy Coriander Dressing (page 215) or reduced-sugar prepared dressing of your choice

MID-AFTERNOON SNACK

Hummous with chicory

DINNER

Two-Bean Chilli Con Carne (page 281)

Cucumber and radish salad

30ml (2tbsp) Ranch Dressing (page 214) or reduced-sugar prepared dressing of your choice

DESSERT

Sugar-free meringue cookie and 240ml (8floz) skimmed milk

DAY 8

BREAKFAST

180ml (6floz) vegetable juice cocktail

Scrambled New York Breakfast Wrap (page 278)

Coffee or tea with skimmed milk and sugar substitute

MID-MORNING SNACK

115g (4oz) reduced-fat cottage cheese with chopped tomatoes and cucumbers

LUNCH

Cobb salad (chopped cos lettuce with 115g/4oz black eyed beans, 1 chopped hard-boiled egg, 30g/1oz grated reduced-fat cheddar cheese, 2 turkey rashers or lean ham slices, diced radishes and yellow pepper/ capsicum

30ml (2tbsp) Spicy Tomato Vinaigrette (page 214) or reduced-sugar prepared dressing of your choice

MID-AFTERNOON SNACK

Chilled prawns with horseradish sauce

DINNER

Sliced Beef with Green Pepper (Capsicum), Onion and Mangetout (page 276); make extra for Day 9 lunch

Baked Sweet Potato Chips (page 283)

DESSERT

2 grilled peach halves with toasted walnuts

DAY 9

BREAKFAST

180ml (6floz) vegetable juice

Breakfast 'pizza' (top a 15cm/6in wholemeal tortilla with 2 scrambled eggs, 30g/1oz reduced-fat cheddar cheese, 30g/1oz crumbled cooked turkey rashers or lean ham slices and diced fresh tomatoes)

Coffee or tea with skimmed milk and sugar substitute

MID-MORNING SNACK

Yogurt Cheese Dip (page 195) with raw vegetable sticks

LUNCH

Clear soup

Asian beef salad cups (fill lettuce 'cups' with leftover beef and vegetables from Day 8 dinner, add extra grated vegetables and drizzle with lime juice)

1 small papaya, cut into cubes

MID-AFTERNOON SNACK

Cream cheese and salmon bagel bite (2tbsp fat-free or light cream cheese and smoked salmon on half a wholemeal bagel)

DINNER

Halibut with Butter Bean and Vegetable Ragout (page 274)

Watercress and red onion salad

30ml (2tbsp) Lime Vinaigrette (page 214) or reduced-sugar prepared dressing of your choice

DESSERT

Baked apple with pistachios (stuff the centre core with crushed pistachio nuts)

DAY 10

BREAKFAST

180ml (6floz) tomato juice

Porridge oats with cinnamon and 90g (3oz) fresh blueberries

Coffee or tea with skimmed milk and sugar substitute

MID-MORNING SNACK

Pizza Wrap (page 278)

LUNCH

Phase 2 soup of your choice (page 265)

Grilled prawns on a bed of baby spinach cooked briefly in olive oil

30ml (2tbsp) Balsamic Vinaigrette (page 214) or reduced-sugar prepared dressing of your choice

MID-AFTERNOON SNACK

Celery sticks with spiced aubergine (eggplant) purée (Baba ghanoush)

DINNER

Herb-Breaded Turkey Escalopes with Mushrooms (page 273)

Steamed Swiss chard

Oven-roasted peppers (capsicum), carrots and onions

DESSERT

Grilled caramel 'rum' banana (cut a banana in half and top with 15ml (1tbsp) sugar-free caramel sauce and a dash of rum essence; grill until heated through)

DAY 11

BREAKFAST

180ml (6floz) vegetable juice

1 small oat bran muffin

115g (4oz) reduced-fat cottage cheese

Coffee or tea with skimmed milk and sugar substitute

MID-MORNING SNACK

1 small Granny Smith apple with 2tbsp wholenut peanut butter

LUNCH

Cos lettuce hearts with 180g (6oz) yellowfin tuna and edamame (young podded soya beans)

30ml (2tbsp) Green Goddess Dressing (page 216) or reduced-sugar prepared dressing of your choice

MID-AFTERNOON SNACK

Hummous on ½ wholemeal pitta bread

DINNER

Grilled sliced skirt steak with grilled onions (make extra for Day 12 lunch)

Courgettes (zucchini) and yellow courgettes cooked in 15ml (1tbsp) olive oil and sprinkled with fresh dill

100g (3½oz) cooked brown rice

DESSERT

Poached plum with flavoured aerosol cream (combine 2tbsp light aerosol cream with 5ml (1tsp) almond essence or flavour essence of your choice)

DAY 12

BREAKFAST

180ml (6floz) tomato juice

Breakfast 'banana split' (cut 1 medium banana in half, top with 115g (4oz) artificially sweetened fat-free or low-fat vanilla yogurt and sprinkle with crushed reduced-sugar wheat flake cereal)

Coffee or tea with skimmed milk and sugar substitute

MID-MORNING SNACK

10 small wholewheat crackers with 2tbsp wholenut peanut butter

LUNCH

Phase 2 soup of your choice (page 265)

Sliced steak (use leftover steak from Day 11) with cucumber rounds and pepper/capsicum slices on a bed of cos lettuce

30ml (2tbsp) Aioli Dressing (page 214) or reduced-sugar prepared dressing of your choice

1 medium pear topped with 30g (1oz) crumbled reduced-fat feta cheese

MID-AFTERNOON SNACK

2 devilled egg halves

DINNER

Stir-Fried Chicken with Soba Noodles (page 271)

Asian cabbage slaw (shredded pak choi/bok choy and Chinese leaves with mung bean sprouts)

30ml (2tbsp) Soy Ginger Dressing (page 217) or reduced-sugar prepared dressing of your choice

DESSERT

Creamy Dreamy Strawberry-Vanilla Shake (page 289)

DAY 13

BREAKFAST

½ pink or red grapefruit

2 poached eggs on a bed of sautéed vegetables

1 slice wholemeal toast with sugar-free fruit jam

Coffee or tea with skimmed milk and sugar substitute

MID-MORNING SNACK

1 small sweet potato cooked in the microwave and topped with 1 small chopped apple and a sprinkling of cinnamon

LUNCH

Endive and Turkey Sausage Soup (page 268)

Mediterranean salad (mixed greens with reduced-fat feta cheese cubes, kalamata olives and 90g/3oz fresh sliced strawberries)

30ml (2tbsp) Mint Vinaigrette (page 214) or reduced-sugar prepared dressing of your choice

MID-AFTERNOON SNACK

Banana bagel bite (top half a toasted wholemeal bagel with 2tbsp reduced-fat cottage cheese, ½ small sliced banana and a sprinkling of sunflower or pumpkin seeds)

DINNER

Prawn and Scallop Sauté (page 275)

Sautéed purple sprouting broccoli with garlic and dried chilli flakes

Roasted red peppers (capsicum) tossed with Balsamic Vinaigrette (page 214)

DESSERT

Sugar-free chocolate-milk ice-lolly with a 240ml (8floz) glass of skimmed milk

DAY 14

BREAKFAST

180ml (6floz) tomato juice

90g (3oz) fresh blueberries

South Beach Eggsadilla (page 262)

Coffee or tea with skimmed milk and sugar substitute

MID-MORNING SNACK

Mango smoothie (blend 90g/3oz peeled and chopped mango, 115g/4oz low-fat natural yogurt, 1tbsp granulated sugar substitute and 6 ice cubes until frothy)

LUNCH

Open-face roast beef sandwich with lettuce, tomato and horseradish on 1 slice wholemeal bread

Cucumber salad with bean sprouts

30ml (2tbsp) Creamy Dijon-Thyme Dressing (page 215) or reduced-sugar prepared dressing of your choice

MID-AFTERNOON SNACK

5 dried apple rings chopped into 115g (4oz) reduced-fat cottage cheese with a sprinkling of cinnamon

DINNER

Pan-Seared Beef Fillet with Creamy Peppercorn Sauce (page 277)

Barley Risotto (page 282)

Endive and radicchio salad

30ml (2tbsp) Blue Cheese Dressing (page 214) or reduced-sugar prepared dressing of your choice

DESSERT

South Beach Diet Tiramisu (page 286)

Recipes
for Phase 2 Meal Plans

Eggs Frijoles

Prep time: 15 minutes • Cook time: 20 minutes

Chock-full of protein, this Mexican egg and bean dish makes for a healthy, satisfying and delicious wake-up meal.

22.5ml (1½tbsp) extra-virgin olive oil

1 large onion, chopped

3 garlic cloves, finely chopped

1tbsp dried oregano

800g (28oz) tinned pinto beans, rinsed and drained

pinch of cayenne pepper

4 wholemeal tortillas

4 large eggs, lightly beaten

225g (8oz) shop-bought salsa

In a large non-stick frying pan, heat 15ml (1tbsp) of the oil over a medium heat. Add onion, garlic and oregano; cook, stirring occasionally, until onion is softened, about 7 minutes. Add beans and cayenne pepper. Simmer, stirring occasionally, until beans are warmed through and flavourful, 10 to 12 minutes. Cover to keep warm.

While beans are cooking, warm tortillas according to package directions.

Five minutes before beans are done, in a medium non-stick frying pan, heat remaining 7.5ml (1½tsp) oil over a medium heat. Add eggs and scramble until just cooked, 3 to 5 minutes; remove from the heat.

Divide beans among tortillas and top with eggs and salsa. Roll up to serve.

Makes 4 servings

Nutrition at a Glance

Per serving: 345 calories, 11g fat, 2g saturated fat, 17g protein, 49g carbohydrate, 10g fibre, 460mg sodium

Wholesome Oat Muffins

Prep time: 10 minutes • Soaking time: 30 minutes • Cook time: 15 minutes

These tasty muffins are so much better than shop-bought; you'll want to bake a supply regularly. Make a double batch and freeze half for later.

225g (8oz)	fat-free natural yogurt	75g (2½oz)	chopped walnuts
75g (2½oz)	porridge oats	5tbsp	granulated sugar substitute
140g (5oz)	wholemeal flour	75ml (2½floz)	rapeseed oil
1½tsp	baking powder	1	large egg, beaten
½tsp	bicarbonate of soda	5ml (1tsp)	vanilla essence
¼tsp	ground cinnamon	2tbsp	porridge oats
¼tsp	salt		

Preheat the oven to 220°C/425°F/Gas 7. Coat a 12-muffin non-stick tin with cooking spray or line with paper cases.

In a small bowl, combine yogurt and 75g (2½oz) of the oats. Let soak for 30 minutes.

Meanwhile, in a medium bowl, combine flour, baking powder, bicarbonate of soda, cinnamon and salt. Stir in walnuts.

In a large bowl, stir together sugar substitute, oil, egg and vanilla essence until well blended. Stir in oat mixture. Stir in flour mixture until just combined. Do not over mix.

Divide batter evenly among the muffin moulds, filling them about two-thirds full. Sprinkle remaining 2tbsp oats over muffins. Bake for 14 to 16 minutes, or until a toothpick or cake tester inserted in the centre of a muffin comes out clean. Transfer the tin to a rack and let cool for 5 minutes. Remove muffins from the tin to the rack to cool completely.

Makes 12 muffins

Nutrition at a Glance

Per muffin: 179 calories, 11g fat, 1g saturated fat, 4g protein, 18g carbohydrate, 2g fibre, 157mg sodium

South Beach Eggsadilla

Prep time: 5 minutes • Cook time: 5 minutes

Quick enough for a weekday morning yet fun enough for a lazy Saturday, this breakfast quesadilla provides an energizing start to the day. Add a spoonful of salsa if you like.

5ml (1tsp)	extra-virgin olive oil
3	large eggs, lightly beaten
20cm (8in)	wholemeal tortilla
	salt
	freshly ground black pepper
60g (2oz)	low-fat cheddar cheese, thinly sliced
	dried chilli pepper flakes or hot pepper sauce to taste

In a large non-stick frying pan, heat oil over a medium–high heat. Add eggs; reduce heat to medium and scramble until cooked but still moist, about 2 minutes. Transfer to a plate and season with salt and pepper.

Carefully wipe the pan with kitchen paper and return to a medium heat. Add tortilla and cook on both sides until warmed through, about 1 minute.

Leaving tortilla in the pan, top half of it with cheese and then with eggs: add chilli flakes or hot pepper sauce to taste and fold the other half over to form a quesadilla. Cook on both sides until heated through, 1 minute longer. Transfer to a cutting board, cut in half and serve.

Makes 2 servings

Nutrition at a Glance

Per serving: 280 calories, 17g fat, 7g saturated fat, 18g protein, 13g carbohydrate, 1g fibre, 580mg sodium

Thai Prawn Soup

Prep time: 10 minutes • Cook time: 30 minutes

This tangy, spicy soup is made with classic Thai ingredients that are easy to find. Look for both garlic-chilli sauce and Thai fish sauce in the foreign food section of most large supermarkets. If you have leftovers, simply whisk while reheating.

960ml (32floz)	low-sodium chicken stock		400ml (14floz)	reduced-fat coconut milk
60ml (2floz)	fresh lemon juice		450g (1lb)	large raw prawns, peeled and de-veined
2	spring onions, white and green parts thinly sliced and kept separate		2	plum tomatoes, quartered and chopped, with juice
2.5cm (1in)	piece fresh ginger, thinly sliced		10ml (2tsp)	chilli-garlic sauce
1	Serrano or jalapeño pepper, quartered lengthways		10ml (2tsp)	Thai fish sauce

In a large saucepan, combine stock, lemon juice, spring onion whites, ginger and pepper. Bring gently to the boil over a medium–high heat; cover, reduce heat to medium–low and simmer for 20 minutes. Stir in coconut milk (it will appear curdled at first), and then add prawns, tomatoes and their juice, chilli–garlic sauce and fish sauce. Return to the boil and simmer until prawns are opaque and cooked through, about 3 minutes. Remove the pan from the heat; divide soup among 4 bowls and sprinkle with spring onion greens.

Makes 4 servings

Nutrition at a Glance

Per serving: 262 calories, 11g fat, 6g saturated fat, 30g protein, 12g carbohydrate, 1g fibre, 616mg sodium

Variation: Try a combination of prawns, scallops and salmon instead of just prawns.

This recipe can also be prepared for Phase 1 meals.

Roasted Tomato Soup

Prep time: 10 minutes • Cook time: 55 minutes

The rich, rustic flavour of this soup comes from slow-roasting the tomatoes (you can do other things while they are in the oven). If you like a little sweetness, add a touch of sugar substitute when adjusting your seasoning. If you're on Phase 2 or 3, add wholemeal tortellini for a satisfying main course.

1.35kg (2½lb) plum tomatoes cut in half lengthways	1tsp dried oregano
1 medium onion, diced	¼tsp salt
4 garlic cloves, smashed and peeled	freshly ground black pepper
1tbsp dried basil	15ml (1tbsp) extra-virgin olive oil
	240ml (8floz) vegetable stock

Preheat the oven to 220°C/425°F/Gas 7.

Line a baking tray with greaseproof paper. Arrange tomatoes, cut side up, on the tray. Scatter onion and garlic in a single layer around tomatoes. Sprinkle tomatoes, onion and garlic with basil, oregano, salt and pepper to taste; drizzle with oil. Bake in the centre of the oven until tomatoes are golden on the bottom and start to collapse, about 40 minutes.

Remove from the oven and carefully transfer the contents of the tray to a blender. Add 120ml (4floz) of the stock and purée until smooth. Transfer puréed mixture to a medium saucepan. Stir in remaining stock and simmer over a medium heat. Remove the pan from the heat and season soup with additional salt and pepper, if desired. Serve warm.

Makes 4 servings

Nutrition at a Glance

Per serving: 100 calories, 4g fat, 0.5g saturated fat, 3g protein, 15g carbohydrate, 4g fibre, 164mg sodium

This recipe can also be prepared for Phase 1 meals.

EASY SOUTH BEACH DIET SOUPS
FOR PHASES 2 AND 3

These easy soups for Phases 2 and 3 include a number of foods like melon, soba and wholemeal noodles, sweet potatoes, carrots and even a touch of dry sherry in the bisque, which you can now enjoy. Great for lunch or dinner, some of these soups are hearty enough for a full meal on their own (with a big green salad, of course), while others make delicious starters for a light meal.

Asian Chicken Noodle Soup: In a large saucepan, heat 10ml (2tsp) extra-virgin olive oil over a medium heat. Add 3 thinly sliced spring onions, 2 diced celery sticks and 2 finely chopped garlic cloves; cook, stirring occasionally, until softened, about 7 minutes. Stir in 450g (1lb) diced boneless, skinless, chicken breasts; 225g (8oz) Chinese greens and a pinch of salt. Add 1.2 litres (40floz)) low-sodium chicken stock, bring to the boil and simmer for 5 minutes. Increase heat and bring stock to the low boil, then add 115g (4oz) soba noodles; cook until noodles are tender, about 5 minutes. Stir in 15ml (1tbsp) low-sodium soy sauce, 10ml (2tsp) sesame oil and 10ml (2tsp) chilli-garlic sauce. Serve hot.

Chilled Melon Soup with Mint: In a blender, purée flesh of 1 chopped honeydew melon until smooth. Add 1 large peeled and chopped cucumber, 115g (4oz) low-fat or fat-free natural yogurt, 2 roughly chopped spring onions, 15ml (1tbsp) fresh lemon juice and 2tsp freshly grated lemon rind; purée until smooth. Transfer to a covered container and refrigerate until chilled. Serve cold with a sprinkling of chopped fresh mint.

Creamy Mushroom and Leek Soup: In a large saucepan, heat 15ml (1tbsp) extra-virgin olive oil over a medium heat. Add 1 small chopped red onion, 2 thinly sliced garlic cloves, 1tsp dried thyme, 1¼tsp salt and a generous pinch of cayenne pepper. Cook, stirring occasionally, until softened, about 7 minutes. Stir in 1tbsp wholemeal flour, reduce heat to low and cook, stirring, until lightly browned, about 3 minutes. Add 450g (1lb) sliced mushrooms and 750ml (25floz) low-sodium chicken stock. Bring to the boil and simmer for 10 minutes. Transfer half of the soup to a blender and purée until smooth. Return soup to pan, add 60g (2oz) fat-free soured cream or crème fraiche and stir to combine. Return to simmer, adjust seasoning and serve hot.

Hearty Minestrone: In a large saucepan, heat 15ml (1tbsp) extra-virgin olive oil over a medium heat. Add 1 small chopped onion, 1 diced carrot, 2 diced celery sticks, 3

(continued)

finely chopped garlic cloves, 1tsp dried Italian herb seasoning and a generous pinch of freshly ground black pepper. Cook, stirring occasionally, until softened, about 7 minutes. Add 850ml (30floz) low-sodium chicken stock, 200g (7oz) chopped spinach leaves and 140g (5oz) thawed frozen mixed vegetables, such as cauliflower, green beans, courgettes (zucchini) and/or broccoli. Bring to the boil, add 2tbsp wholemeal ditalini or small shell pasta and simmer until vegetables are tender and pasta is al dente. Season with salt and additional pepper to taste. Sprinkle each serving with 1tbsp freshly grated Parmesan cheese and serve hot.

Lobster Bisque: In a large saucepan, heat 30ml (2tbsp) vegetable oil over a medium heat. Add 1 small finely chopped onion, 2 diced celery sticks, 1tsp dried thyme and a generous pinch of salt and freshly ground black pepper; cook, stirring occasionally, until softened, about 7 minutes. Stir in 30ml (2tbsp) wholemeal flour; cook, stirring constantly, until lightly browned, about 3 minutes. Stir in 850ml (30floz) low-sodium chicken stock, 115g (4oz) passata and 60ml (2floz) dry sherry; bring to the boil, reduce heat to low, cover and simmer for 10 minutes. Add 450g (1lb) shelled lobster tails, cut into 2.5cm (1in) pieces; simmer, covered, until lobster is opaque, about 6 minutes. Stir in 300ml (10floz) skimmed milk, 1 chopped plum tomato, 2tbsp finely chopped fresh parsley, 1tsp paprika and 1.25ml (¼tsp) hot pepper sauce; simmer and serve hot.

Root Vegetable Soup: Cut 350g (12oz) celeriac, 350g (12oz) turnips and 225g (8oz) carrots into 1cm (½in) pieces. Place vegetables in a large saucepan and cover with 1.2 to 1.4 litres (40–45floz) low-sodium chicken stock. Add ¼tsp dried thyme and a pinch of salt; bring to a low boil and simmer until vegetables are very tender, about 25 minutes. Transfer soup, in batches, to a blender and purée until smooth. Return to the pan, stir in 60g (2oz) fat-free soured cream or crème fraiche and simmer just to heat through. Adjust seasoning and serve hot.

Sweet Carrot-Cumin Soup: In a large saucepan, heat 20ml (4tsp) extra-virgin olive oil over a medium heat. Add 1 small chopped onion and 2 thinly sliced garlic cloves; cook, stirring occasionally, until softened, about 7 minutes. Add 800g (1¾lb) thinly sliced carrots, 2tsp ground cumin, ½tsp dried chilli pepper flakes and ¼tsp salt; stir to coat. Cook, stirring occasionally, for 10 minutes longer. Add 500ml (16floz) low-sodium chicken stock and 240ml (8floz) water; bring to the boil and simmer until carrots are tender, 10 to 12 minutes. Transfer soup, in batches, to a blender and purée until smooth.

Return to the pan and simmer to heat through. Adjust seasoning and serve hot with 1tsp low-fat soured cream or crème fraiche per serving, if desired.

Sweet Potato Soup: In a large saucepan, heat 15ml (1tbsp) extra-virgin olive oil over a medium heat. Add 1 small chopped onion, 2 thinly sliced garlic cloves, 2tsp grated fresh ginger, 1tsp dried thyme, ¼tsp salt and a generous pinch of freshly ground black pepper. Cook, stirring occasionally, until softened, about 7 minutes. Meanwhile, pierce 2 medium unpeeled sweet potatoes all over with a fork. Cook in a microwave until tender, about 10 minutes. Cool briefly, peel and add potato to the pan. Add 360ml (12floz) low-sodium chicken stock and 240ml (8floz) skimmed milk. Bring to the boil, stirring occasionally, and then simmer for 5 minutes. Transfer soup, in batches, to a blender and purée until smooth. Return to the pan and heat through. Adjust seasoning and serve hot.

Sweet Potato Vichyssoise: Pierce 2 medium unpeeled sweet potatoes all over with a fork. Cook in a microwave until tender, about 10 minutes. Meanwhile, in a large saucepan, heat 15ml (1tbsp) extra-virgin olive oil over a medium heat. Add 2 medium chopped leeks, ¼tsp salt and a generous pinch of freshly ground black pepper; cover and cook until leeks are softened, about 5 minutes. Remove potatoes from microwave, cool briefly, peel, then add potato to the pan. Add 240ml (8floz) low-sodium chicken stock, bring to the boil and simmer for 3 minutes. Remove from the heat and let cool briefly. Transfer to a blender and purée for 1 minute. Add 360ml (12floz) skimmed milk and purée until smooth. Transfer soup to a covered container and refrigerate until chilled. Sprinkle each serving with chopped chives and serve cold.

Turkey Noodle Soup: Pierce 2 medium unpeeled sweet potatoes all over with a fork. Cook in a microwave until tender, about 10 minutes. Meanwhile, in a large saucepan, heat 15ml (1tbsp) extra-virgin olive oil over a medium heat. Add 2 medium chopped leeks, ¼tsp salt and a generous pinch of freshly ground black pepper; cover and cook until leeks are softened, about 5 minutes. Remove potatoes from microwave, cool briefly, peel, then add potato to the pan. Add 240ml (8floz) low-sodium chicken stock, bring to the boil and simmer for 3 minutes. Remove from the heat and let cool briefly. Transfer to a blender and purée for 1 minute. Add 360ml (12floz) skimmed milk and purée until smooth. Transfer soup to a covered container and refrigerate until chilled. Sprinkle each serving with chopped chives and serve cold.

Endive and Turkey Sausage Soup

Prep time: 15 minutes • Cook time: 30 minutes

Endive is a hearty green that is just as delicious served raw in salads as it is cooked into soups or sautéed with olive oil and fresh lemon juice. Meatball lovers can replace the sausage with turkey meatballs made with lean white meat.

225g (8oz)	low-fat sweet Italian turkey sausages or turkey mince, seasoned and formed into meatballs		salt
		1	garlic clove, finely chopped
15ml (1tbsp)	extra-virgin olive oil	280 to 340g (10 to 12oz)	endive, cut crossways into 1cm (½in strips, washed and spun dry
1	medium onion, finely chopped		
½tsp	dried rosemary, crumbled	750ml (25floz)	low-sodium chicken stock

Lightly coat a heavy-bottomed non-stick saucepan with cooking spray and heat over a medium–high heat. Add sausage or meatballs and reduce heat to medium; cook, turning occasionally, until browned on all sides, 8 to 10 minutes. Transfer sausages or meatballs to a cutting board.

Add oil to the pan and heat over a medium heat. Add onion, rosemary and a generous pinch of salt and cook, stirring occasionally, until onion is softened, about 6 minutes. Stir in garlic and cook 2 minutes longer.

Meanwhile, if using sausages cut them in half lengthways, then cut crossways into 1cm (½in) pieces.

Add endive to the pan, in batches if necessary and stir just until wilted. Add sausage or meatballs and stock, bring to the boil and simmer until heated through, about 2 minutes. Serve warm.

Makes 4 servings

Nutrition at a Glance

Per serving: 182 calories, 11g fat, 1g saturated fat, 15g protein, 8g carbohydrate, 3g fibre, 513mg sodium

This recipe can also be prepared for Phase 1 meals.

Creamy Chicken Florentine Soup

Prep time: 15 minutes • Cook time: 25 minutes

Reduced-fat cream cheese adds richness to this quick chicken soup. To save time, buy chopped frozen spinach rather than fresh leaves.

15ml (1tbsp)	extra-virgin olive oil
1	small onion, finely chopped
2	garlic cloves, thinly sliced
	pinch of salt
	pinch of freshly ground black pepper
350g (12oz)	boneless, skinless chicken breast, cut into 2.5cm (1in) cubes
280g (10oz)	frozen chopped spinach, thawed, well drained
60g (2oz)	light cream cheese, cubed
750ml (25floz)	low-sodium chicken stock

In a medium heavy-bottomed saucepan, heat oil over a medium heat. Add onion, garlic, salt and pepper; cook, stirring occasionally, until onion is softened, about 7 minutes. Add chicken and spinach; stir for 1 minute. Add cream cheese and stir until melted. Add stock, bring to the boil and simmer until chicken is cooked through, about 5 minutes. Serve warm.

Makes 4 servings

Nutrition at a Glance

Per serving: 197 calories, 7g fat, 2g saturated fat, 24g protein, 6g carbohydrate, 1g fibre, 615mg sodium

This recipe can also be prepared for Phase 1 meals.

Sun-Dried Tomato and Feta-Stuffed Chicken Breasts

Prep time: 20 minutes • Cook time: 25 minutes

Deceptively simple, this tasty chicken dish works just as well for entertaining as it does on a busy weeknight. Make extra for lunch or dinner the next day: thinly slice the chicken and serve it cold over simply dressed salad greens, or roughly chop the chicken and toss it with fresh spinach, a little olive oil and warm wholemeal pasta.

75g (2½oz)	reduced-fat feta cheese		freshly ground black pepper
2	sun-dried tomatoes, finely chopped	4 x 170g (6oz)	boneless, skinless chicken breasts
1	garlic clove, finely chopped		salt
½tsp	dried basil	10ml (2tsp)	extra-virgin olive oil

Preheat the oven to 220°C/425°F/Gas 7.

In a small bowl, combine cheese, tomatoes, garlic and basil. Season with pepper and mash together well with a fork.

Butterfly chicken by carefully slicing horizontally along the long edge of each breast, three-quarters of the way through. Open up each breast and spread inside with one-quarter of the feta mixture. Close breast over filling and press edges together to seal. Season lightly with salt and pepper.

In a large ovenproof frying pan, heat oil over a medium-high heat. Add chicken and cook until browned on both sides, about 2 minutes per side. Transfer frying pan to oven and cook until chicken is cooked through, about 20 minutes. Remove from oven and serve warm.

Makes 4 servings

Nutrition at a Glance

Per serving: 232 calories, 6g fat, 2g saturated fat, 42g protein, 1g carbohydrate, 0g fibre, 326mg sodium

This recipe can also be prepared for Phase 1 meals.

Stir-Fried Chicken with Soba Noodles

Prep time: 20 minutes • Cook time: 15 minutes

Try celery or green or red peppers (capsicum) instead of mushrooms for variety.

115g (4oz)	soba noodles	15ml (1tbsp)	low-sodium soy sauce
675g (1½lb)	boneless, skinless chicken breasts cut crossways into 1cm (½in) slices	10ml (2tsp)	sesame oil
		5ml (1tsp)	vegetable oil
4	spring onions, white and green parts thinly sliced and kept separate	450g (1lb)	Chinese greens, thinly sliced
3	garlic cloves, thinly sliced	170g (6oz)	button mushrooms, trimmed and quartered
1tsp	grated fresh ginger	30ml (2tbsp)	water
½tsp	dried chilli pepper flakes	10ml (2tsp)	fresh lemon juice
	Salt		

Bring a large saucepan of water to the boil. Cook noodles according to package directions.

While noodles are cooking, in a medium bowl, combine chicken with spring onion whites, garlic, ginger and chilli pepper flakes; season lightly with salt.

Drain noodles and transfer to another medium bowl. Add spring onion greens, soy sauce and sesame oil; toss to combine. Season lightly with salt.

In a large non-stick frying pan or wok, heat vegetable oil over a medium–high heat. Add chicken and cook, stirring constantly, until just cooked through, 4 to 5 minutes. Transfer chicken to a plate.

Return the pan to the heat. Add Chinese greens, mushrooms and water. Cook, stirring, until vegetables are wilted, about 4 minutes. Return chicken and noodles to pan, stir and cook to heat through, about 1 minute. Toss with lemon juice and serve warm.

Makes 4 servings

Nutrition at a Glance

Per serving: 359 calories, 6g fat, 1g saturated fat, 46g protein, 29g carbohydrate, 4g fibre, 349mg sodium

Chicken and Lentil Stew

Prep time: 15 minutes • Cook time: 25 minutes

This hearty, quick–cooking stew tastes as if it had been simmered for hours. Double the recipe; it freezes beautifully.

15ml (1tbsp)	extra-virgin olive oil	1tbsp	tomato purée
1	small onion, finely chopped	450g (1lb)	boneless, skinless chicken breasts cut crossways into 1cm (½in) slices
2	garlic cloves, finely chopped	400g (14oz)	tin lentils, drained and rinsed
¼tsp	dried basil		
¼tsp	dried oregano	400g (14oz)	tin chopped tomatoes, with juice
	pinch of freshly ground black pepper	180ml (6floz)	low-sodium chicken stock
	salt	115g (4oz)	baby spinach

In a medium saucepan, heat oil over a medium heat. Add onion, garlic, basil, oregano, pepper and a pinch of salt; reduce heat to medium–low and cook, stirring occasionally, 4 minutes. Stir in tomato purée and cook 3 minutes longer. Stir in chicken and cook for 1 minute. Add lentils, tomatoes and their juice and stock. Bring to the boil and gently simmer, reduce heat to low, cover and cook until chicken is cooked through, 7 to 10 minutes. Stir in spinach, cover and cook 1 minute longer, or until spinach wilts. Season with salt and pepper to taste and serve warm.

Makes 6 servings

Nutrition at a Glance

Per serving: 311 calories, 4g fat, 1g saturated fat, 32g protein, 36g carbohydrate, 17g fibre, 326mg sodium

This recipe can also be prepared for Phase 1 meals.

Herb-Breaded Turkey Escalopes with Mushrooms

Prep time: 15 minutes • Cook time: 16 minutes

Look for wholemeal Italian breadcrumbs, which are flavoured with herbs, in the natural food section of your supermarket or at a health food shop. Or use plain breadcrumbs and add any combination of dried basil, marjoram, thyme and rosemary.

675g (1½lb) turkey escalopes	115g (4oz) wholemeal herb-flavoured Italian breadcrumbs
3 garlic cloves, finely chopped	4tbsp chopped parsley
salt	450g (1lb) button mushrooms, trimmed and quartered
freshly ground black pepper	
1 large egg, lightly beaten	15ml (1tbsp) extra-virgin olive oil
30ml (2tbsp) skimmed milk	

Coat turkey escalopes with two-thirds of the garlic and lightly season with salt and pepper.

In a large shallow bowl, whisk together egg and milk. Spread breadcrumbs on a large plate. Dip escalopes in egg mixture, then dredge both sides lightly in breadcrumbs, pressing to make sure the crumbs adhere.

Coat a large non-stick frying pan with cooking spray and heat over a medium heat. Cook escalopes, in batches if necessary, until lightly browned and crisp, about 2 minutes per side. Transfer to a plate, sprinkle with 2tbsp of the parsley and loosely cover with foil to keep warm.

Add oil to the frying pan and heat over a medium-high heat. Add mushrooms, remaining garlic and remaining parsley. Season lightly with salt and pepper. Cook, stirring, until mushrooms are tender, about 4 minutes. Remove the pan from the heat. Transfer escalopes to a serving plate and top with warm mushrooms.

Makes 4 servings

Nutrition at a Glance

Per serving: 230 calories, 4g fat, 0.5g saturated fat, 40g protein, 8g carbohydrate, 3g fibre, 170mg sodium

Halibut with Butter Bean and Vegetable Ragout

Prep time: 10 minutes • Cook time: 10 minutes

Butter beans add a decidedly creamy texture to this dish. If you can't find them, use haricot beans instead. We prefer vine-ripened tomatoes, sold in most supermarkets, as they tend to be juicier than the standard tomato variety. To save time, ask the fishmonger to skin your halibut fillets for you.

10ml (2tsp)	extra-virgin olive oil	2	medium tomatoes, chopped
1	medium onion, chopped		
2	garlic cloves, crushed	140g (5oz)	frozen peas, thawed
¼tsp	salt	400g (14oz)	tin butter beans, rinsed and drained
	pinch of dried basil	675g (1½lb)	skinned halibut fillet
	pinch of freshly ground black pepper		

Preheat the oven to grill.

In a medium saucepan, heat 5ml (1tsp) of the oil over a medium heat. Add onion, garlic, salt, basil and pepper. Reduce heat to medium-low and cook, stirring occasionally, 4 minutes. Stir in tomatoes and peas; cover and cook 4 minutes longer. Stir in beans, cover and cook 2 minutes longer. Remove pan from heat and leave covered to keep warm.

While ragout is cooking, place halibut fillets on a grill pan, season with salt and pepper and brush with remaining 5ml (1tsp) oil. Grill until opaque and cooked through, 6 to 8 minutes.

Divide ragout among 4 serving plates. Portion fish and serve warm on top of ragout.

Makes 4 servings

Nutrition at a Glance

Per serving: 304 calories, 7g fat, 1g saturated fat, 42g protein, 22g carbohydrate, 6g fibre, 547mg sodium

This recipe can also be prepared for Phase 1 meals.

Prawn and Scallop Sauté

Prep time: 10 minutes • Cook time: 5 minutes

This super-quick dinner main course is great any time of the year. For a change of pace, try coriander, oregano, basil, or thyme instead of parsley. Serve the seafood over wilted greens or toss with brown or wild rice.

350g (12oz)	sea scallops
350g (12oz)	large raw prawns, peeled and de-veined
3	garlic cloves, finely chopped
	salt
	freshly ground black pepper
15ml (1tbsp)	extra-virgin olive oil
10ml (2tsp)	fresh lemon juice
2tsp	finely grated lemon rind
1tbsp	freshly chopped parsley

In a large bowl, combine scallops, prawns, garlic and a pinch of salt and pepper; toss until seafood is well coated.

In a large frying pan, heat oil over a medium-high heat. Add seafood mixture and cook, stirring frequently, until prawns turn pink and scallops are just cooked through, 3 to 4 minutes. Transfer to a large serving bowl, add lemon juice and rind and stir well. Sprinkle with parsley and serve warm.

Makes 4 servings

Nutrition at a Glance

Per serving: 195 calories, 6g fat, 1g saturated fat, 30g protein, 4g carbohydrate, 0g fibre, 326mg sodium

This recipe can also be prepared for Phase 1 meals.

Sliced Beef with Green Pepper (Capsicum), Onion and Mangetout

Prep time: 20 minutes • Cook time: 20 minutes

The combination of green pepper (capsicum), onion and mangetout brings a delicious sweetness to this Chinese-style dish. Alternatively, a red or yellow pepper can be used.

675g (1½lb)	topside of beef (about 2cm/¾in thick), well trimmed	1	medium onion, thinly sliced
	salt	1	garlic clove, finely chopped
	freshly ground black pepper	170g (6oz)	mangetout, strings removed, thinly sliced
5ml (1tsp)	extra-virgin oil	30ml (2tbsp)	water
1	large green pepper (capsicum), thinly sliced	15ml (1tbsp)	low-sodium soy sauce

Season beef with salt and black pepper. Lightly coat a large non-stick frying pan with cooking spray and heat over a medium-high heat. Add beef and cook for 4 minutes per side for medium-rare; remove from heat. Transfer beef to a cutting board and let sit for 5 minutes before slicing.

Meanwhile, heat oil over a medium-high heat. Add green pepper, onion and garlic; cook, stirring constantly, 5 minutes. Add mangetout and water. Cover the pan and cook, stirring occasionally, until vegetables are softened, about 5 minutes. Meanwhile, slice the beef thinly. Uncover the pan, add soy sauce and cook 30 seconds longer. Add sliced beef to pan and toss briefly, just to heat through. Serve warm.

Makes 4 servings

Nutrition at a Glance

Per serving: 333 calories, 15g fat, 6g saturated fat, 40g protein, 8g carbohydrate, 2g fibre, 312mg sodium

This recipe can also be prepared for Phase 1 meals.

Pan-Seared Beef Fillet with Creamy Peppercorn Sauce

Prep time: 10 minutes • Cook time: 10 minutes

Freshly cracked black peppercorns serve double duty in this satisfying main course: first, they're rubbed into the meat for flavour. Then the peppercorns left in the pan after cooking the steaks give body and kick to the sauce. If you don't have a spice grinder or an extra coffee grinder for grinding spices, buy cracked peppercorns or set your pepper grinder to the coarsest setting. Chicken or vegetable stock can be used in place of beef stock.

2tsp	whole black peppercorns		salt
4 x 170g (6oz)	beef fillet steaks about 2.5cm (1in) thick, well trimmed	30ml (2tbsp)	low-sodium beef stock
1	garlic clove, cut in half lengthways	60g (2oz)	reduced-fat soured cream or crème fraiche

In a spice grinder, coarsely grind peppercorns. Rub steaks on both sides with cut side of garlic, then coat with pepper on both sides, pressing to adhere and season lightly with salt.

Lightly coat a large heavy or cast-iron frying pan with cooking spray and heat over a medium-high heat. Add steaks and sear on both sides, about 1 minute per side. Continue to cook to desired doneness, about 3 minutes per side for medium-rare. Transfer to a cutting board and let rest for 5 minutes.

While steak is resting, return the pan to a medium heat, add stock and stir with a wooden spoon to scrape up any browned bits clinging to the pan. Stir in soured cream or crème fraiche and remove the pan from the heat. Serve steaks warm with sauce drizzled on top.

Makes 4 servings

Nutrition at a Glance

Per serving: 284 calories, 13g fat, 5g saturated fat, 38g protein, 2g carbohydrate, 0g fibre, 188mg sodium

This recipe can also be prepared for Phase 1 meals.

SOUTH BEACH DIET WRAPS

Once you're on Phase 2 or 3, you can enjoy a protein- and vegetable-filled wrap made with a wholemeal tortilla. Have one for lunch or for a mid-morning or mid-afternoon snack and account for the good carbs as you think about what other carbs you'll be eating that day. The Scrambled New York Breakfast Wrap is a great alternative to cereal or an omelette for breakfast.

Greek Vegetable Wrap: Combine 1 cos lettuce, chopped, 225g (8oz) halved cherry tomatoes, 60g (2oz) crumbled reduced-fat feta cheese, 1 thinly sliced small red onion, 45g (1½oz) stoned and roughly chopped kalamata olives, 15ml (1tbsp) extra-virgin olive oil, 15ml (1tbsp) red wine vinegar and salt and freshly ground black pepper to taste. Divide mixture among 4 x 15cm (6in) wholemeal tortillas. Roll up burrito-style and serve.

Pizza Wrap: Lay 4 x 15cm (6in) wholemeal tortillas on a work surface. Spread each with 2tbsp pizza sauce or passata. Place 1 slice reduced-fat mozzarella cheese in the centre. Roll up burrito-style and heat in a microwave until cheese melts, 30 seconds to 1 minute. Serve warm.

Pressed Cuban Wrap: Lay 4 x 15cm (6in) wholemeal tortillas on a work surface. Spread each with 1tbsp low-fat mayonnaise and 1tbsp wholegrain mustard. Top each with one-quarter of a thinly sliced large dill pickle, 2 slices ham and 2 slices reduced-fat Emmental cheese. Roll up burrito-style and press with palm of your hand to flatten. Lightly coat a grill pan with cooking spray and heat over a medium-high heat. Place 1 wrap on the pan and press with the back of a large spatula until bottom is golden, 1 to 2 minutes. Turn and cook on the other side until golden. Cook remaining wraps and serve warm.

Reuben Wrap: Lay 4 x 15cm (6in) wholemeal tortillas on a work surface. Spread each with 22ml (1½tbsp) Thousand Island Dressing (page 217) and 1tbsp wholegrain mustard. Top each with 2 slices lean pastrami, 75g (2½oz) sauerkraut or pickled cabbage and 1 slice reduced-fat Emmental cheese. Sprinkle with caraway seeds, if desired. Roll up burrito-style and serve.

Scrambled New York Breakfast Wrap: In a large non-stick frying pan, heat 15ml (1tbsp) extra-virgin olive oil over a medium heat. Add 1 thinly sliced medium onion and a pinch of salt and freshly ground black pepper; cook, stirring occasionally, until just softened, about 5 minutes. Add 6 lightly beaten large eggs and allow to set for about 10 seconds. Sprinkle with 60g (2oz) diced smoked salmon and 60g (2oz) light cream cheese (cut into small pieces). Scramble with eggs just until cheese melts, about 1 minute. Divide egg mixture among 4 x 15cm (6in) wholemeal tortillas. Roll up burrito-style and serve hot.

Smoked Turkey and Asparagus Wrap: Lay 4 x 15cm (6in) wholemeal tortillas on a work surface. Spread each with 1½tbsp low-fat mayonnaise and 1tbsp wholegrain mustard. Top each with 2 slices smoked turkey breast, 2 cooked asparagus spears and 2 thin slices tomato. Season lightly with salt and freshly ground black pepper. Roll up burrito-style and serve.

Tex-Mex Steak Wrap: Rub 1 225g (8oz) skirt steak with Tex-Mex spice mix and grill to medium-rare. Transfer to a cutting board, let rest for 5 minutes, and then thinly slice. Lay 4 x 15cm (6in) wholemeal tortillas on a work surface. Spread each with 1tbsp low-fat mayonnaise and sprinkle with 2tbsp chopped roasted red peppers (bottled). Top each with one-quarter of the steak slices and 30g (1oz) chopped romaine lettuce. Roll up burrito-style and serve.

Spicy Niçoise Wrap: Combine 90g (3oz) chopped red-leaf lettuce, 350g (12oz) tinned drained and flaked water-packed yellow fin tuna, 2 peeled and chopped hard-boiled eggs, 1 chopped large tomato, 45g (1½oz) stoned and chopped Niçoise olives, 15ml (1tbsp) extra-virgin olive oil, 15ml (1tbsp) red wine vinegar and 10ml (2tsp) hot pepper sauce. Divide among 4 x 15cm (6in) wholemeal tortillas. Roll up burrito-style and serve.

Quick Lamb Stew

Prep time: 20 minutes • Cook time: 35 minutes

Since boneless leg of lamb is a tender cut, it can be cooked much more quickly than typical lamb stew meat. Celeriac, also called celery root, is a hearty addition here. And it's easy to prepare: use a sharp knife or vegetable peeler to carefully cut away the thick outer peel before grating or dicing it.

15ml (1tbsp)	extra-virgin olive oil	1	medium onion, chopped
675g (1½lb)	boneless leg of lamb, trimmed and cut into 1cm (½in) pieces	4	garlic cloves, smashed and peeled
¼tsp	salt	2tsp	dried rosemary, crumbled
	pinch of freshly ground black pepper	1tbsp	tomato purée
2	medium carrots, cut into 1cm (½in) dice	75ml (2½floz)	dry red wine
1	medium celeriac, peeled and cut into 1cm (½in) dice	800g (28oz)	tinned whole peeled tomatoes, with juice

In a large heavy-bottomed saucepan, heat 5ml (1tsp) of the oil over a medium–high heat. Add lamb and sprinkle with salt and pepper. Cook, stirring occasionally, 6 minutes, or until lamb is lightly browned on the outside and slightly pink on the inside. Using a slotted spoon, transfer lamb to a plate.

Add remaining 10ml (2tsp) oil to the pan and heat over a medium–high heat. Add carrots, celeriac, onion, garlic, rosemary and a pinch of salt and pepper. Cook, stirring frequently, until vegetables start to brown, about 5 minutes. Add tomato purée and cook, stirring, for 1 minute. Add wine and cook 1 minute longer. Add tomatoes and their juices, breaking up tomatoes with a wooden spoon. Bring to the boil, reduce heat to medium-low and simmer until vegetables are tender and flavours blended, about 20 minutes. Return lamb and any juice to the pan and cook just to heat through. Serve warm.

Makes 4 servings

Nutrition at a Glance

Per serving: 398 calories, 13g fat, 4g saturated fat, 39g protein, 28g carbohydrate, 6g fibre, 568mg sodium

Two-Bean Chilli Con Carne

Prep time: 10 minutes • Cook time: 25 minutes

Two kinds of beans add up to double the fibre in this wholesome beef chilli. We chose black beans and pintos, but you can use whatever types you like best.

15ml (1tbsp)	extra-virgin olive oil	2tsp	dried oregano
450g (1lb)	extra-lean beef mince	1tbsp	tomato purée
2tbsp	chilli powder	800g (28oz)	tinned chopped tomatoes, with juice
¼tsp	cayenne pepper		
1	large green pepper (capsicum), diced	400g (14oz)	tin black eye beans, rinsed and drained
1	medium onion, chopped	400g (14oz)	tin pinto beans, rinsed and drained
4	garlic cloves, finely chopped	225g (8oz)	passata

In a large heavy-bottomed saucepan, heat oil over a medium-high heat. Add beef, 1tbsp of the chilli powder and cayenne pepper. Cook, stirring to break up meat, about 5 minutes, or until browned. Using a slotted spoon, transfer meat to a plate.

Add green pepper (capsicum), onion, garlic, oregano, salt and remaining 1tbsp chilli powder to the same saucepan; cook over a medium heat, stirring occasionally, until onion begins to soften, about 3 minutes. Stir in tomato purée, and then add chopped tomatoes and their juice, black eye beans, pinto beans and passata. Cover and simmer for 10 minutes, stirring occasionally. Uncover, add cooked beef and cook over a medium heat until chilli thickens, about 5 minutes. Serve warm.

Makes 4 generous servings

Nutrition at a Glance

Per serving: 406 calories, 11g fat, 3g saturated fat, 35g protein, 38g carbohydrate, 12g fibre, 639mg sodium

This recipe can also be prepared for Phase 1 meals.

Barley Risotto

Prep time: 5 minutes • Cook time: 55 minutes

Just like classic risotto, this barley version is delicious and creamy. Technique-wise, it's even easier than conventional risotto because it doesn't require as much stirring. This recipe is very adaptable: add mushrooms if you like, or stir in a mix of fresh herbs at the end.

750ml (25floz)	low-sodium chicken stock
10ml (2tsp)	extra-virgin olive oil
1	small onion, thinly sliced
100g (3½oz)	pearl barley
4tbsp	freshly grated Parmesan cheese
¼tsp	salt
	freshly ground black pepper

In a medium saucepan, bring stock to the boil and simmer; remove from the heat and cover to keep warm.

Meanwhile, in a second medium, heavy-bottomed saucepan, heat oil over a medium heat. Add onion and barley; stir to combine. Reduce heat to low and cook, stirring occasionally, until onion is softened and barley is lightly toasted, about 5 minutes.

Add about one-third of the stock, bring to the boil and simmer over a very low heat, stirring occasionally, until stock is almost absorbed, about 12 minutes. Repeat with another third of the stock and then with the remaining stock. Cooking time will be about 50 minutes in total. Remove the pan from the heat and stir in Parmesan, salt and pepper to taste. Serve warm.

Makes 4 servings

Nutrition at a Glance

Per serving: 166 calories, 5g fat, 2g saturated fat, 8g protein, 23g carbohydrate, 4g fibre, 279mg sodium

Make in Advance: Barley risotto freezes well for up to 1 month and reheats easily in the microwave.

Baked Sweet Potato Chips

Prep time: 10 minutes • Cook time: 17 minutes

These healthy low-fat chips get pizzazz with the addition of dried Italian herb seasoning. For 'hot' chips, try Cajun seasoning or add finely chopped garlic.

2	large sweet potatoes, (900g/2lb) sliced into 5mm (¼in) thick wedges
10ml (2tsp)	extra-virgin olive oil
1tbsp	dried Italian herb seasoning
	salt
	freshly ground black pepper

Heat the oven to 200°C/400°F/Gas 6.

In a large bowl, toss potatoes with oil, Italian seasoning and a pinch of salt and pepper. Spread in a single layer on two large baking trays and bake for 10 minutes. With a spatula, turn slices over and continue baking until chips are golden, about 7 minutes longer. Serve warm.

Makes 4 servings

Nutrition at a Glance

Per serving: 216 calories, 2g fat, 0.5g saturated fat, 4g protein, 46g carbohydrate, 7g fibre, 197mg sodium

Kale and Turkey Rasher Gratin

Prep time: 15 minutes • Cook time: 30 minutes

Kale offers an abundance of nutrients, including fibre, vitamin C, vitamin B_6 and beta-carotene. Its hearty texture makes it well suited for a gratin. If you prefer, try other cooking greens, alone or in combination, such as Swiss chard, mustard, turnip or dandelion. For a vegetarian version, simply skip the turkey rashers.

550g (1¼lb)	kale, thick stems stripped and tough ends removed, chopped
4	turkey rashers, cut into 2.5cm (1in) pieces
1	small onion, chopped
2	garlic cloves, finely chopped
120ml (4floz)	fat-free evaporated milk
	freshly ground black pepper
45g (1½oz)	freshly grated Parmesan cheese

Preheat the oven to grill.

In a deep flameproof frying pan, bring a small quantity of water to the boil. Add kale and cook over a medium-high heat until tender, about 6 minutes. Drain and pat dry.

Wipe the frying pan dry and return to a medium-high heat. Add turkey rashers and cook until crisp, 4 to 5 minutes. Transfer to a plate. Add onion and garlic to the pan; reduce heat to medium and cook, stirring, until onion is softened, about 7 minutes.

Return turkey rashers to the pan and add evaporated milk. Bring to the boil and simmer until slightly reduced, about 5 minutes. Season with pepper to taste. Add kale and stir to combine. Sprinkle evenly with cheese. Grill for 2 to 3 minutes, or until cheese is lightly browned.

Makes 4 servings

Nutrition at a Glance

Per serving: 158 calories, 5g fat, 2g saturated fat, 11g protein, 20g carbohydrate, 3g fibre, 345mg sodium

This recipe can also be prepared for Phase 1 meals.

Peanut Butter and Jam Cookies

Prep time: 15 minutes • Cook time: 14 minutes

Who would believe you can get such a delectable cookie out of such a simple process and with so few ingredients? (That's right, there's no flour!) The not-too-sweet, deep, nutty flavour is perfect for children young and old. These cookies are so good that we need to remind you to limit yourself to one serving!

20g (¾oz)	granulated sugar substitute
1	large egg
5ml (1tsp)	vanilla essence
250g (9oz)	smooth trans-fat-free peanut butter
1tsp	bicarbonate of soda
80g (2¾oz)	sugar-free jam, any flavour

Heat the oven to 180°C/350°F/Gas 4. Line a baking tray with greaseproof paper.

Mix sugar substitute, egg and vanilla essence together with an electric mixer on low for 3 minutes. Add peanut butter and bicarbonate of soda. Mix on medium until mixture comes together, about 30 seconds.

Form dough into 24 2tsp balls and place on the baking tray 2.5cm (1in) apart. Gently press your thumb into the centre of each to make an indentation. Fill each indentation with ½tsp jam.

Bake until lightly browned on the bottom, 12 to 14 minutes. Let cookies cool briefly on the tray, and then transfer to a wire rack to cool completely.

Makes 12 (2 cookie) servings

Nutrition at a Glance

Per serving: 140 calories, 11g fat, 2.5g saturated fat, 6g protein, 7g carbohydrate, 1g fibre, 210mg sodium

South Beach Diet Tiramisu

Prep time: 20 minutes • Cook time: 20 minutes • Cool time: 30 minutes

A favourite Italian dessert, tiramisu (meaning 'pick–me–up', referring to the espresso and cocoa it includes) makes a light yet rich conclusion to any meal.

6	large egg whites	115g (4oz)	light aerosol cream
½tsp	cream of tartar	2tsp	granulated sugar substitute
	Pinch of salt	60ml (2floz)	strongly brewed decaffeinated espresso coffee
4ml (¾tsp)	vanilla essence		
5tbsp	granulated sugar substitute	½tsp	unsweetened cocoa powder
45g (1½oz)	wholemeal flour		
120g (4oz)	ricotta cheese, reduced fat if available		Mint sprigs to garnish (optional)

Heat the oven to 180°C/350°F/Gas 4. Lightly coat a 20cm (8in) square baking dish with cooking spray.

In a large bowl, with an electric mixer at high speed, whisk egg whites, cream of tartar and salt until soft peaks form, about 5 minutes. Add 2.5ml (½tsp) of the vanilla essence and whisk to combine. Add 5tbsp of the sugar substitute and whisk until stiff peaks form. Sift 2tbsp of the flour over whisked egg whites and gently fold to incorporate. Repeat twice with remaining flour until all of the flour is incorporated.

Pour batter into the baking dish and gently smooth the top. Bake, turning once halfway through, until cake is golden and a toothpick or cake tester inserted into the centre comes out clean, about 20 minutes.

Cool completely.

In a small bowl, combine ricotta cheese, aerosol cream, remaining 2tsp sugar substitute and remaining 1.25ml (¼tsp) vanilla essence. Cut cake in half vertically down the middle to make two 10 x 20cm (4 x 8in) pieces. Place the halves on a flat work surface. Drizzle 30ml (2tbsp) of the espresso onto each half. Spread half of the ricotta mixture onto one of the halves and dust with half of the cocoa powder. Top with remaining cake half; spread the top with remaining ricotta mixture and dust with remaining cocoa powder. Using a serrated knife, gently cut cake crossways into 4 slices and serve with mint leaves to garnish, if desired.

Makes 4 servings

Nutrition at a Glance

Per serving: 130 calories, 2.5g fat, 1.5g saturated fat, 10g protein, 13g carbohydrate, 0g fibre, 200mg sodium

Coffee Panna Cotta

Prep time: 20 minutes • Cook time: 10 minutes • Chill time: 4 hours or overnight

A traditional chilled Italian dessert, *panna cotta* literally means 'cooked cream'. Our version uses low-fat yogurt and skimmed milk 'cream' for a lighter take on the classic. If you like a stronger coffee flavour, use instant espresso powder in place of ordinary coffee powder.

225g (8oz)   low-fat natural yogurt
¾tsp   gelatine
120ml (4floz)   fat-free evaporated milk
3tbsp   granulated sugar substitute
1tsp   instant coffee powder
    few drops vanilla essence

Lightly coat 4 (180ml/6floz) ramekins with cooking spray.

Line a sieve with kitchen paper and set over a large bowl. Put yogurt into the sieve and set aside for 15 to 20 minutes, or until slightly thickened.

Meanwhile, in a small saucepan, sprinkle gelatine over the evaporated milk; let stand for 10 minutes. Bring to the gentle simmer over a medium-low heat and cook, whisking constantly, until gelatine dissolves. Add sugar substitute, coffee powder and vanilla essence; continue whisking until sugar dissolves. Remove from the heat.

Using a rubber spatula, scrape yogurt into a large bowl. Immediately add milk mixture and stir well to combine.

Divide mixture evenly among prepared ramekins. Cover and chill at least 4 hours or overnight. Serve chilled.

Makes 4 servings

Nutrition at a Glance

Per serving: 69 calories, 1g fat, 1g saturated fat, 6g protein, 9g carbohydrate, 0g fibre, 80mg sodium

This recipe can also be prepared for Phase 1 meals.

Creamy Dreamy Strawberry-Vanilla Shake

Prep time: 5 minutes

Frozen strawberries work like ice cubes to thicken and chill this irresistibly creamy shake. Since strawberries are available year–round, you can enjoy it anytime.

225g (8oz)	fat-free or low-fat yogurt
240ml (8floz)	skimmed milk
280g (10oz)	frozen strawberries
5ml (1tsp)	vanilla essence

In a blender, purée yogurt, milk, strawberries and vanilla until smooth. Serve cold.

Makes 4 servings

Nutrition at a Glance

Per serving: 90 calories, 1.5g fat, 1g saturated fat, 6g protein, 14g carbohydrate, 1g fibre, 75mg sodium

Variation: Use any berry and flavour essence combination you prefer.

Dr Agatston Answers Your Questions about Phase 2

Here are the answers to some of the questions our nutritionists and I are most often asked by dieters on Phase 2.

Can I still eat as much protein now that I'm eating more carbohydrates on Phase 2?

I don't know how much lean protein you were eating on Phase 1, but I'm sure it was enough to keep you healthy and satisfied. As you know, on the South Beach Diet, we don't expect you to count grams of protein or weigh your food on any phase.

Now that you're gradually adding satisfying high-fibre whole grains and fruits to your diet on Phase 2, you'll naturally be less hungry and the amount of lean protein you require to feel full will no doubt be less than you were eating on Phase 1. That said, I encourage you to eat some protein – fish or shellfish, lean beef or pork, white meat chicken or turkey or soya protein, for example – along with these good carbs at most meals.

Protein helps slow down the digestion of carbohydrates, which means that your body will make less insulin, your sugar swings will be reduced and you won't crave more food in between meals.

I also urge you to eat slowly, savour your food and really enjoy the variety of foods you'll introduce on Phase 2. If you do this, your focus will no longer be on how much protein you can have because you'll never be hungry. Another tip: Once you're satisfied, push your chair away from the table. It's fine to leave some food on your plate at the end of a meal.

As soon as I started Phase 2, I regained some weight. Could I be doing something wrong?

Most people move easily from Phase 1 to Phase 2 and continue losing weight (though not as quickly as they did on Phase 1) even when they add good carbs back into their diets. But other people, like you, have trouble. There are several possible reasons why you are putting on weight.

You're eating too many additional carbohydrates too soon. You may be overdoing the new carbohydrates and inadvertently triggering cravings that cause you to overeat. Please review pages 236–240 for advice on how to gradually add more good carbs back into your diet.

You're in a food rut. Sometimes dieters get into the habit of eating the same thing day after day, which can lead to overeating out of boredom. Vary your diet daily and you'll likely start losing weight again. The Phase 2 Meal Plans on pages 244–257 give you plenty of ideas for varied breakfasts, lunches, dinners and even delicious desserts.

You're not savouring every bite. It takes about 20 minutes for your belly to send a message to your brain that you're full and have had enough to eat. If you're eating too fast, you aren't allowing time for this natural feedback mechanism to kick in. You keep eating, thinking you're hungry, when you're actually about to be full. My advice: start with a big bowl of bouillon, stock or vegetable soup, then slow down. Enjoy every bite of your meal. Sip a glass of wine, if you like. Relax after dinner as well with a cup of tea or coffee. Make dining a pleasant, calming experience. You'll notice that you're eating less and enjoying it more.

You're not active enough. I can't emphasize enough the importance of doing regular exercise to keep your metabolism in high gear. The people who run into problems on Phase 2 and ultimately have trouble maintaining their weight loss are often the ones who are the most sedentary. I urge you to take a look at our Supercharged Fitness Programme beginning on page 83. Even if you haven't exercised in a while, this programme will ease you into it. And just because you're on Phase 2 of the diet, you don't have to jump into Phase 2 exercises. Feel free to start with the Phase 1 Interval Walking programme and Total Body Workout to get yourself in shape, then move on to Phase 2 exercises when you're ready.

I lost weight steadily for the first few months on Phase 2, but now I've hit a plateau. I still have about 4.5kg (10lb) to go and am very frustrated. What can I do to start losing weight again?

Some people do extremely well on the diet for the first few months, but at some point during Phase 2, they plateau before reaching their goal. There may be several reasons for this and you need to figure out the cause of the problem before you can solve it.

You've strayed. You need to do some soul-searching. Are you still adhering closely enough to the principles of the diet? After some people have been on the diet for a while, they start taking their success for granted. They get careless and begin eating too many sugary or starchy foods and bad fats. We don't expect you to be perfect, but if you want to continue to lose weight and keep it off permanently, you do have to follow the principles of the diet most of the time.

So give yourself a refresher course. Read over the lists of Foods to Enjoy and Foods to Avoid for Phase 1 and study those you can and can't re-introduce on Phase 2. Review our suggested Meal Plans, which will show you how to put combinations of foods together in appealing ways. Sometimes it's hard to admit it, but if you're starting to indulge in too many of the Foods to Avoid too often, you know you will not continue to get the same good results you had in the past. Try to keep track of what you eat. Some people find that keeping a journal of everything they put into their mouths each day helps them avoid that mindless second handful of nuts or extra nibble of cheese the next time they're tempted.

You're exercising less. Remember, the best way to recharge your weight loss is to get more exercise. When people first embark on a fitness programme, they are wildly enthusiastic and rarely miss a workout. They're scrupulous about fitting exercise into their lives and they schedule their days accordingly. As time passes, the thrill may wear off. Even people who enjoy working out can get lax and start missing sessions. If you've cut back on exercise or stopped working out altogether, yet you're carefully following the diet principles, then your plateau is likely due to the change in your exercise routine. If you want to jump-start your weight loss, you should resume your regular exercise routine and increase the intensity of your workout. Take another look at the Interval Walking programme presented in Part II – it can be your best friend. That's because it's the best way to keep your metabolism in fat- and calorie-burning mode all the time.

You've reached a healthy weight. It's entirely possible that your weight loss has stalled because you've already reached a healthy weight. If your cholesterol and blood sugar levels have normalized and you aren't experiencing cravings, your desire to lose that extra 4.5kg (10lb) may be more a matter of cosmetics than health (see page 33 for more on this). Now is the time for employing more effective exercise rather than restricting calories, which can lead to yo-yo dieting and further weight gain (see 'How Yo-Yo Dieting Affects Your Metabolism', page 41). Instead of zeroing in on the number on your scales, rev up your exercise routine and try to focus on how much better you really look and feel.

I find that when I step on the scales too often, the fluctuations drive me crazy. What's the best way to keep track of my weight?

In the course of a day, your weight may go up and down a few pounds depending on how much you've had to eat or to drink or how much fluid you're retaining (water weight). These hour-to-hour fluctuations can cause anxiety and they are meaningless. Ignore them. The best way to keep track of your progress is to weigh yourself once a week at the same time on the same scale. For most people, first thing in the morning works best.

Is the South Beach Diet safe for children?

I don't recommend that children go on a weight loss diet, except in special situations. In general, if children make healthy food choices most of the time and get a reasonable amount of physical activity, their weight will take care of itself. There's no question that children require ample calories and nutrients to develop properly, but they shouldn't be eating empty calories. What I do recommend is that children, along with their parents, follow the *principles* of the South Beach Diet. As early as possible, children should be introduced to an eating style that emphasizes good carbohydrates (fruits and vegetables), good fats, lean protein, low-fat dairy and high-fibre foods. And, of course, children – like adults – should enjoy an occasional treat. This is a healthy way to eat for life and it is not only safe for children, but will keep them from developing prediabetes, diabetes and so many other ailments we're seeing in epidemic proportions in younger and younger people.

I have problems with gluten. Phase 1 is fine for me because grains are not allowed, but what about Phase 2?

Gluten is a protein found in wheat, barley and rye. A small percentage of the UK population has gluten sensitivity, also known as coeliac disease. When these people eat foods containing gluten, they may experience symptoms ranging from abdominal pain and bloating to unexplained weight loss and neurological problems in severe cases. Gluten sensitivity is caused by elevated levels of antibodies that work against a component of gluten called gliadin. When the antigliadin antibody comes into contact with gluten, it causes an inflammatory response in the body.

Coeliac disease can be diagnosed with a blood test or a biopsy of the small intestine. Anecdotal evidence also suggests that it's possible to get a negative test result for coeliac disease and still have some, if not all, of the symptoms of gluten sensitivity. Interestingly, I've heard numerous stories from people who never realized that they were sensitive to gluten until they began Phase 1 and then found out how much better they felt when they weren't eating grains containing gluten. Many doctors – myself included – believe there may be subtle forms of gluten sensitivity that are often undetected by these diagnostic tests. The real test is how you feel after you eliminate gluten from your diet.

Even if you can't eat foods containing gluten, you can easily follow all the phases of the South Beach Diet. You do have to be careful about choosing the right carbohydrates, but you'd have to do that no matter what diet you were on. Fortunately, many gluten-free products sold today at supermarkets and health-food shops are compatible with the South Beach Diet. For example, you can buy bread, cereal and even pasta made from brown rice flour that taste pretty good and contain a decent amount of fibre. You can also eat brown rice and sweet potatoes, or substitute pasta with julienned courgettes (zucchini). The crustless Vegetable Quiche Cups (page 189) that we recommend on Phase 1 are perfect for you on any phase. Eating lean protein and good fats is also vital, no matter what else you're eating.

But beware – there are also gluten-free versions of processed carbs, so be vigilant about reading labels. Steer clear of products that are high in sugar and low in fibre. Gluten is sometimes used as an additive in foods where you'd least expect it, such as in some brands of vegetable burgers. So if you have a gluten problem, you need to be extra careful about checking all food products before buying.

PHASE 3

Enjoying the South Beach Diet for Life

Congratulations! You have achieved a healthy weight and are now ready to graduate to the maintenance phase of the diet. You can stay on Phase 3 for the rest of your life because at this point it's not a diet, it's a lifestyle. Even if you've never had any extra weight to lose, you'll find that adopting our healthy eating principles is a great way to improve your overall health and well-being.

For those of you who have been on the diet and achieved your weight loss goals, making good food choices is now second nature. The basic principles you learned on Phases 1 and 2 are now ingrained. You will automatically head for the vegetable aisle in the supermarket, readily select wholemeal bread for your sandwich, choose fish and shellfish and lean cuts of meat and poultry and read food labels to check for saturated fats and trans fats as a matter of course.

That's why we haven't included Sample Meal Plans or recipes for Phase 3 in this book. We know from 5 years of talking with our dieters that by now, you are more than capable of putting healthy meals together on your own. That said, we encourage you to use the Sample Meal Plans and all the recipes from Phases 1 and 2 whenever you want and, of course, feel free to refer to the food lists whenever you need a refresher.

Our ultimate goal with the South Beach Diet has always been to show you how to make good food choices for yourself (and your family) most of the time, so you can enjoy a few bites of even the most decadent dessert on occasion and still maintain your weight.

Now that you have reached Phase 3, you will be introducing some new foods, specifically those that you were advised to avoid on Phase 2. This shouldn't present problems. By now you are able to monitor your body's response to particular foods, you know what triggers your cravings and you automatically make the right choices for you. If, given this new freedom, you find that you can't just eat one piece of French bread without practically inhaling the whole loaf or that you can't eat a scoop of ice cream without devouring the entire carton, it's a sign that you should probably avoid these foods altogether, at least for a while.

But the best news of all is that now that you've reached Phase 3, no food is off-limits unless you say it is. The challenge with Phase 3 is learning how to incorporate those occasional sinful treats into your diet without regaining weight. It's also essential that you continue to follow a fitness programme – ideally, one incorporating interval training and core-strengthening exercises. This is the best way to maintain both your weight and your health.

Dr Agatston Answers Your Questions about Phase 3

Here are the answers to some of the questions our nutritionists and I are often asked by dieters who are on Phase 3.

I've been on Phase 3 for 2 months and have started to gain some weight back. What should I do?

The question is, why are you gaining weight? There are two possible reasons: You're no longer adhering to the principles of the diet, or you're not getting enough exercise – or both.

First, let's examine what you're eating. Are you indulging in too many foods that should be eaten only on special occasions? If so, you need to understand that if you revert to your old eating habits, you most certainly will gain weight. If you have put on 4.5kg (10lb) or more, or have started to have food cravings (which I suspect may be causing your problem), you may need to return to Phase 1 for several days until your cravings subside. If your weight gain is minimal and you don't have cravings, simply return to the Phase 2 eating plan that worked for you before. The beauty of the South Beach Diet is that it's flexible enough to accommodate the normal changes of daily life.

Second, I can't overstate the importance of getting enough exercise. Some people believe that once they have achieved their goal weight, they can stop exercising. Nothing could be further from the truth. Exercise is essential to maintaining your weight loss over the long term, especially when you've progressed to a lifestyle that includes those occasional treats. The exciting thing about our fitness programme is that it will keep your metabolism revved up so you can burn more fat and calories. And burning more calories means that you can have that occasional treat without regaining the weight. It's important to integrate your exercise programme seamlessly into your lifestyle, as you have done with the diet. Try to make it a habit, exercising at the same time in the same place every day, or at least on most days of the week.

My food cravings have returned on Phase 3. It's torture for me to eat just one biscuit. I haven't put on any weight, but I'm very worried that I will. What should I do?

The best part about Phase 3 is that no food is forbidden, which means you are allowed to eat virtually anything and that includes the occasional biscuit or a few chips or crisps. (*Occasional* is the operative word.) Phase 3 is a time of experimentation when you'll want to try different foods (ideally, healthy ones) and see which work for you and which don't. If you're unable to include certain sugars or starchy foods without triggering cravings, there's only one solution: don't eat them. Why put yourself through torture? There are plenty of foods you can eat that won't give you trouble. You can also replace those sugary biscuits and fatty chips with healthier options: Try a couple of our famous Peanut Butter and Jam Cookies (page 285) or Baked Sweet Potato Chips (page 283).

Of course there will be those times when you do give in to a craving. When this happens, do have a couple of biscuits or chips, but at the same time think about how much better you will feel if you don't have too many. Or, if a little ice cream will satisfy your desire for a special sweet,

living THE SOUTH BEACH DIET

Jocelyn J., aged 57: We've Changed Our Lives for the Better

I was diagnosed with breast cancer in 2000 and underwent a double mastectomy and a course of chemotherapy. It was very, very rough. After my treatments were over, I was put on tamoxifen to prevent a recurrence of the cancer, and like a lot of women, I started to gain weight because of the medication. Much to my dismay, the weight really started piling on. I had always been slim and suddenly, overnight, I was fat. I zoomed through clothing sizes at record speed. Soon I weighed 80kg (175lb), a lot for my 1.68m (5'6") frame. Needless to say, I was not happy with my situation. Not only had I gone through an ordeal with my treatments, I now had to deal with this new, larger body. I tried cutting back on my food intake, but it didn't help.

I thought I could never get my old body back and resigned myself to being unhappy about my weight. At the time, my husband, who weighed 104kg (228lb), was told by his cardiologist that his cholesterol was bad and he had to lose weight. The doctor recommended that he follow the South Beach Diet. Since I wanted to lose weight, too, we decided to try it together. I wasn't very hopeful, but I felt I had nothing to lose.

I bought the South Beach Diet cookbooks and was intrigued by what I read. Since I had always been thin, I had no idea what triggered obesity. I learned a great deal about how to eat and put meals together. I'm a gourmet cook and I love good food. I got very excited when I started to read the recipes. They were great! My husband, who normally dislikes fish, even enjoyed one of the fish recipes I made.

Over the next few months, my husband lost 12.7kg (28lb) and is now steady at around 90.5kg (199lb). He's always telling me how much better he feels now that he is lighter. His cardiologist is also thrilled. And I'm proud that I lost 16kg (35lb) and have kept the weight off.

The South Beach Diet definitely changed our lives for the better. We are now conscious of what we're putting into our mouths. Occasionally we eat things that we shouldn't, but we haven't regained the weight. I gave away all my fat clothes and swore that I would never get to that point again. Whenever I feel my weight is creeping up, I go back to Phase 2.

We are firm believers in the South Beach Diet and sing its praises whenever we meet someone who is struggling with weight and wondering what diet to go on.

have a few bites. You may find you have more control after a small indulgence. And on those occasions when you just don't stop, let it go and return to making healthier eating choices as soon as possible. You should never feel that you're on or off the South Beach Diet. Eating everything today because tomorrow you know you can't creates an all-or-nothing mentality that's detrimental to making the diet a successful lifestyle.

Do I still need to eat snacks during Phase 3?

It depends on what else you're eating throughout the day. If you're eating three good meals daily and don't get hungry in between, you may not even need healthy snacks. Keep in mind that the purpose of snacking is to prevent drops in blood sugar that cause cravings and leave you feeling famished. On Phases 1 and 2, snacks were particularly important to help wean you off highly processed refined starches and sugar-laden foods and help you adjust to this new style of eating. But now that you're on Phase 3, you're no longer eating the foods that caused your cravings and this makes snacks less critical.

Interestingly, I've had a number of Phase 3 dieters tell me that they prefer to graze or eat smaller meals throughout the day, rather than three larger ones. There's actually an advantage to eating less at a time but more often and it's due to what's called thermogenesis, which is the measure of the amount of calories burned as part of digesting a meal. Not surprisingly, you burn more calories when you digest bigger meals – but, as it turns out, not by that much. Therefore, if you eat the same amount of healthy foods daily, but divide it amongst five smaller meals instead of three larger ones, for example, you'll burn more total calories each day, thanks to engaging your digestive system more often.

Whether you snack, don't snack or graze, do keep in mind that there are times when a strategic snack can be really useful. For example, if you know dinner is going to be late or you're heading to a cocktail party where there will be lots of temptations, have a snack to stave off hunger. If you let yourself become famished, you'll invariably overeat.

The bottom line: By Phase 3, the South Beach Diet becomes a lifestyle that readily adjusts to *your* lifestyle. Only you will know what's best for you in terms of maintaining your new and healthy weight. And now you're free to make those choices.

Should I be taking nutritional supplements?

I recommend taking very few supplements. The reason? We have not yet learned to extract vitamins from foods so that they work as well in supplement form as they do when you eat the foods themselves.

I strongly believe that you should get the nutrients you need from eating a wholefoods diet. This means enjoying a wide variety of fruits and vegetables because they contain thousands of phytonutrients that are critical to good health (see Chapter 7, 'Supercharged Foods for Better Health'). So far the research that has been performed on specific supplements – notably, antioxidants – has been disappointing. To date there is no pill, including multivitamins, that works like a good diet based on healthy foods.

That said, I do recommend that you take an omega-3 fatty acid (fish oil) supplement because it's difficult to get enough omega-3 from foods. I take a fish oil supplement myself and I strongly recommend it to all my patients. The active ingredients in omega-3 are docosahexaenoic acid (DHA) and eicosapentaenoic acid (EPA) and both are listed on the label. A total of between 1,000 and 2,000mg of DHA and EPA a day is recommended. Taking a supplement of the mineral calcium, which many people fail to get enough of from foods, can be helpful for women at risk for osteoporosis.

Can I really eat anything I want on Phase 3?

If you're talking about dessert as an occasional treat, of course. On Phase 3, we don't regulate what you can eat. Yes, you can finally have that small bowl of ice cream or a small piece of chocolate cake, or the white bagel that you couldn't have before. But you shouldn't do it too often and you should continue to watch amounts on desserts. Phase 3 isn't about abandoning the good principles of the diet and suddenly resuming your old eating habits. It's about continuing to make smart, healthy food choices – for life. If you follow the principles of the diet most of the time, we expect you to enjoy anything you want now and then.

living THE SOUTH BEACH DIET

Wendy N., aged 30: It's Simply My New Way of Living

Two years ago, I weighed 168kg (370lb). I'm 1.78m (5'10"), so I'm tall, but even so, I was extremely overweight. I was already on blood pressure medications, and my doctor had been telling me for years that I might develop diabetes if I didn't take off some weight. My mother is diabetic, but I was young and thought I was invincible. In October 2006, my doctor told me I was officially prediabetic. I saw how my mother had struggled with her diabetes, and my immediate thought was, *I'm going to run as fast as I can in the other direction!*

I didn't know where to begin, though, so my doctor recommended that I try the South Beach Diet. I bought the book and the first thing I did was thumb through the recipes. I got scared because I'm not a great cook. But then my doctor told me not to worry so much about the recipes but just read about the principles of the South Beach Diet. That's when it all clicked. I realized that it was easy. I could do this. I saw that I could still eat the same foods I'd been eating, but I'd have to prepare them differently. Once I understood what the diet was about, the recipes didn't seem too complicated. In fact, they were pretty easy.

My first 2 weeks on the diet, I lost 6.8kg (15lb) and I didn't even exercise – I just ate the right foods. I realized that if I started to exercise, I could lose a lot more. I began slowly, exercising just a few days a week. Now I'm working out 6 days a week. Healthy eating and exercise have become a permanent part of my lifestyle. Over the past 12 months on the diet, I have lost 56.8kg (125lb). My co-workers ask me what my secret is and I steer them to the South Beach Diet. In fact, two of them have adopted this lifestyle, too and we exchange tips and keep each other motivated. Of course, I have days when I slip up, but I keep remembering what Dr Agatston says about acknowledging that you've messed up and getting quickly back on track.

During a recent visit to the doctor, I learned that I am no longer prediabetic, and I no longer need medications for my high blood pressure. The South Beach Diet has completely changed my life. Everything is a challenge in the beginning, but when you stick with something long enough, you discover that it becomes easier. The South Beach Diet has been so easy to incorporate into my lifestyle that most of the time I don't even think that I'm on a diet. It's simply my new way of living.

REFERENCES

CHAPTER 1
Changing the Way We Live

Centers for Disease Control and Prevention (CDC). *Behavioral Risk Factor Surveillance System Survey Data*. Atlanta: US Department of Health and Human Services, Centers for Disease Control and Prevention, 2005.

Kivipelto M, Ngandu T, et al. Obesity and vascular risk factors at midlife and the risk of dementia and Alzheimer disease. *Arch Neurol* 2005 Oct;62(10):1556–1560.

Manson JE, Skerrett PJ, et al. The escalating pandemics of obesity and sedentary lifestyle: A call to action for clinicians. *Arch Intern Med* 2004;164(3):249–258.

Ogden CL, Carroll MD, et al. Prevalence of overweight and obesity in the United States, 1999–2004. *JAMA* 2006;295(13):1549–1555.

The President's Council on Physical Fitness and Sports, Department of Health and Human Services. www.fitness.gov/resources__factsheet.htm.

CHAPTER 2
The Basics of the South Beach Diet

Associated Press. "Fainting Dieters Delay New York City Subways." msnbc.com, January 30, 2007.

Brown L, Rosner B, et al. Cholesterol-lowering effects of dietary fiber: A meta-analysis. *Am J Clin Nutr* 1999;69(1):30–42.

Chavarro JE, Rich-Edwards JW, et al. Dietary fatty acid intakes and the risk of ovulatory infertility. *Am J Clin Nutr* 2007;85(1):231–237.

Das S, Powell SR, et al. Cardioprotection with palm tocotrienol: Antioxidant activity of tocotrienol is linked with its ability to stabilize proteasomes. *Am J Physiol Heart Circ Physiol* 2005;289(1):H361–367.

Fuchs CS, Giovannucci EL, et al. Dietary fiber and the risk of colorectal cancer and adenoma in women. *N Engl J Med* 1999;340(3):169–176.

Fung TT, Hu FB, et al. Whole-grain intake and the risk of type 2 diabetes: A prospective study in men. *Am J Clin Nutr* 2002;76(3):535–540.

Ludwig DS. Glycemic load comes of age. *J Nutr* 2003;133(9):2695–2696.

Meyer KA, Kushi LH, et al. Carbohydrates, dietary fiber, and incident type 2 diabetes in older women. *Am J Clin Nutr* 2000;71(4):921–930.

Rimm EB, Ascherio A, et al. Vegetable, fruit, and cereal fiber intake and risk of coronary heart disease among men. *JAMA* 1996;275(6):447–451.

Story JA, Kritchevsky D. Denis Parsons Burkitt (1911–1993). *J Nutr* 1994;124:1551–1554.

CHAPTER 3
A Diet You Can Live With . . . For Life

Aravanis C, Corcondilas A, et al. Coronary heart disease in seven countries. IX. The Greek islands of Crete and Corfu. *Circulation* 1970;41(4 Suppl):I88–I100.

Aude YW, Agatston AS. The National Cholesterol Education Program diet vs a diet lower in carbohydrates and higher in protein and monounsaturated fat: A randomized trial. *Arch Intern Med* 2004;164(19):2141–2146.

Beresford SA, Johnson KC, et al. Low-fat dietary pattern and risk of colorectal cancer: The Women's Health Initiative Randomized Controlled Dietary Modification Trial. *JAMA* 2006;295(6):643–654.

Ebbeling CB, Leidig MM, et al. Effects of a low-glycemic load vs low-fat diet in obese young adults: A randomized trial. *JAMA* 2007;297(19):2092–2102.

Estruch R, Martinez-González MA, et al. Effects of a Mediterranean-style diet on cardiovascular risk factors: A randomized trial. *Ann Intern Med* 2006;145(1):1–11.

Howard BV, Van Horn L, et al. Low-fat dietary pattern and risk of cardiovascular disease: The Women's Health Initiative Randomized Controlled Dietary Modification Trial. *JAMA* 2006;295(6):655–666.

Low-Fat Dietary Pattern and Risk of Breast Cancer, Colorectal Cancer, and Cardiovascular Disease: The Women's Health Initiative (WHI) Randomized Controlled Dietary Modification Trial. http://www.whi.org/findings/dm/dm.php.

Ludwig D, Pereira MA, et al. Dietary fiber, weight gain, and cardiovascular disease risk factors in young adults. *JAMA* 1999;282(16):1539–1546.

Pi-Sunyer FX. Glycemic index and disease. *Am J Clin Nutr* 2002;76(1):290S–298S.

Prentice RL, Caan B, et al. Low-fat dietary pattern and risk of invasive breast cancer: The Women's Health Initiative Randomized Controlled Dietary Modification Trial. *JAMA* 2006;295(6):629–642.

Reaven GM. Banting lecture 1988. Role of insulin resistance in human disease. *Diabetes* 1988;37(12):1595–1607.

Thomas DE, Elliott EJ, et al. Low glycaemic index or low glycaemic load diets for overweight and obesity. *Cochrane Database Syst Rev.* 2007;Jul 18(3):CD005105.

CHAPTER 4
Supercharge Your Metabolism

Bacon CG, Mittleman MA. Sexual function in men older than 50 years of age: Results from the health professionals follow-up study. *Ann Intern Med* 2003;139(3):161–168.

Barrett LA, Morris JG, et al. Effects of intermittent games activity on postprandial lipemia in young adults. *Med Sci Sports Exerc* 2006;38(7):1282–1287.

Billat LV. Interval training for performance: A scientific and empirical practice. Special recommendations for middle- and long-distance running. Part I: Aerobic interval training. *Sports Med* 2001;31(1):13–31.

Billat LV. Interval training for performance: A scientific and empirical practice. Part II: Anaerobic interval training. *Sports Med* 2001;31(12):75–90.

Børsheim E, Bahr R. Effect of exercise intensity, duration and mode on post-exercise oxygen consumption. *Sports Med* 2003;33(14):1037–1060.

Boupland CA, Cliffe SJ, et al. Habitual physical activity and bone mineral density in postmenopausal women in England. *Int J Epidemiol* 1999;28(2):241–246.

Colcombe SJ, Erickson KI, et al. Aerobic exercise training increases brain volume in aging humans. *J Geron A Biol Sci Med Sci* 2006;61(11):1166–1170.

de Groot PC, Hjeltnes N, et al. Effect of training intensity on physical capacity, lipid profile and insulin sensitivity in early rehabilitation of spinal cord injured individuals. *Spinal Cord* 2003;41(12):673–679.

Franco OH, de Laet C, et al. Effects of physical activity on life expectancy with cardiovascular disease. *Arch Intern Med* 2005;165(20):2355–2630.

Frey GC, Byrnes WC, et al. Factors influencing excess postexercise oxygen consumption in trained and untrained women. *Metabolism* 1993;42(7):822–828.

Gibala MJ, Little JP, et al. Short-term sprint interval versus traditional endurance training: Similar initial adaptations in human skeletal muscle and exercise performance. *J Physiol* 2006;575(3):901–911.

Kang J, Robertson RJ, et al. Effect of exercise intensity on glucose and insulin metabolism in obese individuals and obese NIDDM patients. *Diabetes Care* 1996;19(4):341–349.

LaForgia J, Withers RT, et al. Effects of exercise intensity and duration on the excess post-exercise oxygen consumption. *J Sports Sci* 2006;24(12):1247–1264.

McGarvey W, Jones R, et al. Excess post-exercise oxygen consumption following continuous and interval cycling exercise. *Int J Sport Nutr Exerc Metab* 2005;15(1):28–37.

Meston CM, Gorzalka, BB. The effects of sympathetic activation via acute exercise on physiological and subjective sexual arousal in women. *Behav Res Ther* 1995;33:651–664.

Miller AD, Ruby BC, et al. Effects of high intensity/low volume and low intensity/high volume isokinetic resistance exercise on postexercise glucose tolerance. *J Strength Cond Res* 2007;21(2):330–335.

Penhollow TM, Young M. Sexual desirability and sexual performance: Does exercise and fitness really matter? *Elec J Human Sexuality* (Oct 5, 2004).

Puetz TW, O'Connor PJ, et al. Effects of chronic exercise on feelings of energy and fatigue: A quantitative synthesis. *Psychol Bull* 2006;132(6):866–876.

Rozeneck R, Funato K, et al. Physiological responses to interval training sessions at velocities associated with VO$_2$max. *J Strength Cond Res* 2007;21(1):188–192.

Sedlock DA, Fissinger JA, et al. Effect of exercise intensity and duration on postexercise energy expenditure. *Med Sci Sports Exerc* 1989;21(6):662–666.

Smith EL, Gilligan C. Physical activity effects on bone metabolism. *Calcif Tissue Int* 1991;49 Suppl:S50–S54.

Talanian JL, Galloway SD, et al. Two weeks of high-intensity aerobic interval training increases the capacity for fat oxidation during exercise in women. *J Appl Physiol* 2007;102(4):1439–1447.

Thornton MK, Pottciger JA. Effects of resistance exercise bouts of different intensities but equal work on EPOC. *Med Sci Sports Exerc* 2002;34(4):715–722.

Treuth MS, Hunter GR, et al. Effects of exercise intensity on 24-h energy expenditure and substrate oxidation. *Med Sci Sports Exerc* 1996;28(9):1138–1143.

CHAPTER 5
Boomeritis: The New Epidemic!

Bliss LS, Teeple P. Core stability: The centerpiece of any training program. *Curr Sports Med Rep* 2005;4(3):179–183.

Chard MD, Cawston TE, et al. Rotator cuff degeneration and lateral epicondylitis: A comparative histological study. *Ann Rheum Dis* 1994 Jan;53(1):30–34.

Chen AL, Mears SC, et al. Orthopaedic care of the aging athlete. *J Am Acad Orthop Surg* 2005;13(6):407–416.

Felson DT. Weight and osteoarthritis. *J Rheumatol Suppl* 1995 Feb;43:7–9.

Friedland RP, Fritsch T, et al. Patients with Alzheimer's disease have reduced activities in midlife compared with healthy control-group members. *Proc Natl Acad Sci USA* 2001;98(6):3440–3445.

Haskell WL. Physical activity, sport, and health: Toward the next century. *Res Q Exerc Sport* 1996;67(3 Suppl):S37–S47.

Kurtz S, Ong K, et al. Projections of primary and revision hip and knee arthroplasty in the United States from 2005 to 2030. *J Bone Joint Surg* Am 2007;89(4):780–785.

Lanningham-Foster L, Nysse LJ, et al. Labor saved, calories lost: The energetic impact of domestic labor-saving devices. *Obes Res* 2003;11(10):1178–1181.

Levine JA, Lanningham-Foster LM, et al. Interindividual variation in posture allocation: Possible role in human obesity. *Science* 2005;307(5709):584–586.

Messier SP, Gutekunst DJ, et al. Weight loss reduces knee-joint loads in overweight and obese older adults with knee osteoarthritis. *Arthritis Rheum* 2005;52(7):2026–2032.

Pennington, B. Baby boomers stay active, and so do their doctors. *New York Times* 2006 April 16.

Thompson WG, Cook DA, et al. Treatment of obesity. *Mayo Clin Proc.* 2007;82(1):93–102.

Willardson JM. Core stability training: Applications to sports conditioning programs. *J Strength Cond Res* 2007;21(3):979–985.

Wilson JD, Dougherty CP, et al. Core stability and its relationship to lower extremity function and injury. *J Am Acad Orthop Surg* 2005;13(5):316–325.

CHAPTER 6
Bye-Bye Belly Fat

Banks J, Marmot M, et al. Disease and disadvantage in the United States and in England. *JAMA* 2006;295(17):2037–2045.

Cruz ML, Bergman RN, et al. Unique effect of visceral fat on insulin sensitivity in obese Hispanic children with a family history of type 2 diabetes. *Diabetes Care* 2002;25(9):1631–1636.

Dériaz O, Tremblay A, et al. Non linear weight gain with long term overfeeding in man. *Obes Res* 1993;1(3):179–185.

Fontana L, Eagon JC, et al. Visceral fat adipokine secretion is associated with systemic inflammation in obese humans. *Diabetes* 2007;56(4):1010–1013.

Ford ES, Capewell S. Coronary heart disease mortality among young adults in the US from 1980 through 2002: Concealed leveling of mortality rates. *J Am Coll Cardiol* 2007;50(22):2128–2132.

Fox CS, Pencina MJ, et al. Trends in the incidence of type 2 diabetes mellitus from the 1970s to the 1990s: The Framingham Heart Study. *Circulation* 2006;113(25):2914–2918.

Giannopoulou I, Ploutz-Snyder LL, et al. Exercise is required for visceral fat loss in postmenopausal women with type 2 diabetes. *J Clin Endocrinol Metab* 2005;90(3):1511–1518.

Hong Y, Rice T, et al. Familial clustering of insulin and abdominal visceral fat: The HERITAGE Family Study. *J Clin Endocrinol Metab* 1998;83(12):4239–4245.

Irwin ML, Yasui Y, et al. Effect of exercise on total and intra-abdominal body fat in postmenopausal women. *JAMA* 2003;289(3):323–330.

Jensen MD. Is visceral fat involved in the pathogenesis of the metabolic syndrome? Human model. *Obesity* (Silver Spring) 2006; 14 Suppl 1:20S-24S.

Katcher HI, Legro RS, et al. The effects of a whole grain–enriched hypocaloric diet on cardiovascular disease risk factors in men and women with metabolic syndrome. *Am J Clin Nutr* 2008;87(1):79–90.

Neel JV. Diabetes mellitus: A "thrifty" genotype rendered detrimental by "progress"? *Am J Hum Genet* 1962;14(4):353–362.

Okura T, Tanaka K, et al. Effects of aerobic exercise and obesity phenotype on abdominal fat reduction in response to weight loss. *Int J Obes (Lond)* 2005;29(10):1259–1266.

Park SK, Park JH, et al. The effect of combined aerobic and resistance exercise training on abdominal fat in obese middle-aged women. *J Physiol Anthropol Appl Human Sci* 2003;22(3):129–135.

Seddon JM, Gensler G, et al. Association between C-reactive protein and age-related macular degeneration. *JAMA* 2004;291(6):704–710.

Slentz CA, Aiken LB, et al. Inactivity, exercise and visceral fat. STRRIDE: A randomized, controlled study of exercise intensity and amount. *J Appl Physiol* 2005;99(4):1613–1618.

You T, Murphy KM, et al. Addition of aerobic exercise to dietary weight loss preferentially reduces abdominal adipocyte size. *Int J Obes (Lond)* 2006 Aug;30(8):1211–1216.

Yusuf S, Hawken S, et al. Obesity and the risk of myocardial infarction in 27,000 participants from 52 countries: A case-control study. *Lancet* 2005;366:1640–1649.

CHAPTER 7
Supercharged Foods for Better Health

Aviram M, Rosenblat M, et al. Pomegranate juice consumption for 3 years by patients with carotid artery stenosis reduces common carotid intima-media thickness, blood pressure and LDL oxidation. *Clin Nutr* 2004;23(3):423–433.

Casagrande SS, Wang Y, et al. Have Americans increased their fruit and vegetable intake? The trends between 1988 and 2002. *Am J Prev Med* 2007;32(4):354–355.

Chong EW, Wong TY, et al. Dietary antioxidants and primary prevention of age related macular degeneration: Systematic review and meta-analysis. *BMJ* 2007;335(7623):755.

Christen WG, Liu S, et al. Dietary carotenoids, vitamins C and E, and risk of cataract in women: A prospective study. *Arch Ophthalmol* 2008;126(1):102–109.

Church DF, Pryor WA. Free-radical chemistry of cigarette smoke and its toxicological implications. *Environ Health Perspect* Dec 1985;6:111–126.

Elwood PC, Pickering JE, et al. Milk and dairy consumption, diabetes and the metabolic syndrome: The Caerphilly Prospective Study. *J Epidemiol Community Health* 2007;61(8):695–698.

Forest CP, Padma-Nathan H, et al. Efficacy and safety of pomegranate juice on improvement of erectile dysfunction in male patients with mild to moderate erectile dysfunction: A randomized, placebo-controlled, double-blind crossover study. *Int J Impot Res* 2007;19(6):564–567.

Hu FB, Stampfer MJ. Nut consumption and risk of coronary heart disease: A review of epidemiological evidence. *Curr Atheroscler Rep* 1999;1(3):204–209.

Kesse-Guyot E, Bertrais S, et al. Dairy products, calcium and the risk of breast cancer: Results of the French SU.VI.MAX prospective study. *Ann Nutr Metab* 2007;51(2):139–145.

Lau FC, Shukitt-Hale B, et al. Nutritional intervention in brain aging: Reducing the effects of inflammation and oxidative stress. *Subcell Biochem* 2007;42:299–318.

Lin J, Manson JE, et al. Intakes of calcium and vitamin D and breast cancer risk in women. *Arch Intern Med* 2007;167(10):1050–1059.

Liu L, Zubik L, et al. The antiatherogenic potential of oat phenolic compounds. *Atherosclerosis* 2004;175(1):39–49.

Liu RH. Health benefits of fruit and vegetables are from additive and synergistic combinations of phytochemicals. *Am J Clin Nutr* 2003;78(3 Suppl):517S–520S.

McGuire SO, Sortwell CE, et al. Dietary supplementation with blueberry extract improves survival of transplanted dopamine neurons. *Nutr Neurosci* 2006;9(5–6):251–258.

McMichael AJ. Integrating nutrition with ecology: Balancing the health of humans and biosphere. *Public Health Nutr* 2005;8(6A):706–715.

Mellen PB, Liese AD, et al. Whole-grain intake and carotid artery atherosclerosis in a multiethnic cohort: The insulin resistance atherosclerosis study. *Am J Clin Nutr* 2007;85(6)1495–1502.

Nagao T, Hase T, et al. A green tea extract high in catechins reduces body fat and cardiovascular risks in humans. *Obesity* 2007;15(6):1473–1483.

Schulze MB, Schulz M, et al. Fiber and magnesium intake and the incidence of type 2 diabetes: A prospective study and meta-analysis. *Arch Intern Med* 2007;167(9):956–965.

Sumner MD, Elliot-Eller M, et al. Effects of pomegranate juice consumption on myocardial perfusion in patients with coronary heart disease. *Am J Cardiol* 2005;96(6):810–814.

Taubert D, Roesen R, et al. Effects of low habitual cocoa intake on blood pressure and bioactive nitric oxide: A randomized controlled trial. *JAMA* 2007;298(1):49–60.

van der Gaag MS, van Tol A, et al. Alcohol consumption stimulates early steps in reverse cholesterol transport. *J Lipid Res* 2001;42(12):2077–2083.

Walker AR. Are health and ill-health lessons from hunter-gatherers currently relevant? *Am J Clin Nutr* 2001;73(2):353–356.

Whelton SP, Hyre AD, et al. Effect of dietary fiber intake on blood pressure: A meta-analysis of randomized, controlled clinical trials. *J Hypertens* 2005;23(3):475–481.

Wu JM, Wang ZR, et al. Mechanism of cardioprotection by resveratrol, a phenolic antioxidant present in red wine (Review). *Int J Mol Med* 2001;8(1):3–17.

Zampelas A, Panagiotakos DB, et al. Fish consumption among healthy adults is associated with decreased levels of inflammatory markers related to cardiovascular disease: The ATTICA Study. *J Am Coll Cardiol* 2005;46(1):120–124.

Zhao H, Lin J, et al. Dietary isothiocyanates, GSTM1, GSTT1, NAT2 polymorphisms and bladder cancer risk. *Int J Cancer* 2007;120(10):2208–2213.

Zibaeenezhad MJ, Shamsnia SJ, et al. Walnut consumption in hyperlipidemic patients. *Angiology* 2005;56(5):581–583.

PART II

See references for Chapter 4.

PART III

Bazzano LA. The high cost of not consuming fruits and vegetables. *J Am Diet Assoc* 2006; 106(9):1364–1368.

Daviglus ML, Liu K, et al. Relationship of fruit and vegetable consumption in middle-aged men to Medicare expenditures in older age: The Chicago Western Electric Study. *J Am Diet Assoc* 2005 Nov;(11):1735–1744.

INDEX

Headings in *italic* indicate recipes.

A

ab circle exercise 126
abdominal fat *see* belly fat
acne 4, 63
aerobic activities (cardio) 43, 45, 66
aerobic metabolism 43
ageing
   injuries and 50
   muscle loss with 35
   premature 74
aioli dressing 214
alcohol 152, 153, 162
   see also wine
Almon, Marie 26
alternating leg kick 141
Alzheimer's disease 4, 14, 50, 74
   studies of mice with amyloid
      plaques 75–6
American Heart Association Step II
   Diet 27
anaerobic exercise 43–4
anaerobic metabolism 43
anthocyanins 75
antioxidants 12, 74, 75
arm reach exercises
double 137
single 122
arthritis 4, 50, 63, 74
   rheumatoid 81
artichoke 'tortilla', Spanish 188
asparagus and smoked turkey wrap 279
atherosclerosis 24, 60, 63, 77
ATP (adenosine triphosphate) 42–3,
   44, 46
attention deficit disorders 4, 82

B

baked goods 12, 21
   Phase 1 avoidance 152
Balance of Good Health plate model
   20–1
balsamic vinaigrette 214
barley risotto 282
beach kneel 127
beans
   black bean soup 192
   to enjoy in Phase 1 diet 166
   halibut with butter bean and vegetable
      ragout 274
   Provençal white bean soup 194
   red bean mash/cakes 218
   turkey meatloaf with mushrooms and
      white beans 200–1
   two-bean chilli con carne 281
beautiful biceps exercise 123
beef 165, 170, 241
   pan-seared fillet with creamy peppercorn
      sauce 277
   roast beef and horseradish roll-up 197
   sliced with green pepper, onion and
      mangetout 276
   South Beach Diet Shepherd's pie 208
   Tex-Mex steak wrap 279
Belding, Kris 47
belly fat 26–7, 40, 59–66, 70
   prediabetes and 23
bikini swirl 109
bladder cancer 76
blood sugar levels
   carbohydrates and 12–13, 22
   prediabetes and 23–4

exercise *continued*

    functional 55–6

    injuries from 51 *see also* boomeritis

    interval training 34–46

    as a lifestyle 144–6, 299

    prevention of injuries through
        52–8

    Total Body Workout *see* Total Body
        Workout

    see also specific exercises

exercise equipment 92–3, 95–6, 161

F

fab abs exercise 125

fast food 6–8, 61, 63–5

    tips on eating out 159

fat, visceral *see* belly fat

fat reduction 33–40, 44–6

    by NEAT (non-exercise activity
    thermogenesis) 57

    shrinking belly fat 66, 70 *see also*
    South Beach Diet

fatness *see* obesity

fats

    avoiding the bad fats 15–16, 78

    choosing the good fats 13–15,
        80–2

    Phase 1 limitations 153, 168

    see also polyunsaturated fats;
    saturated fats; unsaturated fats

fibre

    carbohydrates and 11–13

    in fruit and vegetables 73

    high fibre diets 17–18

    soluble and insoluble 12

    supplements 233–4

fish 81

    chowder 193

    grilled salmon with tomatoes, spinach
        and capers 203

    halibut with butter bean and vegetable
        ragout 274

    Mediterranean cod 202

    oil 80–1

pecan-crusted trout 204

fitness programme *see* Interval
    Walking Programme; South Beach
    fitness programme; Total Body
    Workout

flan, maple-almond 225

flour 152

free radicals 74

French cuisine 157

fruit

    anthocyanins in 75–6

    good carbohydrates in 73

    nutrients bred out of 5

    Phase 1 limitations 153, 170

    Phase 2

        increase 238–9

        limitations 241, 243

fruit juice 74–5

functional fitness 55–6

G

game meats 165

gazpacho, green 190

gluten 294–5

glycaemic index 12, 22

gout 60

grains

    refined 77–8

    whole *see* whole grains

Greek cuisine 157

Greek vegetable wrap 278

Greek yogurt 78

green goddess dressing 216

H

halibut with butter bean and vegetable
    ragout 274

Haskell, William L. 57

HDL (high-density lipoprotein) 15,
    23, 75

headaches 234

heart disease/attacks

lifestyle *continued*
    health and 3–8, 50, 54, 63–5
    sedentary 4–5, 50, 54, 56–7, 63–5
    South Beach Diet Phase 3 as a
        lifestyle 296–7
lime vinaigrette 216
lobster bisque 266
Ludwig, David S. 30
lutein 75
lycopene 75

M

macular degeneration 4, 75
magnesium 77
maple-almond flan 225
meat
    choosing lean protein 17
    Phase 1 avoidance 153
    see also specific meats
Mediterranean diet 30, 81
melon soup, chilled, with mint 265
metabolic rate 67
metabolic syndrome *see* prediabetes
metabolism 42–3, 44
    yo-yo dieting and 41
Mexican food 156
Middle Eastern food 157
milk 78
minerals 5, 73, 77, 233, 239, 302
mint vinaigrette 216
monounsaturated fats 14, 17, 80
monounsaturated oils 168
mood 82
moussaka, vegetable 210–11
mousse 242
    cocoa-nut 224
muffins, oat 261
muscle strengthening 35–7, 55–7
mushroom and leek soup, creamy 265

N

NEAT (non-exercise activity
    thermogenesis) 57–8

Niçoise wrap, spicy 279
noodles
    Asian chicken noodle soup 265
    chicken stir fry with soba noodles 271
    turkey noodle soup 267
nutrients
    good carbohydrates 11–13, 73
    in meat 17
    missing in the modern diet 5, 73
    nutritional supplements *see*
        supplements
    phytonutrients 12, 73, 74–6
    vitamins *see* vitamins
nuts 80, 167–8
    nutty granola topping 228

O

oat muffins 261
obesity 3–4, 20–1, 54
    apple-shaped 59–61
    hunger and 22
    and low-glycaemic diet 30–1
    pear-shaped 59–60, 66–7
    saturated fats and 15
    stress not main cause of 24
oils
    fish 80–1
    Phase 1 limitations 153, 168
omega-3 fatty acids 14, 80–2
omega-6 fatty acids 14
orange-cumin vinaigrette 216–17
osteoporosis 4, 302

P

panna cotta, coffee 288
pasta 20, 22
    Phase 1 avoidance 10, 152
    Phase 2 re-introduction 76,
        242
    wholewheat 77, 78
peanut butter and jam cookies 285
peas 166

vitamins 17, 80, 233, 239, 284
    in fruit and vegetables 73
    removed in refined grains
        77
    supplements *see* supplements

W

waist measurement 59, 64
    waist-to-hip ratio 64
wall sit 135
weight, optimal 64
weight gain
    metabolic rate and 67
    in Phase 3 diet 298–9
    at start of Phase 2 diet 291–2
weight loss
    exercise for 33–40, 44–6, 70 *see
    also* South Beach fitness programme
    through the South Beach Diet
        10–11, 70, 163, 236, 292–3

'You Can Never Be Too Thin'
    syndrome 67–70
    through yo-yo dieting 41
whole grains 12, 18, 22, 77–8
    Phase 1 avoidance 162
    Phase 2 re-introduction 241–2
wine 239
    red 73, 75
wraps 278–9

Y

yogurt 78
'You Can Never Be Too Thin'
    syndrome 67–70
yo-yo dieting 41, 293
Yucatan prawn roll-up 197

Z

zeaxanthin 75